BARBARA PYM AND THE NOVEL OF MANNERS

Barbara Pym and the Novel of Manners

ANNETTE WELD

MACMILLAN

First published 1992 by
MACMILLAN ACADEMIC AND PROFESSIONAL LTD
Houndmills, Basingstoke, Hampshire RG21 2XS
and London

Companies and representatives
throughout the world

Edited and typeset by Grahame & Grahame Editorial, Brighton

ISBN 0–333–562844 (hardcover)

A catalogue record for this book is available
from the British Library

Printed and bound in Great Britain by
Billing and Sons Ltd, Worcester

Contents

List of Abbreviations

All references are to the Macmillan editions of Pym's novels and are cited parenthetically in the text as the following acronyms.

Some Tame Gazelle	STG
Crampton Hodnet	CH
Jane and Prudence	JP
Excellent Women	EW
A Glass of Blessings	AGOB
Less than Angels	LTA
No Fond Return of Love	NFRL
An Unsuitable Attachment	AUA
The Sweet Dove Died	TSDD
An Academic Question	AAQ
Quartet in Autumn	QIA
A Few Green Leaves	AFGL
Civil to Strangers	CTS
A Very Private Eye	AVPE

Acknowledgements

For permission to quote from the collection of Pym papers I thank Hazel Holt, Hilary Walton, and the staff of the Department of Western Manuscripts, Bodleian Room 132. Colin Harris of that library provided much help, both long-distance and on-the-spot, over a period of several years and my thanks go to him for his patience.

Thanks are due to Macmillan London Ltd, E.P. Dutton Inc, and the Estate of Barbara Pym for permission to quote from the novels, and to Faber & Faber Ltd and Farrar, Straus and Giroux Inc for permission to include Philip Larkin's 'Posterity' from *High Windows* © 1974, Philip Larkin. I am also grateful to the representatives of the Philip Larkin Estate for their permission to quote from the Larkin-Pym correspondence.

Other of Pym's correspondents granted their kind permission to include extracts from their letters, including R. S. Smith, Paul de Angelis, and the estate of Lord David Cecil. Kate Heberlein graciously allowed me to quote from her fine dissertation on Pym, and several others including Geoffrey Holt, Colin Harris, P. T. Baxter, and Alfred Harris contributed their remembrances.

My grateful appreciation and sincere thanks are owed to many for the completion of this work, but especially to Hazel Holt and Hilary Walton for their kindness and inspiration; to professors J. W. Johnson and Bette London for their advice and encouragement in its early stages; to the Susan B. Anthony Center for Women's Studies at the University of Rochester for the grant enabling me to visit Oxfordshire and the Bodleian Library; to my friend Lotus Snow for her superb editing skills and unwavering confidence in me.

Most of all I thank Chip and our children, for their patience, their computer, and their love.

ANNETTE WELD

1

Manners and Comedy

Two years before her death in 1980, Barbara Pym described to a radio audience her ideal of artistic immortality:

> One of my favorite quiz games on television some years ago was the one in which panelists were asked to guess the authorship of certain passages which were read out to them, and then to discuss various features of the author in question. There were no prizes for guessing, no moving belt of desirable objects passing before their eyes, just the pleasure and satisfaction of recognizing the unmistakable voice of Henry James or Henry Greene, or whoever it might be. I think that's the kind of immortality most authors would want – to feel that their work would be immediately recognisable as having been written by them and by nobody else. But of course it's a lot to ask for. (MS Pym 98, fol. 125)[1]

As well as admiring Pym's candor here, we can congratulate her success. In twelve novels, a posthumously issued autobiography, and numerous unpublished stories and journals, Pym's voice is 'immediately recognisable', witty, dry, perceptive. Popular and literary acclaim for her work was late, swift, and appropriately ironic, but complete enough to warrant inclusion in both best seller lists and college curricula. So familiar and distinctive is her imagined world that only a few years after Pym's death a fictional narrator can complain, 'Encounters like that . . . make me feel like a character in Barbara Pym. Perhaps that's what I am: *anima naturaliter Pym'*,[2] and feel no further need for explanation. Her work has engendered popular success and survived close critical examination.

Pym's world of solitaries and small comforts is, as she hoped, 'unmistakably' her own. Curates, spinsters, academics, and librarians lead lives circumscribed by indecision; small worlds collide, characters converge and recoil, much conversation and little action

1

occur, and the social scene is barely altered. Her readers have come to expect the tightly controlled evocation of postwar Britain, the exposition of characters slightly threadbare but of good family, and the working out of a plot with less than world-shattering consequences. She never disappoints them.

Yet seldom in contemporary fiction do we find an author whose canon is simultaneously so homogeneous and so distinctive. Never straying far from the self-imposed restrictions of place and person, Pym within that limited frame creates in each novel a social mosaic that both comforts and disturbs, as familiar as an old lace tablecloth and as difficult to lean on. Loneliness and self-doubt go hand in hand with cozy cups of tea and printed silks; the reassurance of the recognisable is often undermined by the price paid for stasis. The What Ifs of life haunt these works, and while the social comedy is broad, the doubting persists.

And what of the woman behind the authorial voice? A cursory glance reveals an Oxford-educated editor of a small but respected anthropological journal whose life, if not measured out in coffee spoons, at least weathered none of the female upheavals of marriage and family. To dismiss Pym as a character from her own collection, however, is to overlook the rich sensuousness of her college days, the passions of several unrequited loves, and the efforts of work in the wartime WRNS or at her writing and editing. As her friend and literary executor, Hazel Holt, has noted, 'her shyness and reticence concealed much of the variety and complexity of her personality'.[3] Pym's family and friends, war work and professional life moved her in and out of a series of contained communities which provided rich material for a novelist concerned with social behavior.

Shy and reticent Barbara Mary Crampton Pym may have been, but these qualities did not deny her a headstrong plunge into life. Born during the first world war to supportive parents and middle-class comfort, Barbara and her younger sister Hilary led what Hilary calls 'a happy, unclouded childhood' (AVPE, 2). They learned Gilbert and Sullivan from the local operatic society, shared the organ-stool while their mother played parish hymns, and enjoyed encouragement from an extended family in their separate talents. Indeed, Barbara's first public success came at the age of nine: an operetta, *The Magic Diamond* (MS Pym 98, fols 1–12) written for an Easter reunion with favorite cousins. Separated only during their school and university days, the sisters remained close confidantes and friends throughout their lives. Barbara, Hilary relates, even based her first fully rounded characters, Belinda and Harriet Bede, on her speculaions about the aging Barbara and Hilary Pym.

> It was never our particular intention, in spite of the prophetic circumstances of *Some Tame Gazelle*, which she had started in 1934, to live together, but it somehow turned out that from about 1938 right up until the time of her death in 1980 we were never apart for more than a year or so at a time. (AVPE, 4–5)

Amiable and tolerant, both the sisters Bede and Pym radiate the warmth of mutual affection and support.

Entering St. Hilda's College, Oxford, in 1931, Pym set out eagerly to discover the pleasures and passions of Oxford social and, secondarily, academic life:

> 15 January. A new term in a new year – golden opportunities (and how!) to get a moderator – a peer's heir – a worthy theological student – or events change entirely; But Oxford really is intoxicating. (MS Pym 101, fol. 5)

The early journals record with adolescent breathlessness rounds of sherry parties, cinema dates, and a succession of young men. Subsequent entries detail plots or single scenes for novels, quotations from favorite authors, or observations of human behavior that might bear later development. Journals and notebooks became a lifelong habit beginning in these years – 'mercifully less personal and introspective as the years go on' – a sixty year old Pym will later admit.[4] While the reader may grow impatient with the schoolgirl sections, later ones follow the growth of the mature woman and the accomplished author. When collected along with selected correspondence in *A Very Private Eye*, they chart the ebb and flow of Pym's personal and artistic life.

Perhaps predictably, the central section of this collection, entitled 'The Published Novelist', is also the briefest. After too generously detailing Oxford and the war years, the book offers disappointingly few details of her most productive period.

> February 20, 1946: There is so much that I want to write now, that I hardly know where to begin. But I feel I must also have a job, not only because of earning money but because I find routine work soothing (as long as it is not too boring) and the best way of

keeping out that Angst, from which we all suffer in some degree nowadays. Though creative work is better still. (AVPE, 179)

Working for twenty-eight years at the International African Institute, first as proof-reader and then Assistant Editor, she oversaw publication of anthropological and linguistic monographs for its journal, *Africa*. Anthropologists and their milieux would later become worthy targets for her comic darts and add an exotic element to her novels of manners, but on the job her 'hawk eye for a misplaced comma'[5] and gentle good humor won her many friends:

> . . . it is by her dedicated work for *Africa* that Barbara will be so fondly remembered, and especially for the warmth of her welcome to unheralded callers . . . . she would quickly charm them into believing the unlikely story that in no way could their visit be an interruption to her coping with the yards of galley proofs or the mountains of books for review on her desk.[6]

The workload itself may partly explain the scarcity of journal entries or notebook jottings for this period, but six novels produced in thirteen years are better justification. The Pym papers collected at the Bodleian Library, Oxford, contain multiple drafts, seminal short stories, efforts begun and tabled, rewrites conducted at editors' requests – all evidence of a woman successful with two full-time jobs.

It was also during this period that Pym and the poet Philip Larkin began a lifelong correspondence (indeed, her Christmas card to him is the final entry in *A Very Private Eye*). Offering in his first letter to write a review article for her sixth novel, he would play a major role in her artistic future. Even their early letters are filled with mutual admiration and appreciation:

25 February 1962

Dear Mr. Larkin,

> Thank you for your letter which gave me the rather disquieting picture of you sitting, pen-in-hand – before a daunting pile of my novels. You will be relieved to hear that progress on the seventh is very slow, but perhaps sure – I sometimes wonder. In any case, I don't think I've written to you since seeing your very charming tribute in the *Guardian* which gave me so much pleasure that it really absolves you from doing anything else. (AVPE, 205)

During their years of correspondence they traded opinions on contemporary writers, sent travel postcards, even exchanged snapshots – 'Philip Larkin sent me a photograph of his new Library extension. Was ever a stranger photo sent by a man to a woman (in a novel she might be disappointed)' (AVPE, 246). A letter to him in 1963 admits the 'bitter blow' of her seventh novel's rejection, and although they were not to meet for twelve more years, Larkin's support was steadfast during this frustrating period of non-publication.

When her publisher, Jonathan Cape, refused *An Unsuitable Attachment*, Pym began a fourteen-year effort to recover her literary equilibrium. She tried other publishing firms for the work – 'twenty-one publishers is surely enough' – consulted with friends and colleagues on changes, and finally laid it aside, suffering a self-doubt that would feed on further rejections. She contemplated a pseudonym, a change of style, a new subject:

> What sort of novel could I write now? A gothic novel . . . Why shouldn't it be a *modern* gothic novel. What are the ingredients. A heroine, but much more of a heroine than Mildred or Wilmet. A setting. A hero. Mystery. A modern version of Jane Eyre? (AVPE, 258)

Although she never abandoned her writing altogether, production slowed during these years until, refusing to compromise her artistic sense, she retired to the Finstock cottage to write a book for herself, 'as churchy as I wished to make it'.[7]

In large part Philip Larkin engineered Pym's artistic resurrection. The *Times Literary Supplement*, for a 1977 anniversary article aptly entitled 'Reputations Revisited', solicited fifty writers, scholars, and artists to name their favorite underrated novelist of the past seventy-five years. Larkin and Lord David Cecil concurred:

Philip Larkin

Underrated: the six novels of Barbara Pym published between 1950 and 1961 which give an unrivalled picture of a small section of middle-class post-war England. She has a unique eye and ear for the small poignancies and comedies of everyday life.

Lord David Cecil

Underrated: Barbara Pym, whose unpretentious, subtle, accomplished novels, especially *Excellent Women* and *A Glass of Bless-*

ings, are for me the finest examples of high comedy to have appeared in England during the past seventy-five years.[8]

The reversal of her literary fortune was rapid and complete. Within months a new publisher, Macmillan, printed *Quartet in Autumn*, which was nominated for Britain's prestigious literary honor, the Booker Prize. Requests for interviews, American publishing contracts, and even a television biography followed; the escalation of her reputation was as unexpected as its previous nosedive. With an ease that belied the publishing difficulties of the previous decade, she was able to see three more novels into print in as many years. But the cancer that had precipitated an earlier mastectomy reappeared and she died three years after the *TLS* article. Although Pym produced short stories, radio scripts, personal essays, and hundreds of journal and notebook sketches, it is with twelve similar, slender novels that she claims her audience.

'Good books for bad days' – as she often referred to her work – these comic worlds, though not what the 'Swinging Sixties' were demanding, have proved their staying power. They continue a literary convention that defines the world by its detail, that considers manners as a measure of morals, and that has long been a part of what F. R. Leavis calls 'the great tradition' of English literature: the novel of manners.

Easily identified in practice but more difficult to define in theory, this slippery sub-genre remains, in the hands of such deft practitioners as Pym, a vital force in modern fiction. The comic spirit lies at its heart, but its tonal variations can range from the affectionate to the acerbic. Pym, aligned in this traditional form with a unique group of novelists – masters like Austen, Trollope, and Waugh, as well as such lesser lights as E. F. Benson, Elizabeth Taylor, and Kingsley Amis – borrows and reshapes the conventions of the novel of manners for her own use.

Her versions of the form, crammed with masses of detail and finely sketched characters, wry humor and gentle irony, carry the traditions of social comedy into the crowded arena of contemporary fiction. Eschewing violence and random sexual encounter, avoiding narrative disjunctions and the conventions of black humor, limiting space and time frames to small and familiar settings, Pym's work in the novel of manners simultaneously continues the tradition of her predecessors and adds an uniquely feminine and personal perspective.

Before considering the Pym novels themselves, however, it seems useful to examine this sub-genre, to catalogue its varieties and vagaries, and to delineate the factors that define the novel of manners. For in the broadest sense every novel concerns itself with the relationship between a character and his social world and therefore qualifies as a novel of manners. With the genre itself provoking mostly broad-brushed description – 'a fiction in prose of a certain extent'[9] – how can we best characterise this restrictive version? Unlike its gothic, romantic, science fictive, or mythic form, the novel, when primarily concerned with the effects of social intercourse on character development, resists definition and classification, and the difficulty in discussing the outwardly ordinary may be the reason: Lionel Trilling calls manners 'a nearly indefinable subject'.[10] Even though we recognise that social assumptions in large part determine individual and group behavior, a close inspection of a society's manners may prove as evanescent and ultimately as deflating as overexplaining a good joke.

Nevertheless, certain conventions prevail and can be broadly defined. Whenever a character's actions or attitudes grow out of or respond to the expectations of his fictional society and the microscopic detailing of that society becomes the basis for moral and ethical measurement, there is fertile ground for the novel of manners. In his book *The Novel of Manners in America*, James Tuttleton offers the following definition:

> By a novel of manners I mean a novel in which the manners, social customs, folkways, conventions, traditions and mores of a given social group at a given time and place play a dominant role in the lives of fictional characters, exert control over their thought and behavior, and constitute a determinant upon the actions in which they are engaged, and in which these manners and customs are detailed realistically – with, in fact, a premium upon the exactness of their representation.[11]

Many of the great American novels of adventure and self- discovery fall outside the confines of this definition and Tuttleton focuses his discussion on Wharton, Howells, and O'Hara rather than Hawthorne, Melville, or Twain. His criteria, on the other hand, achieve greater validity when applied across the Atlantic.

Curiously, the most recent edition of *The Oxford Companion to English Literature*,[12] compiled by novelist Margaret Drabble, contains no entry for the term 'novel of manners'. Whether Anglo or American in definition, in practice the British version of the social novel examines just this conjunction of manners and character. It relies on social patterns to explicate behavior, and adds to Tuttleton's formula an established class system, geographic insularity, and a thousand years of cultural history. It looks to relationships between individuals, among families, and within neighborhoods to define the common body of belief. It requires communal experience to establish the principles and taboos of human life, relying on manners to outline the ethical and moral underpinnings of the social fabric. It assumes that an analysis of the public world will explain the private, and therefore amasses the details of daily existence: food, clothing, shelter, occupations, leisure activities, religious practices, and social traditions. Unrestricted by the requirements of statistics or empirical data, the novel of manners becomes a kind of fictionalised sociology, faithful to its place and time.

The roots of the novel of manners lie deeply buried in the comic mode: Greek and Roman comic drama, Restoration and Shakespearean comedy, indeed, the whole of the English comic tradition. Although some have discussed the possibility of the 'tragedy of manners',[13] it is from the archetypes, characters, and patterns of comedy that the novel of manners usually draws its life. No single definition will accommodate all the various forms that comedy assumes, and each theoretician begins by refuting his colleagues' most recent assertions. Nevertheless, in its classic form certain characteristics persist, and central to the mode is stability: into a calm and ordered world, an irritant is introduced, a complication arises only to be resolved by the central character, and a new harmony is restored. The universe is ordered, safe, and reliable.

The appeal of this stability to a modern audience cannot be underestimated. When all of ethics, religion, politics, family life, even the continuation of the race seem questionable, comedy serves as antidote. As one critic notes, the comic response is most appropriate for our century:

> . . . our greatest novelists and playwrights are comedians (Shaw, Joyce, Beckett, Brecht, Ionesco, Saul Bellow, Joseph Heller, Kingsley Amis, Anthony Burgess, Philip Roth, and so on), and . . . the comic, ironic reaction of twentieth-century literature is an understandably human, reasonable, and healthy response to

the devastating chaos of twentieth-century life, politics, morality, and science.[14]

The predictable provides necessary solace in an often unpredictable world, and no fictional form seems more stylised and predictable than the novel of manners. It offers traditional plot patterns, conventional, even stereotypical, characterisations, constricted settings, and familiar themes – all packaged in the comfortable wrappings of an attractive, recognisable, often aristocratic, social scene.

Along with stability, comedy offers further comforts, appealing to our intellect, our sense of the humane, and our finest communal instincts. Comedy needs company. Both object and audience are essential for the shared experience, not only of laughter but of the comic in general. Even when directed at one of the group, and temporarily disruptive of the status quo, the natural end of comedy is socially restorative. It may create situations of pain as well as pleasure, and allow much that is neither light nor laughable, and still the pervasive atmosphere affirms the individual within the group. Richard Poirier, in his work on Henry James, discusses this phenomenon:

> There is nothing extraordinary about the use of comedy at the culmination of a series of distressing and very uncomic actions . . . . It is a way of reminding oneself that existence goes on beyond the periphery of one's own disaster. It is a way of affirming that though your situation is killing you, you still have the capacity to recognize that life is going on outside it.[15]

The realisation that 'life is going on outside', permits the willing reintegration of the self into a reformed society, creates a comic release, and allows us to embrace the resolution wholeheartedly.

The appeal of the communal comic world resides not only in this fulfillment of expectations, but also in its assumptions about our intellectual capabilities. Seldom will the novel of manners contain the broad gestures of farce or the grotesque exaggerations of more raucous comedy, relying usually on the tacit agreement of certain givens between the reader and his fiction. It will provide a logical, rational milieu, admitting only those characters and situations whose existence is verifiable in the observed world. It will operate within limits, relying on understatement, constriction, and wit rather than overemphasis and hyperbole to achieve its ends.

And it will insure that rather than from symbol, myth, or archetype, the world is knowable from the tangible.

The reader agrees, in return, to engage his intellect in a game where the smallest gesture or turn of phrase encapsulates a larger condition. He will forgo frenetic energy in these novels in favor of the subtler pleasures of the ironic twist of phrase or the implications of an incorrectly chosen tie. He acknowledges the conjunction of the socially correct and the morally right.

Extending his full cooperation in this fictional 'contract', the reader aligns himself with the author and other readers in a seemingly elite community. In assumed prepossession of the rules of the social game, and incapable of his own transgressions, he observes the action secure in his role as initiate. Necessarily, and due in large part to this aura of elitism, the territory of the novel of manners is tinted by blue blood and silver spoons; vicarious participation in a homogeneously upper-crust society accounts for much of the genre's popular appeal. Rationally, the reader assumes that the truth is discoverable in the observable clues; emotionally, he relishes the rarified air of exotic and, for most of us, unobtainable luxury. The novel of manners, then, provides both intellectual and emotional satisfaction.

Along with this gratifying sense of superiority that the form provokes comes a more altruistic response. Appreciation of and sympathy for the human condition lie at the heart of comedy, especially in a genre so closely concerned with group behavior as the novel of manners. In his seminal essay 'Manners, Morals, and the Novel', Lionel Trilling applauds the form for engendering this moral compassion:

> For in our time the most effective agent of the moral imagination has been the novel of the last two hundred years. It was never, either aesthetically or morally, a perfect form and its faults and failures can be quickly enumerated. But its greatness and its practical usefulness lay in its unremitting work of involving the reader himself in the moral life, inviting him to put his own motives under examination, suggesting that reality is not as his conventional education has led him to see it. It taught us, as no other genre ever did, the extent of human variety and the value of this variety. It was the literary form to which the emotions of understanding and forgiveness were indigenous, as if by the definition of the form itself.[16]

We recognize the human capacity for gross injustice, misunder-
standing, or intolerance, but buried within our laughter at others'
comic follies and foibles is the dual recognition of our mutual frailty
and our mutual worth. Hoping for the best, appreciating the 'value
of variety', holding out realistic expectations for human behavior,
the novel of manners asks us to be both human and humane.

Along with this essential quality – the overriding comic climate of
the field of action – the novel of manners exhibits other identifiable
characteristics. Signifying manners as 'a culture's hum and buzz
of implications', Trilling advises that we find in the choice of
setting, character, structure, style, and theme indications of what
the novelist of manners need never articulate.

> . . . in the tone of greetings and the tone of quarrels, in slang
> and popular songs, in the way children play, in the gesture the
> waiter makes when he puts down the plate, in the nature of the
> very food we prefer . . . . [these are] half-uttered or unuttered or
> unutterable expressions of value. They are hinted at by small
> actions, sometimes by the arts of dress or decoration, sometimes
> by tone, gesture, emphasis, or rhythm, sometimes by the words
> that are used with a special frequency or a special meaning.[17]

The reader of the novel of manners must be alert to nuance, sensitive
to culturally shifting mores, and appreciative of the consequences
of proper behavior. These sensibilities put him in touch with the
writer's version of reality and allow his imaginative participation
in this most stylised of fictional worlds.

Because social environment is largely responsible for shaping
character, the setting, whether at an Austen country ball or in
a Jamesian formal drawing room, is crucial for establishing and
controlling the atmosphere of these works. Unlike the romance
or adventure novel which demand space and expansiveness, the
novel of manners operates in tightly compressed, often pastoral,
quarters: small towns, out-of-season resort hotels, rural parishes.
It requires a manageable geography, familiar enough to envision
at a glance and preferably encompassable in the course of an
after-dinner stroll. Strangers and dangers enter from outside, since
inside is a close-knit, inbred, almost claustrophobic familiarity. Far
enough from the city to avoid its speed, variety, and anonymity,
be it London, Paris, or New York, the scene of action nevertheless
provides life's essential goods and services. The form's setting is

self-contained, intensely personal, and slow to admit change.

Since environment shapes destiny to such a large extent in these works, rights of property and material possessions take on moral worth. Land, country estates, family artifacts, great-grandmother's silver – all must be acknowledged and enumerated, with special homage paid to long-standing wealth. Central to the British novel in all its forms, a sense of history and an appreciation of the past often lead in the novel of manners to comic ends: tradition and stability become top-heavy targets.

Set character types grow naturally from these settings; materially conscious, of good family, often stereotypical, they are products of their environment, shaped by its values. Although characters shaped from social pressures tend to repeat familiar patterns, this reliance on types need not be considered a handicap; there are always new variations within the confines of the familiar. Each new society contains slightly altered versions of the social groups that preceded it, and the joy of rediscovery can outweigh a reader's desire for innovation. Indeed each reworking of recognisable characters permits the economy or spareness so characteristic of the novel of manners. Each befuddled clergyman, hysterical ingenue, or wise fool draws strength from previous literary incarnations, and author and audience are able to recognise stereotypical characterisation as a kind of literary shorthand. Stock characters neatly provide a peopled cosmos in a small space. In his now famous discussion of 'round' versus 'flat' characters E. M. Forster recognises the virtues of the stereotype:

> One great advantage of flat characters is that they are easily recognized whenever they come in – recognized by the reader's emotional eye, not by the visual eye, which merely notes the recurrence of a proper name . . . . It is a convenience for an author when he can strike with his full force at once, and flat characters are very useful to him, since they never need reintroducing, never run away, have not to be watched for development, and provide their own atmosphere – little luminous disks of a pre-arranged size, pushed hither and thither like counters across the void or between the stars; most satisfactory.
>
> A second advantage is that they are easily remembered by the reader afterwards. They remain in his mind as unalterable for the reason that they were not changed by circumstances; they moved through circumstances, which gives them in retrospect

a comforting quality, and preserves them when the book that produced them may decay.[18]

Like the omnipresent fast-food drive-in, a flat character satisfies a basic need in a speedy and reliable, if not totally original, fashion.

Stock characters in the novel of manners also allow the novelist to people his limited world economically. Within the homogeneous society that he creates there must be variation enough for differences in manners to be apparent and for subtle gradations of social class to be weighed, all within the confines of the restricted setting. Representative types, both likeable and ridiculous – absent-minded academics, distressed gentlewomen, mysterious exotics – allow us to peek at the world from odd angles and permit the inclusion of a wide world of characters who need little or no introduction or explanation.

These stock types move away from mere decoration in the novel of manners as they take on more realistic characteristics in appearance, dialogue, and activity – as they become plot movers. The most successful engage our sympathy for their efforts, regardless of how their fictional society views them, and the key to their success is self-awareness. The more self-conscious, the more aware of self-delusion a character is, the less likely he is to arouse audience antipathy or scorn. Caricatures or types, locked into one-dimensional views of the world, lack the necessary introspection that a genre devoted to behavior requires of its heroes. The counterpoint of inward doubts and outward hopes creates characters with complex personalities, 'capable of surprising in a convincing way', satisfying Forster's criteria for roundness. It is his public behavior – the traditions, rituals, and ceremonies of social intercourse – that identify a character type for the comic novel of manners; a character's private behavior – self-scrutiny, moral code, and consciousness of good and evil – insures him our empathy.

This melding of characters – both types and true – in the novel of manners directly affects the structure or shape of the form. As one might expect, the traditional complications of comedy provide the skeleton. Sometimes these complications create an episodic, tableau-plotting that leads the reader trippingly from situation to situation with only the repetition of the stock characters to sustain it. More commonly, the practice results in the contrapuntal weaving of similar plots, the duplication or inversion of action, repetition, or the intentional disruption of established repetition.

With the material world as its touchstone, violations of space, time, and balance are rare in this genre, making it one of the last strongholds of realism in the contemporary novel. Education, betrothal, marriage, the occasional death (reported from offstage and necessary for removing obstacles to happiness), inheritance – the empirical rather than the theoretical – shape the form; theory is generally cloaked in social relationships. There is little room for multiple levels of meaning or symbolic obscurity when social phenomena determine value. Fascination with social differences and reliance on sharp detail could indicate a relation to the genre of travel literature (the limitations of setting notwithstanding) and the longevity of the form reveals both historical and contemporary variations, as different as the chronicles of Regency etiquette and the whodunits of Agatha Christie.

In each instance the language, style, or tone of the novel of manners may be more indicative than its subject. It is a world of absolutes: precise, factual, and morally encased, where language reveals what action might not. Dialect, repetition, and cadence create character, and dialogue often bears much of the weight of narrative. We can assess a character's social position, family history, and moral worth from his speech patterns.

The authorial voice as well distinguishes the form, shimmering with a slightly ironic tone, suggesting to its reader that he is party to an elite joke and shares with the writer a certain level of taste or suitability. The elusive term 'wit' is usually applied to this sort of treatment, this mutual elbowing by author and audience. Henri Bergson draws an important distinction between wit and comedy: 'A word is said to be comic when it makes us laugh at the person who utters it, and witty when it makes us laugh at a third party or at ourselves.'[19] This ability to provoke self-directed laughter may finally be the *raison d'etre* for the novel of manners, allowing us to recognise ourselves in the ridiculous.

The final identifying trait for these novels is a characteristic set of ideologies and themes, the most over-riding of which is their essential Britishness. History, politics, religion, education – in short, all the veneer of civilisation and empire are polished to a rich patina and presented as the foundation on which the literature is built. On the negative side, a stifling class system, a bourgeois self-satisfaction, and a narrow world-view can also be contributing elements.

As in all comedy, domestic history explains the past and

generational conflicts provide the source of much of the action. It is expected that true love will overcome most social obstacles. Wealth and family position mean both power and prestige; tradition and stability are valued over innovation and mutability. Like the Gothic novel, the novel of manners casts a wary eye on foreigners – Italians and Americans being the most suspect – and sexually assertive types are usually expelled from the final festivities. The players and the playing fields of the social game are the focus for these works which meticulously record every victory or defeat.

And how do the twelve novels of Barbara Pym measure up against these criteria? Her contemporary versions of the novel of manners both resurrect and renew the genre, creating a female, post-war perspective on a world where manners and social behavior are more often bypassed by popular writers in favor of the graphically violent or sexually explicit. Isa Kapp, reviewing Pym in *The Washington Post*, acknowledges her singularity in her chosen form:

> In the world of modern fiction, where only sin is guaranteed to spellbind and our prominent authors come most alive in the moments they conjure up death or evil, Pym is a lone sturdy figure, bent on making virtue entertaining.[20]

Pym's middle-class, mid-century milieu lends itself more to tea than titillation, and the conventions of the novel of manners fit her like a pair of yellowed kid gloves. Everything from her choice of setting and character to her consistent ideologies and themes aligns her in the tradition; even the substitution of a middle- for the upper-class world usually characteristic of this form is appropriate for her carefully detailed Britain of the 1950s and 1960s.

Pym's is an historically accurate England of rationing, paraffin heaters, and queues, of services held cheerfully in half-bombed churches, of cafeterias and train schedules. The world outside one's bus route is a source of amusement and mild curiosity, but not a cause for longing or discontent. If she ventures to a pastoral village, it differs from a London suburb only in its choice of altar flowers, or in the speed with which its neighbors learn each other's business. So consistent is she in her limitations of setting that even when an intrepid parish group makes a visit to Florence, they seek on their first excursion the safe haven of an English tearoom.

Like her predecessors, Pym peoples her social comedies with a small community of characters, homogeneous enough to co-exist in close quarters yet with enough differences to provide surprise. In several instances a familiar character will make a cameo appearance in a later novel (a practice which Philip Larkin dubbed 'coincidence rather than Barchester') providing a satisfying linking device for the faithful reader. She writes of solitary women living on reduced incomes, clergy both young and old, and foggy academic types as her typical favorites. She gives us only a handful of children and few extremes of rich or poor. Occasionally she will attempt a 'modern' – a seductive female student, a randy antique dealer, or a homosexual or two – but her trademark characters are the excellent women, 'capable of dealing with most of the stock situations or even the great moments of life – birth, marriage, death, the successful jumble sale, the garden fête spoilt by bad weather' (EW, 6). They harbor few illusions, make few demands, and scrutinise themselves and others with a clarity of vision only occasionally clouded by the appearance of an eligible man.

Although relations between the sexes are more often cerebral than physical, the search for companionship structures most of Pym's comedies. Speculation on the advantages and disadvantages of marriage occupies much of her characters' time, and even though unrequited love or the solitary life are not ideal, they are often preferable to the shared life with the wrong partner. Episodic and lightly plotted – two marriages, no births, several deaths but only off-stage – each novel works through to some resolution for the heroine that offers consolation and comfort, if not conjugal bliss.

Pym's style is hallmarked by this search for consolation and comfort: sharp-edged dialogue combines with a generosity of tone to characterise her authorial voice. Yet in the midst of sharply detailing the mundane or trivial, she can deliver a caveat: life's pain is real, but relieved by small pleasures that should be savored. Pym controls the conventions of the novel of manners, asking us to recognise ourselves in the ridiculous, to redirect our laughter inward, to make moral touchstones of sympathy, kindness, and honesty. Never bitter or acerbic, she humanises her prose with acute observations of social behavior, lingering lovingly over the language and detail of her circumscribed, churchy world.

In ideology and choice of theme, Pym is consistent with most of the traditions of the novel of manners. Steadfastly rooted in her heritage, she cultivates only native soil: the Anglican church, the greater and lesser English poets, the cosy cup of tea. Atypically for the form, however, the issues of social rank focus on the middle rather than the upper class, with little outright wealth and fewer poor. Pym's cities collect immigrants from all corners of the empire and her country villages are crowded with representative types, causing one claustrophobic heroine to worry, 'One wouldn't believe there could be so many people, and one must love them all' (EW, 78).

The search for love, or at least companionship, occupies most of Pym's heroines. Her young women pursue men less vital and adaptable than they; those already married busy themselves with planning unsuitable attachments for their friends; aging unmarrieds reminisce about lost possibilities. In this pre-feminist world, female fulfillment is closely tied to male attention, however feckless those males may be.

When love proves fleeting or, more often, futile, Pym's women show their resiliency, proving that the solitary life is necessarily neither lonely nor unproductive. Possibility is always lurking and until it appears there is much pleasure to be gained from the physical comforts of food, second-hand clothing, cosy bed-sitters, and a variety of fond if not intense friendships. If love does not always prevail in her versions of the novel of manners, the consolations are serenity and a familiar routine.

In its mid-twentieth century guise, the novel of manners remains fundamentally unchanged in Pym's hands. It is still closely bound by the constraints of economics, social class, and ethical behavior, operating on its own conventions of character, setting, and theme, and documenting the taste, decorum, and social mores of its period. Like any of her predecessors, Pym consistently paints her world in these characteristic hues, drawing upon sixty years of her own observations and experiences.

2
The Early Work –
Poems, Stories, Radio Plays

Once she discovered her niche in the genre Pym would remain faithful to the comic novel of manners, but a few early efforts collected with the Bodleian manuscripts show her experimenting with style and form, searching for the voice that would satisfy both the comic and the ironic strains of her creative personality. With a nod to the past she tries an eighteenth-century standby: 'Satire – (Pope and BMCP) Concerning a Few of My Acquaintances.' A beast fable in rhyme, 'Tame Donkey: A Sequel to 'Midland Bank', similarly allows her to disguise character assessments in fictive costumes. Even in these overly self-conscious and self-dramatizing efforts, the young author seems to recognise her need for establishing a more familiar milieu: in the cautionary fantasy, 'The Sad Story of Alphonse: A Warning to Would-Be Poets', a ghost speaks to the narrator about the dangers and drawbacks of attempting poetry.

Ignoring that ghost's good advice, the young Pym was usually driven to poetry by unrequited love. Novelist Shirley Hazzard considers poetry one of the well-springs of Pym's talent as a novelist:

> I have the impression that poetry formed her. Poetry flows through her books – not only in outright quotations, but in suggestions, in allusions concealed not merely for the appreciative but for the loving. She is herself the poet of the lonely, the virtuous, the ironic; of the unostentatiously intelligent and witty; of the angelically self-effacing, with their diabolically clear gaze.[1]

The young Pym's plaintive laments, neatly transcribed in fine ink into a copybook and sandwiched between hand-drawn ornamental patterns, document undying and eternal attachments to at least three young men. She was as fond of elaborate titles, 'Sonnet written to a Dear Young Friend on the Third Day of December Nineteen Thirty-Eight, it being the first Anniversary of our Meeting', as of coy dedications to the young man of the moment 'with the author's fondest love. (But without his permission)' (MS Pym 97). The poetry itself seems to demand her own immediate acknowledgment of its literary debts, as in:

'Fragment Inspired by Tennyson'

O that t'were possible
After long grief and pain,
To find the arms of the younger son of the
Rt. Hon. L. S. Amery, M.P.
Around me once again.

(MS Pym 97)

Even as she bares her soul, albeit in heavily borrowed metaphysical language, she is never far from artistic self-evaluation, signaling in post-script the alternate version of a love sonnet's closing line:

My Gothick Spirit obstinately lingers
In long-forgotten Places, Haunts of ours
Where we, who loved in a proctorial* way
Did twine our Hands and for a Moment stay.

*some versions have 'poetic'

This insistence on accurate and elegant transcription, the careful choice of ink, of position on the page, of decorative borders and ornamental design, demonstrate in these early copybooks not only her respect for the effort but also her attention to detail. The look of the art was important, from the most private to the most public: a plain cardboard folder entitled 'Short Stories, etc – Ideas and Beginnings' has pasted to its front an incongruous picture of an exotically dressed senorita presenting the Lippizaner stallions (MS Pym 99, fol. 3); in later years, she would choose Jonathan Cape as her publisher 'largely because she always liked the look of their books' (MS Pym 98, fol. 25).

Reading Aldous Huxley's *Crome Yellow* convinced the sixteen-year-old Pym to begin her first (unpublished) novel.

I don't suppose for a moment that I appreciated the book's finer satirical points, but it seemed to me funnier than anything I had read before, and the idea of writing about a group of people in a certain situation – in this case upper-class intellectuals in a country house – immediately attracted me. (MS Pym 98, fol. 4)

Since the young Miss Pym had little personal experience of this fictive world, 'clothes, makes of cars, golf, and drinks – (especially descriptions of cocktails – which I'd certainly never tasted)', _Young Men in Fancy Dress_ bears little resemblance to her later style. Fifty years after its writing she would comment, 'Reading the manuscript again, I detect almost nothing in it of my mature style of writing, except that the Bohemian young men aren't taken entirely seriously, and that there's a lot of detail' (MS Pym 98, fol. 5). At sixteen though, with Huxley as her guide, she had begun to stake out some of the territory of the novel of manners, and recognised that her literary strength lay in that 'group of people in a certain situation'. Her eye for detail was beginning to focus.

At Oxford in 1931, she began to confide sporadically to a diary: at first, the tear-stained problems of her latest romance; later, more self-analytical observations of her actions and emotions. The impression of Pym drawn from these pages is not entirely flattering: a giddy, scatterbrained schoolgirl, absorbed in every aspect of Oxford life except the study of English literature. Apart from the occasional mention of 'an amusing lecture in the morning – Professor Tolkein on Beowulf' (AVPE, 28), or an isolated hour of study between social engagements, the diaries provide a fully documented panorama of Oxford's non-academic diversions in the 1930s. Fashion, films, popular music, cocktails at local pubs, punting on the river, evenings of sexual experimentation – all are lovingly preserved in the pages of the diaries; only the academic experience is missing.

This may be less disconcerting if we remember that the fashion of the day dictated an appearance of casualness toward, if not the direct neglect of, one's studies. As Hazel Holt suggests, an apparent indifference to approaching deadlines, the ability to 'dash back from a late evening's social engagement, spend a brief hour or two at one's desk, and produce by morning an acceptable essay or exam, was an admired skill'.[2] With an undergraduate's unassailable logic, as pervasive in our day as in Pym's, success without obvious effort was the best indicator of excellence. Awarded her degree in 1934 with second-class honors, she crowed, *'I got a 2nd.* With comparative ease too' (AVPE, 44).

Pym stands with good company in this studied nonchalance. The contemporary novel's portrayal of the academic experience generally bears out this attitude, so obvious in Pym's undergraduate journals. Evelyn Waugh's Charles Ryder minimises the value of his Oxford lessons compared with those learned in the glittering world of Sebastian Flyte. Kingsley Amis's Lucky Jim laughs at the posturings of an academic community and learns more about creativity and the development of the human spirit from drink than from dons. The learned literary critics in David Lodge's *Small World* who criss-cross the globe attending professional conferences recognise to a man that as the valuable academic commodity 'the American Express card has replaced the library pass'.[3] In Pym's own novels the serious scholar rarely appears; instead dedicated academics come in for ridicule or, at best, bemused tolerance. They are isolated from the community by their esoteric and ultimately worthless efforts. Commitment to an academic life creates the fatuous Aylwin Forbes of *No Fond Return of Love*, the anemic Alaric Lydgate of *Less Than Angels*, and the larcenous Alan Grimstone of *An Academic Question.*

To give voice to this anti-scholastic breeziness, Pym develops in the Oxford days the fictional persona Sandra, a glamorous and devil-may-care alter ego. Sandra appears regularly in these early diaries, her name even carefully embroidered onto a lounging pillow in Pym's rooms at St. Hilda's. She provides an opportunity for the young Pym to experience the lush, dramatic, and hedonistic side never exploited in her novels. The origin of the name, writes Hazel Holt, 'may have been (as her friend Robert Liddell suggests) short for Cassandra, but it seems possible that it was simply a name she considered glamorous and sophisticated, being short for Alexandra and thus having overtones of Russian and Central European aristocracy' (AVPE, 9).

Pym maintained these confessional and often overly dramatic diaries throughout her Oxford years, detailing experiences so faithfully that later she would prudently excise some of the more explicit pages. 'Today I must always remember I suppose. I went to tea with Rupert . . . and he with all his charm, eloquence and masculine wiles, persuaded . . . . [missing pages]' (AVPE, 17) Whether discretion demanded this propriety, or the older writer simply rued the predictable seduction scene, is difficult to determine.

In addition to the poetry and the diaries, much of what Barbara Pym was learning about her craft was practiced in letters to friends. Although she insisted in 1978 that, 'Any letters I have written are much the same as the diary and (of course) I don't keep copies' (MS Pym 98, fol. 88), fortunately the recipients did. Robert Liddell regrets the loss of some early letters in a hurried move:

> I am very sorry about this, for she was an extremely good letter-writer, and her letters to me would have been a valuable addition to those of Henry Harvey, Robert Smith and Philip Larkin which form what is perhaps the best part of [*A Very Private Eye*].[4]

Hazel Holt recalls her difficulty, when assembling this auto-biographic volume, in gathering enough material to document Pym's later years. After the letters from these three correspondents were offered, she remembers that the book came together quickly.[5] The lost Liddell letters would have made an interesting addition, based on their lifelong friendship and the imitative styles they affected:

> With a pen in her hand and a correspondent in her mind, Barbara was an adult writer, and English gentlewoman, who never whined or complained. She was witty and funny and no doubt had private jokes with most of her intimates. She and I often wrote deliberately stylised letters, influenced by the novels of Ivy Compton-Burnett, or by Stevie Smith's *Novel on Yellow Paper*. There would be references no one but myself can now understand.[6]

Her frankness in letter-writing is evidenced by the numbers in the Bodleian collection 'reserved from use' by request of the owners: 'mainly on the grounds of confidentiality', notes librarian Colin Harris. Letters from Julian Amery as well as Robert Liddell are restricted, almost certainly because of personal material they include. In granting permission to view his correspondence from Pym, Robert Smith wrote 'I am afraid that as most of the people mentioned in the letters are still alive, I must ask to see extracts which you use in any publication or thesis.'[7] Fortunately, many of the observations, meditations, or descriptions that Pym shared with her correspondents appear first as brief notations to herself in a personal diary or notebook.

Ultimately the confessional college diaries gave way to a lifelong habit, the keeping of a literary notebook. From 1948 until her death, Pym carried a series of small, spiral notebooks, some tiny enough to record only a single thought per page. Judging from the dog-earred condition of the collection at the Bodleian, the one in current use was continually at hand, jammed into a coat pocket, stuffed into a handbag or catchall, always available whenever a passing pedestrian or view from a bus-top warranted preserving for later use. For the Pym devotee these annual inventories present a touchingly accurate, if naturally fractured, portrait of the artist.

The method of the notebooks matches their purpose: methodically, Pym worked from front-to-back observing the world around her and from back-to-front documenting the details of her daily life. When the two streams met in the middle, uncannily often at the start of a new year, she began anew. The back sections should bring joy to future sociologists or anthropologists researching mid-century Britain and middle class life. Here, Pym tallied expenses for the year: clothes (those purchased and those coveted), groceries (gin often the most expensive item), and debts ('Poopa [family nickname for sister Hilary] owes me £10, 3p'). She made lists for holiday packing, kept addresses of absent friends, and included newly discovered recipes.

For the reader more interested in Pym the writer, the front sections of these notebooks provide a kaleidoscopic vision of her artistic method. We learn that in addition to her powers of observation, the daily newspapers provided a handy source of comedy:

> I have a collection of newspaper cuttings on a variety of subjects – A stuffed crocodile found on a beach – 25 deer knocking over a car in Epping Forest – a woman who annoyed her neighbors by playing the harp and banging on a tin tray – a woman who fell in love with a clergyman she saw on television and proposed marriage to – those are just a few that have taken my fancy, but what use they will ever be I can't possibly imagine. (MS Pym 98, fol. 62)

Often, however, the items that take her fancy are put to immediate use, and a single idea or brief character sketch entered into the notebook reappears as the springboard for a novel. 'Novels don't come to me in a tidy package,' she wrote in 1977 to her Macmillan editor, 'often a single incident gives me an idea' (MS Pym 165, fol. 100). Weeks or months later the initial entry may begin to gather a group of characters around itself, and soon the notebook records short chapter descriptions or narrative strategies scattered in among new observations for future writings. This leap-frogging technique means that any one notebook may contain incidents from several of the finished novels, and that Pym could always return to even the oldest for unused comic inspiration.

Since they provide the germination for many scenes from the longer works, and especially since they reflect experimentation with styles and attitudes, the collection of some thirty short stories and fragments of stories contributes much to our knowledge of Pym's novels of manners. Uneven and often unsuccessful, many of these stories will remain quietly buried in the Bodleian collection; a few, however, receive fine critical analysis in Anthony Kaufman's article 'Pym's Short Fiction',[8] and four are included in Hazel Holt's edition of *Civil to Strangers and Other Writings* .

Only a handful of stories were accepted for publication during her lifetime, and many were repeatedly rejected by magazines. Pym researched the short fiction requirements of a variety of publications, especially those aimed at a popular women's audience. In a 1953 letter to literary agents Curtis Brown Ltd, she demurs, 'My stories aren't good enough for a highbrow magazine, even if such things existed which they hardly do, and were in fact written with women's magazines in mind' (MS Pym 147). Among her papers is a handwritten alphabetical listing of the word limits or special preferences of a variety of magazines for choosing fiction.

> Adelphi – up to 5000 w
> Argosy – 2-7000
> Blackwoods – strong in plot and characterisation
> [etc.]
>
> (MS Pym 99, fol. 4)

Poignantly, in the upper right corner of some of these short story typescripts Pym handwrites two dates, submission and rejection. One editor, Anita Christopherson of *Women and Beauty*, complains in her rejection letter that Pym needs stronger plots instead of 'situations' and is 'just a shade too objective, too watchful' (MS Pym 163, fol. 10). Responding the next day, a rueful Pym explains 'I am afraid that all my stories tend to be of the 'situation' rather than the 'movement and action' type – it is just the way one sees things which is very difficult, probably impossible, to alter very much' (MS Pym 163, fol. 11).

Most of the stories are difficult to date, with the exception of those she saw published: 'The Jumble Sale' (later retitled 'The White Elephant') for *Woman and Beauty* in 1949; 'Across a Crowded Room', July 1979, commissioned by the *New Yorker* magazine at the height of her resurrected popularity; and 'A Christmas Visit', written in 1977 at the request of *Church Times*. This ecclesiastical commission, says Holt, 'gave her great pleasure since she enjoyed quoting items from this publication in her novels' (CTS, 327). Indeed, a diary notation two months before the request notes,

> And a very nice thing – I had a letter from the Editor of the *Church Times* saying that although they didn't now normally have space for novel reviews he was going to review mine in November (the new one and the reprints) if only because I had given so many splendid free commercials. (AVPE, 307)

These short fictions contain many of the same conventions that Pym would later develop in full-blown novels: recurring characters, autobiographical detail, and her characteristic themes of love, loss, and making do. Kaufman's article recognises this pattern, and he structures his argument around eight stories which for him best embody 'her most central concerns': 'The Day the Music Came', 'English Ladies', 'The White Elephant', 'Back to St. Petersburg', the radio play 'Something to Remember', 'Goodbye, Balkan Capital', 'So, Some Tempestuous Morn', and 'Across a Crowded Room'. The last three along with 'A Christmas Visit' make up the four stories chosen by Hazel Holt for *Civil to Strangers*. Unarguably these are among the best the collection contains.

The less successful stories, however, – the fragments, rejections, and discarded efforts – though sometimes wooden, artificial, or underdeveloped, contain moments of brightness. At their worst, they reveal an unpracticed voice struggling for a mature style; at their best they reflect Pym's special polish, with familiar themes and recurring characters. Miss Doggett and her much put-upon companion Jessie Morrow of 'So, Some Tempestuous Morn' will make further appearances in *Crampton Hodnet* and *Jane and Prudence*; Mark and Sophia Ainger and cat Faustina are borrowed for 'The Christmas Visit' from the then unpublishable *An Unsuitable Attachment*; Ned, the manipulative homosexual of *The Sweet Dove Died*, becomes a priggish dinner partner in 'Across a Crowded Room'. Excellent women searching for 'something to love' are the focus of 'The Day the Music Came', 'English Ladies', and 'Goodbye, Balkan Capital', and receive fine discussion in the Kaufman article.

Hazel Holt has pronounced the four stories included in *Civil to Strangers* 'a final selection' from the unpublished material in the Pym collection, so it seems unlikely that the lesser pieces will reach the Pym public. Holt recognises that Pym 'never felt comfortable in the more rigorous confines of the short story. She needed space to develop her characters and 'to load every rift with ore', with detail and observation' (CTS, 4). But the more obscure pieces have their moments of comic success and bear witness to alternate moods and techniques attempted along the way to her novels of manners.

Oddly enough for a writer who often mined her own experiences for her novels, the most directly autobiographical of the short stories are the least satisfying. 'Trivial Rounds and Common Tasks' (MS Pym 94, fols 230–46) presents a disjointed series of set-pieces, usually conversations between a character named Barbara, recently disappointed in a love affair with Henry Harvey, sister Hilary as naif, and Mrs Pym as peacemaker. In brittle dialogue patterned after the 'precise, formal conversation' Pym admired in Ivy Compton-Burnett, family discussions reveal Barbara's bitterness in being excluded from a holiday abroad with friends while the scenes shift rapidly from meals, to social gatherings, to shopping trips. The tone alternates between Hilary's teasing and Barbara's complaining, and the few comic moments grow out of her own unhappiness:

> 'No,' said Barbara, 'I am not in very good spirits. I have had a letter from Jock [her friend Robert Liddell], and I feel I should be with them in Italy. They did not ask me if I would care to go. It did not occur to them. No, I must stay in Oswestry, writing novels that no publisher will take. I must not see the beauties of Italy. I must not enjoy the sunshine there. They did not think that I might like to have accompanied them. Yes, Henry might have thought of it, but he would not wish me to be there. No, I understand that. Jock might have thought of it too, but he knew it would be more than I could bear. One does not want to go about the continent bearing a burden, he could see that.'
>
> 'Surely you would not have had to carry your own luggage?' said Hilary, who had come into the room.

'Are Henry and Jock not even gentlemen enough for that?' asked Mrs Pym.
'Would they have made you carry their luggage as well as yours?' asked Mr Pym with rising indignation in his voice.
(MS Pym 94, fols 236–7)

The comedy suffers under the thinly disguised pain, and the jumpy nature of the shifting scenes allows the reader little time to develop sympathy.

'Mothers and Fathers' (MS Pym 94, fols 1–15) also borrows characters directly from Pym's life but places them in a more fictionalised situation, inexplicably 'in the year eighteen eighty seven'. Here we see 'Miss Pym . . . forty three years old, with a vague face whose expression might once have been kind. Now she looked somehow withdrawn as if she had already lived her life and were merely marking time for the years that remained to her.' As in *Some Tame Gazelle*, Pym here imagines her circle of friends grown older, and she delights in private jokes, often at their expense. Taking belated revenge on her old love Henry Harvey (as she will again in her first published novel) she presents him as a tiresome academic, 'Twenty years of lecturing in foreign Universities had given him an emphatic way of speaking and an overbearing manner which made him much disliked.' Robert Liddell's 'precise' habits and his brother Donald's 'absent-minded' look are included, and Hilary becomes 'a handsome woman in the full bloom of middle age. Her husband was thin and dried up like a stick and seemed to live in his wife's shadow'. The story quickly disposes of Henry's Swedish wife, Elsie, and her indomitable mother, one by accident and one by suicide, and the plot rushes on to include the possibility of an incestuous marriage, a series of confessed indiscretions which realign parents and offspring, and the final reconciliation of Barbara and Henry – all in thirty pages.

'Mothers and Fathers' is noteworthy, however, for an uncharacteristic and poignant reference to the value of children, buried in a comic exchange between the sisters and concerning the Harveys' progeny:

'Well, seven is too many,' said Hilary. 'One is quite enough. None is better still.'
'I think we all like to hand ourselves on to the future,' said Barbara rather urgently.

> 'Yes, but not seven times. And anyway, I do not think there
> is much worth handing on in Henry and Elsie.'

Sexual and competitive undercurrents ebb and flow throughout the often stilted conversations and situations, culminating in the illegitimate daughter's incestuous attraction to her natural father. Not until late in her career would Pym include such overt sexuality in a full length novel, and seldom again such autobiographical characterisation.

Before leaving such characterisation behind, though, Pym would write her way out of another unhappy emotional engagement. Shortly after receiving the news of Henry Harvey's marriage, Pym met in December 1937 the handsome, intelligent, and highly ambitious Julian Amery. Six years younger than she, he was far less anxious to pursue a long term romance, and the relationship ended, as far as he knew, within two years. For Amery, today a prominent British statesman, prize-winning author, and Member of Parliament, the attachment was brief and forgettable. For Pym its romanticised memory pervaded much of her life and work. A handful of poems (MS Pym 97), periodic remembrances in diaries or notebooks, and several short stories attest to her compulsive interest in a young man who quickly outgrew their relationship. For nearly thirty years her notebooks commemorate such dates of importance as 'This time last year I met Julian again' (MS Pym 106) or '27. 3. 63 Julian Amery's 43rd birthday' (MS Pym 57).

Pym's lingering, even obsessive, attraction to Julian Amery has proven an uncomfortable subject to the friends and family of both. Hazel Holt discreetly disguised his identity in *A Very Private Eye* (calling him simply 'Jay') but later in *A Lot to Ask* includes a discussion of this brief and tentative relationship. The Bodleian staff prohibits circulation 'on the grounds of confidentiality' of that portion of Pym's memorabilia relating to Amery, and consequently several items listed in the Bodleian's catalogue are currently 'reserved from use'.[9] These include 'Reflections by Barbara Pym concerning herself and Julian Amery, *c*. 1939–1952, with (fol. 29) an envelope containing a pressed flower and a blue handkerchief. 29 leaves' (MS Pym 146), her letters from Amery (MS Pym 147, fols 1–36), and the short story 'The Love of a Good Woman' (MS Pym 93). Before these restrictions were imposed, Kate Heberlein included in her dissertation a synopsis of this story, the only one of the collection now unavailable to scholars.

The first section, set in 1873, shows Julian Avery (not Amery) as a spoiled, selfish, cruel ten-year-old. In the next section, set in 1883, Julian rejects the love of Barbara Pym because she is six years older than he and very plain. His father tells him to value the love of a good woman, and his friend Simon sees the nobility in her character and marries her. The third section, set ten years later, shows Barbara and Simon, very happily married and the parents of a daughter, discussing Julian's nine children and failure to get into Parliament.[10]

Heberlein calls this semi-autobiographical three-part story 'almost unadorned and unmediated wish fulfillment' on Pym's part.

A similar but unrestricted story, untitled, undated, and probably inspired by these unrequited feelings, sets forth a common theme for Pym: the older woman in love with and spurned by a younger man. MS Pym 98, fol. 38 tells of a governess in love with the eldest son of the household where she is employed. He marries briefly but when that marriage dissolves, he proposes to the still devoted heroine. The story ends when cruelly he changes his mind. The age difference between the characters, the difference in their social class, and the double rejection clearly grow from Pym's emotional involvement with Julian Amery.

The single work, apart from 'The Love of a Good Woman', that most obviously owes its genesis to this one-sided relationship is the bittersweet 'Something to Remember' (MS Pym 96 fols 217–29) begun as a novel in 1940 and cited in her diary as 'for Julian' (MS Pym 106). Rewritten as a radio play and transmitted February 1, 1950, 'Something to Remember' owes much to Pym's imagined rejection by Julian Amery, but takes on the special aura of myth or fairy tale as well.

A paid companion to the formidable Miss Lomax, Edith Gossett as a young woman had a brief association with the dashing, if somewhat callow, Simon Sheldonian. When Simon, like Amery destined for Vienna and the Diplomatic Service, spouts some shop-worn bit of flattery, 'what lovely eyes you have', the young Edith knowingly responds ' . . . it's a safe thing to tell anybody. You can usually say a person has fine eyes even if they have no other good features.'

Simon's mother and a friend watch this anemic flirtation from the sidelines and they provide the social commentary on the suitability of the match, predicting its outcome correctly:

Lady Sheldonian: Simon's so *naughty*! I don't know what he's been saying to the vicar's girl. She's really looking quite pretty. He's probably been telling her what lovely eyes she has. Dear Simon, his compliments are all rather obvious ones.

Lady R.:   She's a very nice girl. Brought me a cup of tea at the garden party – young people often don't trouble to show any consideration for their elders. She'll make a good wife for somebody – some clergyman or schoolmaster, of course. Most suitable.

Lady S.:   But not for a budding diplomat. It would be a pity if she got any ideas about Simon. Not that she would, I'm sure, she seems such a very sensible girl, but I'm afraid Simon is rather naughty sometimes.

                                                           (MS Pym 96, fol. 220)

Besides undercutting his moral worth as Edith's suitor from this early point in the story, Pym builds this bittersweet comedy of manners around the social position of the paid companion and her society's expectations that she will fulfill a predetermined role. Edith, certainly a Cinderella derivative, describes this role in self-deprecating terms, 'There's certainly nothing special about me. I buy the wrong wool for Miss Lomax. I decorate the window that nobody will notice at Harvest Festival. I iron dresses for other people to wear at parties.' She tolerates her dim life with Miss Lomax and even manages a comic-ironic self awareness: 'If I were an object you might send me to a rummage sale.'

When years later Simon returns to stand as MP for their district, he approaches Edith at a political gathering, a nameless, nearly faceless, envelope-stuffer for his campaign. He senses that they have met before, but of course cannot remember when, and like Cinderella at the prince's ball, Edith slips away before he learns her name. He must search to find her at her employer's house and the reunion, minus a glass slipper, is predictably awkward. When Simon suggests that they meet the next day, Edith coolly rebuffs him: 'Oh, you wouldn't have time and I don't suppose I would either. Besides, what would be the use?' Puzzled by this response he leads up to what should be the fairy tale's climax: 'The use? Well, I don't really know, but ever since I saw you again I knew that you were just the person I'd been looking for. So I may as well say what I have to say now.' With an ironic twist, Edith's Prince Charming offers his proposal: his mother needs a companion – a 'nice, sensible person, and not too young.' Edith, he suggests, would be perfect.

The Cinderella effect is underscored in this radio piece by the many clocks and chimes striking and by the fade-ins of waltz music which clue the radio audience to scene changes. The rapid shifting from vignette to vignette that seems awkward in some Pym stories here effectively reinforces the theme of time passing Edith by. The large number of characters, eleven in all, provides a cacophony of demanding voices all calling for Miss Gossett's service.

Pym handles the problems of setting that radio presents by having two young voices, the niece and nephew of Miss Lomax, frame Edith's story, recreating and romanticizing the confrontation for the audience as they imagine the final scene in the hallway of their aunt's house:

> *Christopher*: Exquisite! The meeting again after all those years in that pitchpine hall with the stained glass in the front door and the encaustic tiles. And the elephant's foot umbrella stand with Aunt Maud's stick and the umbrellas . . . James could have made something wonderful out of it.

The stuffy cloistered house, the diplomat arriving home from years of service abroad, the patient, long-suffering woman living a circumscribed life on society's fringes – 'Something to Remember' reflects Pym's debt to James's novel of manners and allows her to deal artistically with disappointment in her personal life. Speaking to this issue of autobiographical characterisation, in a lecture given in the 1950s (MS Pym 98, fols 56–73) Pym told her audience:

> I think authors very seldom take a character straight from life, they are nearly always composite figures and the greatest source of material for character drawing is probably the author's own self. Even when a novel isn't obviously autobiographical one can learn a good deal about a novelist from his works, for he can hardly avoid putting something of himself into his creations. (MS Pym 98, fol. 66)

The stronger stories, like 'English Ladies', 'The White Elephant', or 'The Day the Music Came' draw familiar composite types but avoid direct correlations to her personal world. The fictional mask, however transparent, would hereafter disguise her family, friends, and lovers in the mature works, and would permit Pym necessary artistic distance.

In addition to autobiography, many of the stories draw upon established styles from familiar popular fiction. Among the un-published stories are some with O. Henry-like final twists, ('Poor Mildred') or parallel plotting ('The Day the Music Came'). In 'The Table' (MS Pym 94, fols 211–17) Pym offers a hallucinatory trick – a retired governess experiences a psychic time shift as she tours the stately home where she was once employed – and although the story itself is unsuccessful, Pym reuses the incident in her final novel. She borrows the conventions of the detective-mystery story in 'The Unfinished Flower' (MS Pym 94, fols 247–59) and the spy thriller in 'So Very Secret' (CTS, 271–324). Sex, murder, coincidence, and romantic retribution all appear to a degree rarely attempted in her later work.

One of the collection's grislier stories, 'The Unusual Ornament' (MS Pym 94, fols 270–91), oddly combines comedy and macabre suspense, with one element often undermining the other. The overly complicated plot, in somewhat longer than Pym's usual ten-to-fifteen page format, shifts from a small village setting to mountain climbing in Scotland and back again, only to end without resolution. Although the alternation of comedy and suspense seems sometimes out of balance, the technique is not inappropriate for Pym's biting wit. When the story opens we meet Honor Malden, widowed on her honeymoon in Scotland when her bridegroom stumbled (or was pushed?) over a precipice:

> What made it worse was that his body was never found, although a search lasting many days was organised. The natives thought that it had probably been sucked into a bog, as it had been known for the body of a sheep to disappear so completely as to leave no trace of its whereabouts. So there was really no reason why the body of a husband shouldn't vanish in just the same way. Indeed, some of the more frivolous people who had known Ernest Maldon said that he had looked so exactly like a sheep that they couldn't see what the difference was. (MS Pym 94, fol. 271)

Beatrice Newton, the timid narrator, is unusually dense for a Pym heroine and blind to the designs that Honor has on her husband, even when confronted directly. Already tiring of her recently acquired second husband, Honor confides to her friend that she 'had no idea Laurence was so nice', and that she was 'just *crazy* about him'. Surface appearances deceive Beatrice easily and she cannot conceive of Honor as a sexual threat:

> . . . it was difficult to know what to say when another woman declared that she was just crazy about your husband. Besides, Honor looked so stout and sensible in her tweeds, with little ends of mouse-coloured hair escaping from her bun, that it was hard to imagine her being crazy about anything. (MS Pym 94, fol. 284)

When the two couples set off to replicate the late husband's climb, Pym injects an unusual attempt at sexual dalliance, and hints obliquely at the possibility of some wife swapping. Watching their spouses walking arm-in-arm ahead on the trail, Honor's husband is about to suggest to Beatrice that 'exchange is no robbery' when all too coincidentally they spy a bleached skull on the edge of the bog and the moment is lost. The sexual suggestion is so timid on the part of both the would-be adulterer and the author as to go nearly unnoticed, and it disappears entirely as the identity of the skull becomes the story's focus.

Is it indeed the first husband? Is Herbert destined for the same fate on this climb? Is Honor held in check only by the presence of witnesses? The unanswered questions might make a fine denouement under other circumstances, but returning home, Beatrice's ambivalence about 'the unusual ornament', the skull now decorating her bedroom mantlepiece, only leaves the reader feeling similarly. The mixed intentions of the story, its comedy, suspense, and titillation, muddy its effect and the reader's response. Its whisper of sexual nonconformity, however, must reflect Pym's deliberate attempt to speak in a contemporary tongue, however subdued.

Several of these little known stories are useful comments on Pym's novels of manners for the aberrations they include rather than for the confirmation of already established characteristics. 'Unpast Alps' (MS Pym 94, fols 270–91), sent off to *London Mercury* magazine in November 1935 and rejected a month later, centers on a would-be poet cosseted in self-exile to create an epic, or at least a metaphysical, masterpiece. Pym buries this rare male protagonist under an avalanche of literary references and snippets of poetry, but redeems the story with two landladies. In the generous Mrs Horrocks and her 'hard faced' sister Pym creates comic gatekeepers for the dreamy poet in the attic. These two, clad in curlers and bedroom slippers, 'except on Sunday when [they] blossomed out in great glory', fiercely protect their gentleman lodger from suspicious callers, especially young attractive ones:

> . . . she couldn't help feeling that this young woman was up to no good. Why should she be coming to see Mr Cooley if not to blackmail him? It was absent-minded gentlemen like him that always got had. Besides she had red finger-nails, and in Mrs Horrocks' opinion that explained everything. (MS Pym 94, fols 266–7)

When they discover by eavesdropping that the young lady in question calls Mr Cooley 'Father', Pym skillfully records their disappointment in dialect laced with indignation:

> 'You could've knocked me down with a feather,' she said afterwards to her sister, 'I'd never've thought it of Mr Cooley.'
> 'You never know with lodgers,' said the sister, in a melancholy but none the less triumphant voice. 'Even those as seem most respectable has their skellington in the cupboard.'
> (MS Pym 94, fol. 267)

In the circumscribed world of the novels, few working class and almost no lower class characters exist, but Pym will continue to delineate character and class by minor shifts in their word choice and pronunciation. Important male characters play major roles in Pym's later work, but after 'Unpast Alps' none gets center stage.

In 'Poor Mildred' (MS Pym 94, fols 58–75) Pym experiments with convoluted plot machinations. Helena Tillotson is the adamantly devoted sister of the vicar:

> Miss Helena's admirers always implied that Gabriel had been utterly destitute before she came to live with him, but it was questionable whether he was as happy under her rule as he had been when he lived alone. (MS Pym 94, fol. 59)

To protect her domineering position in the vicar's life Helena must dispose of the threat posed by the attractive new neighbor, Mrs Felicity Ireby. Borrowing from *Jane Eyre*, Pym has Helena invent for her unknowing brother a mentally deranged wife, confined to an institution in the north. All too predictably and without further question the lady suitor decamps at this revelation with a contrived promise never to communicate with the confused vicar.

Offstage and after several weeks, the lovers discover Helena's deception, and arrange for their solution to arrive in the morning's post. The telegram provides the story's first climax as Gabriel pronounces to his scheming sister: 'She passed away yesterday morning, very suddenly. Poor Mildred, it was a happy release. But every sorrow has its compensation. I am a widower now, and a free man.' If all this plot twisting were not enough, Pym provides a double climax and ends the story by assuring the reader that Helena's talents will not be wasted:

> . . . a few days later she saw in the same *Times* that contained the announcement of her brother's engagement to Mrs Ireby, the news that her elder brother's wife had died suddenly. Almost before the unfortunate widower had time to realise his loss, his sister Helena was on the doorstep with all her luggage. She had come to make a home for him. (MS Pym 94, fol. 75)

The story suffers on several accounts: from overplotting, from shop-worn characterisation, and from jarring breaks in the framework that provide rapid but clumsy plot-moving information.

Several of the weaker stories show Pym relying on the same or similar formal devices that she attempted in 'Poor Mildred'. 'The Rich Man in his Castle' (MS Pym 94, fols 121–31) compresses time in a three-part story that attempts too much for its limited space, juggling parallel scenes over a seventy year flashback. Three narrative disjunctions allow Pym more space than the short story usually provides, but still not enough room for the detailed pictures she draws best. Little character development occurs between the sections and the technique seems merely to alter setting and time.

One of the better stories, 'The Day the Music Came' (MS Pym 92, fols 116–26), is also sectioned although more justifiably than 'Poor Mildred' or 'The Rich Man in his Castle'. Its shifting narrators and mirrored behavior convey themes of isolation and timidity. Pym chooses for its settings grey London sidewalks, dimly-lit food shops, and gloomy basement cafeteria lines to reflect the sort of hidden embarrassment we all experience when detected in our foibles. Juliana, another of her familiar single women, lunches daily at a large downtown cafeteria, and her story provides a study in the art of eating alone: 'it could be very pleasant if you had an interesting book, but sometimes people got in the way and you couldn't concentrate, but would wonder about them, who they were, why they came here and what they talked about.'

Her favorite restaurant is 'a vast high-ceilinged room with baroque-style decorations of white and gold, now a little shabby'; real privacy was impossible at the closely packed tables, and the 'great expanse of the place . . . made you feel peculiarly separate and alone'. The usual crowd – solitary clergymen, sober-suited bank clerks, and dim typists, 'talking in low voices as if ashamed of their very ordinary conversations' – provides little to interest her until Juliana spies a tall gentleman accompanying an elderly woman. She immediately likens him to a favorite painting in the National Gallery of an unknown eighteenth century gentleman. His regular Friday appearances allow Juliana to build a fantasy life for him: ' . . . by taking out her mirror and pretending to attend to her face, Juliana could see him quite well, eating fish or drinking a glass of water. Not very romantic or interesting really, but her imagination was able to make stories out of very little.' Through the winter months she fantasises about his family, job, and suburban commuter life, while peering from behind the imitation marble pillars or discreetly tailing him down the sidewalk.

The seasons pass until, without warning one spring day, musicians arrive to entertain the lunch hour patrons, making the situation seem to Juliana 'at once romantic and ridiculous'. The combination of springtime and romantic music upsets her and after lunch she follows him aimlessly. Distracted, she pauses before an elaborate display of prepared food, contemplating 'a tray of cold meats, whose centrepiece was a cold bird of some kind, covered with aspic jelly and elaborately decorated'. When she turns to find herself face-to-face with her quarry, 'He was smiling – he was obviously going to speak to her', she flees in panic before any words can be exchanged. Taking refuge in yet another cafeteria, she dazedly fills her second lunch tray with a comic array of unwanted and unattractive food: 'a small salad full of beetroot, a plate of fish covered in a kind of yellow sauce, and a piece of steamed pudding.'

Growing calmer, she begins to rationalise, turning the non-event from defeat into victory: 'For whatever could they have said to each other? . . . She had made such a fool of herself that she could probably never come here again . . . . She drank some coffee and began to feel a little better. How stupid of him to think that she was interested in him. The conceit of men was something quite astonishing.'

The narration shifts abruptly here from Juliana's to the gentleman's point of view, and we learn that much of what she has imagined is reality – the wife, the job, the commuter train. Initially imbued with the glamour and elegance of the mysterious portrait in the National Gallery, he becomes demystified, even gains a name, Geoffrey. As we step into his consciousness for the story's denouement, instead of secretive trysts and romantic subterfuge, we find a bland suburban existence, a distracted wife, and company coming for dinner. Riding home on the evening train he probes his motives for approaching the mysterious lady of the restaurant. 'She had looked rather interesting, but whatever could they have said to each other? That was no way to begin an acquaintance and how could it have gone on? Madge and the children . . . quite impossible.' His rationalisation for not pursuing the encounter mirrors hers, even to the purchasing of unwanted food. Disconcerted by Juliana's flight he has grabbed the nearest available option to carry home for the evening's dinner party: the jellied decorated bird. Their dual responses, buying inappropriate food and resolving not to return for more unsuitable music, are finally their only connection.

At least two more stories, 'The Funeral' (MS Pym 92, fols 214–28) and 'A Few Days Before Winter' (MS Pym 92, fols 166–82), seem patently written for the women's magazine trade, providing the expected happily-ever-after pattern. Pym recognised that although there was a market for this sort of fiction, it was not her natural mode. Her stories, she heard from her literary agent, Graham Watson, were often 'unsalable', and what most women's magazines 'really do mainly want [is] the Boy meets Girl kind of thing which I am not at all good at' (MS Pym 147e, fol. 172). But she consciously tailored these two stories to meet the demands of those women's magazines.

In the first, Helen, elegant and urbane, returns from living abroad to attend her father's funeral and to help her spinster sister close up the family home. Nostalgia sets in as she remembers 'only the good things, the huge log fires in winter, carol singers coming into the hall, spring flowers in the wild part of the garden, peaches ripening against the sun-warmed bricks of the south wall.' When Roger, an ex-beau, arrives, old flames rekindle. Pym masterfully draws the opposing characterisations of the two sisters, each unaware of the other's insecurities and dreams. Meg misinterprets Helen's

unhappiness as boredom; Helen feels like a stranger, left out of a
select group:

> Being with a group of older women who had known her when she
> was a child took away her self-confidence and made her, a poised
> woman of thirty-two, feel like an awkward schoolgirl . . . some-
> how she did not seem to belong. She lacked the comfortable
> security, the cosy dullness, even, of their background. (MS Pym
> 92, fol. 217)

Meg has always assumed that in Naples seven years earlier
Helen had rejected Roger's proposal. Explaining with the careful attention to word choice that characterises the Pym heroine,
Helen replies: 'It was *he* who jilted *me*, you know, or rejected
me, perhaps. You can only be jilted if you're actually engaged,
I believe.' Uncharacteristically both for Pym and for this usually
reserved protagonist, Helen recreates the romantic balcony scene in
a detailed confession:

> 'We had a long talk at a party one evening, on a balcony
> overlooking the Bay of Naples. One of those long tortured sort
> of conversations – I expect that particular balcony had seen a
> good many of that kind . . . ' she paused, remembering the
> dark shining water below them, the glow of their cigarettes
> in the darkness, and the strong scent of some flowering shrub
> – all the trapping of the most obviously romantic kind and not
> Roger's background at all, nor her's either, though he had not
> believed it. She went on talking almost to herself. 'He said we
> were seeing each other in falsely glamorous surroundings, and
> that it wouldn't work when we were back in England.'

Pym too was stationed in Italy during the war and her diaries contain nearly a dozen ideas or incidents 'for Naples Poems or Stories'
(AVPE, 176), none as developed or as sentimental as this scene.
Reversing the sisters' roles to end the story, Pym frees Meg to leave
the village for London social work, concerts, and art galleries. Helen
will marry Prince Charming and repopulate the family home.

'A Few Days Before the Winter' (MS Pym 92, fols 166–82) also
ends with its heroine falling happily into the arms of her beloved,
but the exposition is shared with a pair of quintessentially Pym
schoolmistresses on September holiday. At the same hotel where

Lavinia Sedgwick has retreated to mope about the staleness of her eleven-year marriage, Miss Potter and Miss Dokes measure their own predictable lives against the glamour they imagine for her.

> 'She's certainly very *smart*,' went on Miss Potter, 'and that dress, almost the colour of blackberries, very unusual. I'm sure she does something to her hair, a blue rinse, perhaps, rather distinguished, she looks sad, doesn't she, and yet amused, as if she were remembering some joke . . . ' Miss Potter's voice trailed off undecidedly. The stranger disturbed her a little, made her feel dowdy and provincial in her flowered rayon afternoon dress, and her gin and lime a girlish, unsophisticated drink, the kind of thing women accustomed to drinking only with other women might order. (MS Pym 92, fol. 167)

The pictures of mealtime rituals, evenings in the hotel lounge, tonic walks along the beach or about the moor – all the typical behaviors of the middle-class tourist hotel – are lovingly detailed and grow out of Pym's familiarity with this scene. Visits both to family and to the Holts' West country home took her near many prototypes of what Lavinia labels an 'indifferent hotel in an obscure little Somerset town'; Hazel Holt can point out several candidates for this particular hotel or for the original Eagle House of *No Fond Return of Love*, and she recalls Barbara's fascination with the wide variety of their guests, like the many who appear in this story. Lavinia, who had 'forgotten that such types existed or that they could herd together in such numbers', is only dimly aware of her fellow vacationers as she hopes for the romantic reconciliation she has fantasised. The romance plot notwithstanding, Pym best uses 'A Few Days Before Winter' to catalogue a comic society grouped to observe and be observed on holiday, a cast she will reassemble in *No Fond Return of Love*.

The best stories of the collection, like the novels, are lightly plotted and manifest their energies in careful characterisation and elaborate detail. Instead of rapid movement, murder motives, or romantic climaxes, she presents in 'The White Elephant' (MS Pym 94, fols 292–300) a character and a scene as fully realised as any from the mature novels. In fact, Miss Edith Bankes-Tolliver, here of St. Mildred's parish, will reappear in *Excellent Women* as one of the distressed gentlewomen for whom Mildred Lathbury does her social work.

Lamenting to the young curate who visits, 'Oh, the district has gone down so . . . I don't know what my poor father and mother would have said,' Edith nevertheless preserves a shabby gentility around her. Unselfpitying and stiffly proud, she and her small flat epitomise the world of the Edwardian spinster.

> He gazed round the room, which was as full of objects as the room of an elderly lady must be, when she has only a small space in which to crowd a lifetime's possessions. The grand piano was covered with a piece of oriental embroidery and dotted with silver-framed photographs of heavy-moustached men in military uniform, full-bosomed Edwardian ladies and prim groups of young girls in flat straw hats. In one corner a bed was disguised with a paisley shawl, while a Japanese screen evidently hid cooking or toilet arrangements. (MS Pym 94, fol. 294)

This abundance of possessions, the accumulation of a lifetime, yields not a single donation for the Jumble Sale: 'You see,' she responds to the new curate's inquiry, 'I have all my treasures around me here – I couldn't part with them now.'

But she attends the sale, lured by the news that an old rival, now Lady Alice Hogarth, has contributed some 'good things.' Among the discarded jumble Edith discovers a tarnished silver picture frame containing the photo of the young clergyman lost years before to Alice's affections:

> Oh yes, he had fallen in love with her – one could admit it after all these years – and many people said that Alice had loved him too, even though she had married somebody else. Mr Gorringe wouldn't have been considered a *good* marriage, although he had been so handsome, dear Arthur, people didn't look like that in these days. (MS Pym 94, fol. 297)

The joy of the story resides in Pym's skillfully dramatizing 'that crucial moment when memory must be revised, personal history rewritten'.[11] When she returns home weak-kneed but purchase in hand, Edith's mood turns a mocking reverse as she examines the curate's photograph, 'the smooth hair, the high collar, the expression of almost sickly piety. Perhaps it served Mr Gorringe right.' Sweet revenge, fed on forty years of living alone, envisions the solemn-faced clergyman as the White Elephant he has become:

Miss Bankes Tolliver suddenly smiled to herself as she looked again at the pale, ponderous face, the small eyes, the rather large ears. (MS Pym 94, fol. 300)

Casting aside romance for economy she realises that the frame, on the other hand, will 'polish up nicely.' No doubt she can find another use for it.

This intrusion of reality onto cherished memory or fantasy will recur throughout Pym's works and force more heroines than Edith to reconstruct familiar fictions. When a private illusion is shattered by a contradicting revelation, the Pym woman will often compensate by denying the importance of the fiction, as in 'The White Elephant', or by ignoring the reality in favor of the fiction. Pym, says Kaufman, repeatedly explores,

> . . . the centrality of memory and fantasy, and dramatizes the opposition of past and present, youth and age, opportunity and loss, the romantic and the familiar. Her most interesting characters, all women, typically treasure- up memory or elaborate present experience into fantasy. At the moment when reality intrudes, there is crisis and then a variety of response: either flight, or determined restoration of memory, or resignation, or release.[12]

A variation on the pattern occurs in 'They Never Write' (MS Pym 94 fols 218–29) in which we watch the young heroine's unreciprocated yearnings for a reluctant suitor abroad gradually shift to the less glamorous but more available curate at home. Learning Icelandic to please one man is displaced by teaching in the Sunday School for another; the fantasised ideal is rescaled to accommodate reality.

Two minor stories, 'The Pilgrimage' (MS Pym 94, fols 44–57) and 'An Afternoon Visit' (MS Pym 92, fols 40–50), employ similar coming of age themes, as young female protagonists give up romantic paradigms for more realistic points of view. This convention recurs throughout Pym's work, but usually with older protagonists who are forced to rescale favorite hopes or expectations in light of dwindling possibilities. Neither of these two stories is particularly well developed in character or setting, and each returns its heroine to her appropriate young man, wiser from her experience yet undamaged by the loss of a favorite fiction.

Closely related to these stories, 'Goodbye, Balkan Capital!' (MS

Pym 92 fols 245–261), included in the volume *Civil to Strangers and Other Writings*, offers a heroine, Laura Arling, who in the course of the story must also readjust a lifelong fantasy. Like Edith of 'Something to Remember', Laura has shaped a life of memory on the basis of a single romantic evening with a young Oxford student, Crispin, another Julian Amery type. They have neither met nor corresponded since the night of the Oxford Commemoration Ball decades before, but Laura has filled her life with imagining Crispin's glamorous career of foreign embassies, affairs of state, and wartime service to his country.

As in the earlier stories, autobiography grows into fiction for 'Goodbye, Balkan Capital', here inspired by war time. A diary entry for 23 April 1941 notes, 'After tea began writing a story about the Balkans and me (perhaps) which I thought might do for *Penguin New Writing*.' The initial inspiration seems to have been a radio news report suggesting that the staff of the British legation to Belgrade (possibly including Julian Amery) had disappeared under mysterious circumstances. Besides adding another element of intrigue and impending danger to the heroic image of Amery that Pym adored, the incident provided another chance to link their lives fictionally, and this time, ironically.

Crispin, like Amery for Pym, never ages in Laura's imagination, 'For she could not think of him as fat or bald, the brightness of his hazel eyes dimmed or hidden behind spectacles, his voice querulous and his fingers gnarled with rheumatism', and she always plays her memories of him before a romantic backdrop strewn with flowers to accentuate 'his dark good looks.' She has followed his career, poring over encyclopedia pictures of each new locale to which he is posted, 'as familiar to her as if she had really trudged round them on a wet afternoon'.

The plot of the story turns on Laura's accidental discovery of Crispin's obituary in the local newspaper. Instead of the wartime life of codebooks and secret documents that she had imagined, Crispin had retired from the diplomatic corps five years before to live quietly with his sister in a nearby village.

> When she had recovered from the first shock Laura found herself grieving not so much for his death, as that could make no practical difference to her, but for the picture she had of him. The remembrance of her wonderful imaginings about his journey made her feel foolish and a little desolate, when all the time he

had been perfectly safe in an Oxfordshire village, his life as dull as hers. He might even have been an Air Raid Warden. She paused, considering this possibility for Crispin with amusement and dismay. (CTS, 354)

The fantasy must be abandoned, it would seem, in light of this new information. But the idea that her own small dangers are greater than those she had lovingly imagined for Crispin is unpalatable. For Laura the fiction proves more durable than the reality and she makes a conscious decision to continue it: she will deny the Oxfordshire graveyard, and remember him always in the Balkans, 'in the dangerous places. There would always be something of him there.'

More interesting than this romantic fantasy, however, is Pym's recreation of what Laura calls 'all the rather ludicrous goings-on of a country town that sees nothing of the war'. The long central section, detailing Laura's night of volunteering at the village First Aid Post, allows Pym to construct this story on the conventions of the novel of manners. The claustrophobic setting, the cast of eccentric personalities, the small details that determine mood and define character, all shape a story more like her familiar novels and less forced than most of her short pieces. For this evocation of wartime country life, rather than for the romantic plot, the story deserves attention.

The accoutrements of wartime caution are all here: the blackout curtains, the tin helmets, the gas mask's 'cool rubbery smell and tiny space of unbreathed air'. Evacuee children arrive for a brief stay, 'labels tied to their coats, haversacks and gas masks trailing on the ground'. Laura shrouds her flashlight for an evening walk to avoid its detection by enemy aircraft, but the act evokes childhood memories of more peaceful times – 'The bulb was swathed in tissue paper and tied as on a pot of jam, so that she wanted to write on it "Raspberry 1911" as their mother used to.' Food shortages mean fewer options, not starvation, and Laura and her sister resort to creative menu-planning with locally available resources:

Lord Woolton had said that we must make more use of oat-meal . . . and they were going to have savoury oatmeal for supper tonight. One couldn't honestly say that it was very nice, but it was filling and made one feel virtuous and patriotic, especially when eggs or something out of a tin would have been so much more tasty. But Janet had banned all tin opening and the eggs were being pickled for next winter, when they would be scarce or *difficult*, that was the word she had used. (CTS, 348)

Pym here employs one of her favorite combinations for this household: two sisters, Janet, like Hilary Pym Walton, strong and competent; Laura, like Barbara, 'dreamy and introspective.'

Their village, like Oswestry where Pym spent the early war years at her family home, was near enough to Liverpool for them to hear the 'sinister purring' of enemy planes on bombing raids. The town has the usual share of petty rivalries – Janet has 'resigned from the ARP after a disagreement with the Head of the Women's Section. It had started with an argument about some oilcloth and had gone on from strength to strength, until they now cut each other in the street' – but war has cut across social boundaries and created a rare classless community. With almost dreamlike reverie Pym describes the warm feelings of camaraderie and companionship during evenings at the civil defense shelter as the volunteers wait for casualties that blessedly never come.

The most unlikely people were gathered together, people who would otherwise never have known each other, bound as they were by the rigid social conventions of a small country town. Conversation was animated and ranged over many topics, horrible stories of raid damage, fine imaginative rumours, titbits about the private lives of the Nazi leaders gleaned from the Sunday papers, local gossip and grumblings about ARP organisation. Time passed quickly, an hour, two hours. The throb of enemy planes was drowned with voices until everything was quiet, except for the chatter and the welcome hissing of the Primus from another room. Everybody began to get out their little tins of biscuits, rare blocks of chocolate were broken up and shared, like the Early Christians, Laura thought, having all things in common. At last somebody came round with cups of tea on a tray and thick triangular slices of bread and margarine, with a smear of fish paste on each. No banquet was ever more enjoyed than this informal meal at one o'clock in the morning. (CTS, 350)

The volunteers settle down to Bridge or knitting, some smoking cigarettes or dozing fitfully in the hazy, crowded warmth of small, dimly lit rooms: 'The scene would have made a good subject for a modern painter; there was nothing in Dali and the Surrealists more odd than this reality . . . . As still life garnishings there were the tables covered with dressings, bottles and instruments, with all that their presence implied . . . . In a hundred years' time this might be a problem picture. What were these people doing and why?' (CTS, 351).

Pym loads this story with images of the Eastern European cities she loved, of trains rushing through the darkness, and of the excitement and intrigue of foreign service, but she grounds the work by alternating Laura's imaginings of these scenes with the reality of the citizens on the home front. A flight of fancy is interrupted by the sounding of the local siren:

> A beautiful note sounded through the room, piercing and silvery as the music of the spheres must sound. It was the All Clear. In a surprisingly short time the blanket covered shapes became human and active, everything was put away and they walked out into the sharp, cold air, their voices and footsteps ringing through the empty streets. They were all much jollier and noisier than they normally would have been, because they were up at such an odd hour of the morning and they felt the flow of virtue which comes from duty done. (CTS, 352–3)

Penguin New Writing, 1941 rejected 'Goodbye, Balkan Capital', as Pym records without comment: 'Did a little writing and washed my hair. Had 'Goodbye Balkan Capital' back' (CTS, 328). She pencilled the rejection onto the front of the manuscript, but also notes the word count – 'c. 4,300 words', a self-reminder for the day she would submit it again.

Her writings for the radio in the late 1940s and 1950s proved more saleable than the short stories. Besides 'Something to Remember', she wrote radio scripted adaptations of H. Rider Haggard's *She* and of her own novels *No Fond Return of Love* and *Excellent Women*. Three short comic pieces fared less well. 'How I Distempered a Room' (MS Pym 96, fols 16–19), a comic meditation on the trials of home-decorating, and a play about anthropological superstitions, 'Parrots' Eggs' (MS Pym 96, fols 129–52) went unsold. For 'The Rectory' (MS Pym 96, fols 153–66), a radio play of parish rivalries, Pym was only partially paid since the series was cancelled before her work could be produced.

None of these radio pieces breaks new ground for Pym and

often the characterisation is sketchy, but the medium seemed more compatible to her style than the compression of the short story. Of her lack of success with publishers for her stories she wrote, 'Shall I ever succeed – I begin to doubt and now is a hopeless time to try . . . It seems that the best stories nowadays are more atmospheric than anything else – incomplete rather than rounded off – anyway they mustn't be too long as my things generally are' (CTS, 328). Radio offered the chance for developing characters and plot solely through rapid narrative shifts and the tonal interplay of dialogue. It was a challenge that she met, but all the while most of her energy went toward the novels, where she would find the unconstricted space and leisurely tempo more suited to her style.

3

The Early Novels

Perhaps not surprisingly, given the abrupt caesura in her publishing career, Barbara Pym's novels group themselves handily into categories: the earliest, most broadly comic – *Crampton Hodnet, Some Tame Gazelle, Civil to Strangers*, and *Excellent Women*; the 'middle' novels, confident, literary, and brimming with detail – *Jane and Prudence, Less Than Angels, A Glass of Blessings*, and *No Fond Return of Love*; and the final, more problematical group – *An Unsuitable Attachment, An Academic Question, The Sweet Dove Died, Quartet in Autumn*, and *A Few Green Leaves*. The eight novels comprising the first two groups share a lightness of spirit and tone and inhabit such similar comic worlds that they can be examined together as Pym's earliest efforts in the novel of manners. These are the works that first enlist Pym's fans, the ones which establish her consistency and satisfy all the criteria for something 'very Barbara Pym'.

Examined chronologically, this group exhibits characteristic themes and intents, but shows little evidence of artistic growth or change, or of labored efforts toward perfecting her craft. As Philip Larkin notes:

> All six of Barbara Pym's novels (published between 1950 and 1961) open on to [her] world from different angles: England in the 1950s, and the lives of youngish middle-class people, educated rather above the average and sometimes to a background of High Anglicanism, who find for the most part that the daily round, the common task, doesn't quite furnish all they at any rate do ask. As novels they exhibit no 'development'; the first is as practiced as the last, the observation, the social comedy, the interplay of themes equally expert.[1]

These novels do not evolve in a Darwinian fashion, each progressively better or more complex than the previous; rather, they accumulate, piling up their attributes to form a unified, if disjunctive, whole.

Although her confidence in her own talent was severely shaken during the long years of rejection and non-publication, Pym from her earliest days never doubted that she would be a writer, or that the extended form of the novel would suit her style. The juvenilia show an early self-confidence and the presumption of success. Hilary Walton has stated that their parents championed each girl's artistic talents, nurturing and encouraging public performance: art was to be shared, a gift or bond that extended the social group. Whether as a child directing and performing in her own Easter operetta or as a young Oxford graduate sharing her first novel with the friends it parodied, Pym perceived of herself as a writer and sought an audience for her talent.

An awareness of this audience pervades even the diaries, as though Pym assumed that their musings would not always be private. 'February 20, 1941: This evening I was looking for a notebook in which to keep a record of dreams and I found this diary, this sentimental journal or whatever you (Gentle Reader in the Bodleian) like to call it' (AVPE, 104). Surely only half in jest, the diaries refer several times to future scholars poring over her not-yet-written 'works', and she makes early plans for disposing of her literary remains: 'Wouldn't it be marvelous if you could give all your love letters to the Bodleian and then go and read them 30 years later!' (AVPE, xiv). Missing diary pages, admittedly ripped out and burned, attest to her awareness of possible public inspection of private papers. A consummate saver, she carefully preserved multiple drafts of most of her writing, even the discarded attempts that she had no plans for reworking, always conscious of future readers.

As early as three years before her death she began seriously to consider the disposition of her work, after receiving several inquiries from interested purchasers. An anonymous request through a reputable agent prompted her to seek Larkin's advice:

> I have had a letter from Rota, the antiquarian bookseller, acting on behalf of an American University (he doesn't say which) wanting to buy some or any of my manuscripts or typescripts of my immortal novels! . . . Ought one to bequeath one's MSS to some English University (much to their dismay)? I imagine you must always be having requests for the scraps of paper you

keep by your bed to write down things. What do you do about it? (AVPE, 314)

Larkin and Pym shared a distaste for the idea of over-eager (usually American) graduate students building their careers on the shards of another's reputation. Several letters refer to the horror of being 'done' by the sort of archetypal academic that Larkin parodies in one of Pym's favorite poems:

Posterity

Jake Balokowsky, my biographer,
Has this page microfilmed. Sitting inside
His air-conditioned cell at Kennedy
In jeans and sneakers, he's no call to hide
Some slight impatience with his destiny:
'I'm stuck with this old fart at least a year;

I wanted to teach school in Tel Aviv,
But Myra's folks' – he makes the money sign –
'Insisted I got tenure. When there's kids – '
He shrugs. 'It's stinking dead, the research line;
Just let me put this bastard on the skids,
I'll get a couple of semesters leave

To work on Protest Theater.' They both rise,
Make for the Coke dispenser. 'What's he like?
Christ, I just told you. Oh, you know the thing,
That crummy textbook stuff from Freshman Psych,
Not out for kicks or something happening –
One of those old-type *natural* fouled-up guys.'
(from *High Windows*)

Sharing this distrust of American scholars – 'Wouldn't like any of my MS handwritten material to go to USA to be pored over by earnest Americans (not even Jake Balokowsky)' (AVPE, 315) – Pym follows the first of six alternatives suggested by Larkin for disposing of her papers – '(1.) Do nothing.' Having made that decision, she replies with relief, 'And now my literary remains are all in a large cardboard box in my bedroom' (AVPE, 317). At her death, faced with an expanded collection of Pym manuscripts in even more cardboard boxes, Hazel Holt and Hilary Walton offered to move the whole group to the Bodleian, confident that she would have approved: ' if there was any chance of a British Library or University being interested I would gladly leave the whole lot to them, even without getting money' (AVPE, 316).

Ironically perhaps, the most frequent visitors to the Department of Western Manuscripts, according to the Library staff, have been American. Colin Harris writes 'we are expecting another 'invasion' of Pym scholars from the U.S. . . . It will be interesting to see how we manage to cope with the demand. At one point last year we had four scholars consulting the Pym manuscripts at the same time. Strangely there is, as yet, no great interest from English scholars.'[2] To date, nearly all the critical work published on Pym's life and work, apart from Larkin's appreciation and some brief periodical reviews, has come from Americans.

Beyond the careful preservation of the product, Pym's work habits and methods show a consistency that her publishers did not. The methodical notebook and diary keeping were only a part of the process which led to the generation of thousands of pages of script over her lifetime. Her creative urge was intense, and even when future publication seemed unlikely, she wrote steadily and regularly. The overwhelming need to write is probably most apparent during the publishing dry spell. When the publisher Longman's rejected *The Sweet Dove Died* with the faintly damning comment 'well written', she attempted to alter and constrict her writing methods: 'Don't actually *write* anything for a year, but go on making "copious" notes about everything.' The very next diary entry shows her frustration with this self-imposed regime: 'Writing 'copiously' in notebook – don't think I can wait a year' (MS Pym 65, fol. 20). Observations and ideas continue to be recorded in her usual fashion, and she never again seriously considers abandoning her craft. 'The worst of writing is that you get addicted to it – you might say that it is habit-forming' (MS Pym 98, fol. 82).

The luxury of writing full time would not be hers until retirement. As a young woman, heady with the success of *Some Tame Gazelle*, she considered and then quickly rejected the financial uncertainty of earning a living by one's typewriter:

> I don't know of anything to equal the thrill for a novelist at having a first novel accepted. A literary career now stretched before me! I wrote a short story for a woman's magazine and that was accepted. I was paid 30 guineas for it – just about what I was

earning per month at my job. I even thought of giving up my job and becoming a full-time writer . . . Dreams are wonderful things but I have always been prudent, even unadventurous, certainly not rash . . . The next story was rejected and the one after that . . . I haven't the sort of temperament to be able to write something to pay the rent – I had to have the peace of mind that a regular salary, however small, brings, and so I kept on working, and writing novels in my spare time. (MS Pym 98, fol. 80)

No aristocratic life of international travel and leisure for this novelist of manners, but rather the kind of nine-to-five job that many of her characters would hold. Working at the International African Institute from 1958 until her retirement in 1974, she was unable to follow 'the ideal pattern of starting to write first thing in the morning, after breakfast say, and on a weekday' (MS Pym 98, fol. 75). In a letter to Philip Larkin she imagines the delightful decadence of the full-time writer: 'What would one do for the rest of the day, having spent the morning writing? Lead a worthless life, I suppose, and how pleasant it might be for a bit. Then one would get involved with the English church – there would be no escape' (AVPE, 205). Instead she spent her days in the tiny office she shared with Hazel Holt, editing the 'scrupulously produced, prestigious, and prized-by-the budding-scholar journal, the IAI's *Africa*'.[3]

Here, between intense periods of work and with quarterly publication deadlines to meet, Pym occasionally managed to borrow time for her own work. Attesting to her office creativity are letters to friends written from her desk, and notes for novels jotted on secretarial pads or on the small, 4' x 5' *While You Were Out* or *Don't Forget* memos provided by the institute. For the original drafts of her novels she often carried home old abstracts from *Linguistic Studies* or carbon copies of letters to *Africa*'s contributors, to type her stories on their reverse sides. Commenting on this recycling habit, she stresses its frugality over its possible breach of privacy:

I don't think we spend so much on stationery now – my first drafts are usually done on the back of old office scrap paper with the carbon copies of letters to anthropologists on the other side. (MS Pym 98, fol. 74)

Juggling office responsibilities and novel writing often required compromise. When she sat down to work it was 'mainly at week-ends and on holiday – sometimes even in the very early morning, trying to get in a couple of hours before I went to the office. (But that meant I sometimes used to fall asleep in the middle of the day, so I couldn't keep it up for long)' (MS Pym 98, fols 75–6). Working methodically, usually 'straight on to a typewriter with a hand written draft or a few notes or nothing' (AVPE, 315), she completed six novels in eleven years, all the while editing monographs, letters, and reviews of 'irritating authors' for the upcoming issue of *Africa*.

Writing in the early morning or snatching a few moments during the work day, Pym mastered a technique that was methodical, productive, and usually private. Hilary remembers few occasions on which Barbara consulted her on a developing novel or discussed unfinished work, preferring instead to present a polished version for her sister's perusal. She recalls that they seldom conferred on work in progress: 'People ask "what I thought *when* . . . ?" or "what was she thinking *when* . . . ?", and I really don't know. Of course, she often showed me finished manuscripts to read for my opinion but not when she was still at work on a project.'[4] Hazel Holt, too, was offered nearly completed manuscripts, for her opinion or advice, 'largely technical', and most of her assistance during Pym's lifetime was as proof reader. Holt credits Pym with teaching her the 'craft of editing',[5] but with raw material drawn from the imperfect offerings of anthropologists, not from the writer's own hand.

With Larkin she consulted by mail on her artistic bottlenecks, even sending him the rejected *An Unsuitable Attachment* for his evaluation. The distance provided by their epistolary friendship, coupled with her confusion concerning the merit of this seventh novel, permitted this breach of her ususal practice. Larkin com-miserated, sharing his own embarrassment when once seeking professional approbation: 'I remember the tremendous trepidation and trembling with which I put my most cherished critical ideas to Mary McCarthy: Had she intended, etc. She listened to the end and then said, "No." That was all. Moments with the Mighty' (MS Pym 151, fol. 6). Larkin was more generous.

If she did not easily share the germination of her novels with friends and family, she did fill pages of the literary notebooks with her theories of how novels develop, mature, and change. Chief among her methods was what she called her observational tech-nique: 'the deliberate seeking out of experience to use in fiction' (MS

Pym 98, fol. 64). Whether this fondness for 'research' into the lives of ordinary people was her most or least attractive personality trait, it lay at the heart of her method. Recognizing that the researcher in this game approached her subject 'cold-bloodedly and consciously', and might well be considered an 'alarming, unpleasant sort of person', she was nevertheless seldom deterred when her curiosity was piqued.

The tools of this trade were varied. Public libraries provided such sources of information as telephone books, street maps, and contemporary reference books. *Who's Who* and *Crockford's Clerical Directory* listed genealogies, employment, addresses, and social and professional clubs for her subjects, and *Kelley's Directories* provided the street guides to follow up the investigation outside the library walls. She would search indexes of the anthropological books that crossed her desk for new characters' names, 'Gems From Crockford: de Blogue (formerly Blogg)' (MS Pym 44, fol. 3), or for comic conjunctions of information 'pottery, prawns, pregnancy, proverbs – I know I shall enjoy this' (MS Pym 48, fol. 3). Hazel Holt remembers joining the hunt and spending enjoyable lunch hours away from IAI in search of new material. Her husband Geoffrey smiles as he notes that while visiting them in Somerset, 'Barbara was never just "on holiday"; there was always something (or somebody!) to be looked into.'[6]

This fondness for 'detective work' contributes to all the novels, but comes to fruition with the character of Dulcie Mainwaring in *No Fond Return of Love*. Although this novel, published in 1961, appears chronologically in the middle of Pym's work, it explains much about Pym's technique for constructing the comic novel of manners and about her penchant for transposing 'ordinary' lives into her fictions.

It presents a protagonist whose kinship with her creator is undeniable: 'Clearly, Dulcie is Barbara – the most like her of all the heroines', says Hazel Holt, to whom Pym dedicates this work. Early in the novel Dulcie seeks approbation for the sort of genteel voyeurism in which Holt sometimes participated and on which Barbara doted:

> Perhaps the time will come when one may be permitted to do research into the lives of ordinary people . . . people who have no claim to fame whatsoever . . . . I love finding out about people, I suppose it's a sort of compensation for the dreariness of everyday life. (NFRL, 18)

It is on these lives of ordinary people that Pym constructs her canon, and with this heroine she demonstrates the technique. Nominally, Dulcie is a free-lance indexer, one who can ask: 'Do we all correct proofs, make bibliographies and indexes, and do all the rather humdrum thankless tasks for people more brilliant than ourselves?' (NFRL, 13). But her seemingly minor job fulfills a valuable social function: creating order out of chaos, overlaying the concrete on the abstract, and providing the means by which the efforts of one become useful to the group.

Apart from her functionary role, Dulcie's passion is for the details of others' lives. Unbeknown to her subjects, she dedicates all of her research skills to fleshing out the bare-boned scraps of information which capture her imagination. Reversing the process of the creative artist who develops character inductively, Dulcie deduces that anybody's world is knowable from empirical evidence, and the more challenging that evidence is to discover, the better.

> It was most satisfactory if the objects of her research were not too well known, either to herself or to the world in general, for it was rather dull just to be able to look up somebody in *Who's Who*, which gave so many relevant details. *Crockford* was better because it left more to the imagination, not stooping to such personal trivia as marriages or children or recreations. (NFRL, 44)

Preferring more left to the imagination, Dulcie becomes not the 'woman manquee' she fears, but the artistic developer of her own world. In dogged search of information about an attractive gentleman scholar whom she encounters in the novel's opening scene, Dulcie stakes out Aylwin Forbes's neighborhood. Under an assumed name, she crashes a jumble sale to check out both the inhabitants and their belongings, attends an evening church service where Aylwin's brother, Fr Neville Forbes, officiates, checks into a West country hotel owned by his mother, and prowls both a castle and a cemetery. She manipulates 'accidental' encounters, eavesdrops on private conversations, fibs discreetly to conceal her own identity, and generally stage-manages the course of several characters' lives – all with a disarming geniality that prohibits our disapproval.

Pym's playfulness in this novel shows up especially in its attempted plot intricacies. Plots generally are not Pym's strong suit, and most of the novels rely on an episodic or linear method of storytelling. Anita Brookner complains of her 'hasty improvisations of plot',[7] and even those critics who appreciate her talent agree with novelist Anne Tyler that 'in all of Barbara Pym's novels, character is everything',[8] and with critic Lotus Snow that 'Her conviction that the importance of trivia in the individual life matters more than dramatic or historical drama does not accommodate the cause-and-effect progression of plot.'[9] Pym herself recognised that her strength lay in character development and that for plots she should rely only on her best instincts and her narrow world.

> I am well aware that plots are not my strong point but I do feel that the everyday happenings of life are in their way as interesting as the more exciting things. I have sometimes been criticised for my love of triviality but I like detail in other people's novels and try to provide it in my own. (MS Pym 98, fol. 84)

> I suppose everyone who has ever written anything has had people come up to him and say 'I've just heard or seen something that would make a wonderful plot for you to write a book about' or words to that effect – but how very seldom can a writer use other people's ideas. For the writer, like the singer, has a range and if he is wise he will keep within that range. There is the well known story of Jane Austen when it was suggested to her by the Prince Regent's librarian that she should write a historical romance on the fortunes of the German royal family. Her reply was that although such a book might well be more popular than her pictures of domestic life in country villages, she could no more write a romance than an epic poem. 'I must keep to my own style and go on in my own way', she said. Of course it was sensible of her to reject the suggestion, but how interesting it would have been to see what she made of it! (MS 98 fols 57–8)

Pym's own plots are derived from the world she sees around her, employing the same talents with which she endows Dulcie Mainwaring. In creating this most Barbara Pym-like of heroines, the novelist presents in a fictional character the method by which she creates her comedies of manners, a method of observation borrowed, she says, from another:

> I also like Denton Welch's words, even though they make the novelist sound an alarming, unpleasant sort of person. (which

perhaps he is!) He says: 'Now as I write, I wonder if many of us ever think that, while we are talking, moving about our daily business, some stranger may be near us, listening, watching, melting away to write our words down in his little book at home, there to fix them as long as the ink and paper last, or longer still if they are found, printed and scattered broadcast all over the land.' Somebody may also be watching the novelist, of course! (MS Pym 98, fol. 56)

Before this observational technique becomes ingrained, Pym constructs her first two novels from other sources, relying on the autobiographical and the mythic for *Some Tame Gazelle* and on the near farcical for *Crampton Hodnet*.

Just weeks after finishing her degree, Pym left Oxford for Oswestry, resumed living with her family, and began her first full length novel, *Some Tame Gazelle*. This return was not uncommon for an unmarried daughter, since women of her age, education, and class often did not seek employment or independent living arrangements upon completing their schooling. Hazel Holt reminds us, 'At that period there was no pressure on girls to take up any sort of job or career, many of her social class simply remained at home until they married or as "the daughter at home" if they did not' (AVPE, 11). Barbara's return to her family satisfied them all.

I am staying at home this autumn [October, 1934] and not taking a job. I think I am going to enjoy it very much, being naturally contented. (AVPE, 45)

She wrote regularly in her journal, busied herself with domestic pleasures, and traveled a little. In July of that year she had drafted a short story 'about Hilary and me as spinsters of fiftyish', circulating it among the Oxford friends who were also included as characters. Encouraged by their approval, she spent the fall expanding the story into a 'novel of real people', revising and editing in accord with each rejecting editor's suggestions: 'They [Chatto] think it's too long and my character drawing too detached, but I have a style which is a pleasure to read, etc. I wasn't as depressed as I thought I'd be and even looked forward to cutting and improving it' (AVPE, 55).

The manuscript collection contains little documentation of these revisions, offering only an early draft of 604 folio leaves (MS Pym 2, 1–2), a notebook with 'Notes for . . . [the] 'Second version' (MS Pym

3), and the final printer's copy (MS Pym 4), a briefer 303 leaves. In the shorter second version, Pym removes the references to Germany and Finland and sharply reduces the overwhelming number of literary allusions (although retaining more than in any other of her published novels), asking herself in her journal, 'If you want quotations, why not have them at the beginnings of the chapters?' (MS Pym 3, fol. 2). A self-admonition to 'Go over all the characters and make them *worse* – as Proust did. Especially the Archdeacon. (and Mr Parnell)' results in sharpening those characters as well as that of her own Belinda, who becomes less sentimental and more wryly perceptive in the second version.

Revising the novel proved therapeutic as well as profitable. As was often the case for Pym, the creative drive sustained her in emotionally trying times and re-thinking *Some Tame Gazelle* was no exception. 'I can remember finding some solace in revising it when my mother was dying at the end of 1945 – it took my mind off what was happening in a way that nothing else could' (MS Pym 98, fol. 80).

Although they too had rejected the 1936 *Some Tame Gazelle*, the publishing firm of Jonathan Cape, Ltd. agreed fourteen years later at the urging of Robert Liddell to reconsider the novel and this time accepted it for publication. Liddell remembers:

> Jonathan Cape held out some hopes of publication in 1936, but 'falser than false Cressid', he disappointed those hopes. In 1945, when I was back in England from Egypt (where I had been for four years), I called on him in Bedford Square . . . . He spoke of Barbara's book, and I reacted warmly to his good opinion of it. He suggested that I should urge her to revise it, and send it in again. Thus I made my humble contribution to its ultimate appearance. When it did appear, and I reviewed it in Cape's journal *Now and Then*, I could say that my feelings on opening it may have resembled Cassandra's on receiving *Sense and Sensibility*: 'has she spoiled it? No', for despite every little change it was the book I had cherished in memory for more than fifteen years.[10]

Perhaps because of the autobiographical connections or the years of revision or the enthusiasms of a first novelist, *Some Tame Gazelle* is the gentlest, most sweetly comic of all Pym's works.

She says she wrote it 'for Henry' (MS Pym 103, fol. 5), also called 'Lorenzo' or 'Gabriel' in her diaries, and the 'great love of her life', according to Hazel Holt and Hilary Walton. Henry Harvey's affection for Barbara Pym during his university days was anything but consistent – days and nights of concentrated attention followed closely by a deliberately cruel, sometimes disdainful, distance. Her early devotion to him, however, never completely waned. At Oxford she darned his socks, typed his manuscripts, slept on his leopard-skin couch, read to him in his bath, and when he married Elsie Godenhjelm, wrote regularly to his wife as 'my darling sister'. Occasionally she balked at the one-sidedness of their friendship, 'I am beginning to feel the weest bit hostile towards Henry, and to think that the glamour of being his doormat is wearing off some' (MS Pym 102, fol. 54); but for many years Harvey epitomised for her the masculine ideal.

The pain of this relationship is reflected forthrightly in Pym's diaries and autobiographical short stories, and satirically in the life-long correspondence she maintained with Harvey, throughout his several marriages. A few of the longer works reflect her continued fascination: an early, unpublished novel, *Beatrice Wyatt,* also called *The Lumber Room,* (MS Pym 6, fols 1–3) takes a self-absorbed Henry Harvey figure for its hero; *Civil to Strangers,* begun in 1936, depicts 'a loving wife and a selfish husband'; *Some Tame Gazelle* recasts the pain of this unsatisfactory infatuation into comedy.

In a 1950 review a *Times Literary Supplement* critic misreads this novel as centering on the Henry Harvey character, the Archdeacon Henry Hoccleve, and complains that it 'is as restrained as its title suggests, and describes the relation of an archdeacon in a small country town with his wife and female parishoners. Apart from an excellent parody of a "literary" sermon, the book flows cheerfully on with little wit and much incident, and many readers will compare it unfavorably with the earlier novels of Mrs Thirkell.'[11] Most of the reviews, however, were complimentary, and Pym would later make comic use of this one, characteristically turning her own rejection into comedy.[12] Although the archdeacon may be one of Pym's most memorable clerics, the *Times* critic fails to see that this novel focuses squarely on the Barbara Pym character, Belinda Bede.

Philip Larkin in a letter dated 14 July 1964 wrote Pym, '*Some Tame Gazelle* is your *Pride and Prejudice,* rich and untroubled and confident, and very funny. John Betjeman was here a few weeks ago and we rejoiced over your work' (MS Pym 151, fol. 22). Hazel Holt calls this first novel, 'a considerable achievement . . . The observation and language were already mature, the cadences of speech were idiosyncratic and the handling of character wholly assured' (AVPE, 12). The twenty-two year old Pym imagines sister Hilary and herself thirty years in the future, settled happily in an unnamed village (remarkably like Finstock where the two would actually retire.) An assortment of unmarried women make up the majority of the town's inhabitants, spending their days in gossip and gardening, and catering to the whims of the local clergy – a married archdeacon and a series of anemic curates. A parade of intruders into this isolated setting provides the plot complications, minor as they are, and the resolution reaffirms the status quo. On this seemingly slight framework Pym constructs a study of the manners and morals of a community of women seen mainly through the eyes of its most representative member, Belinda – Barbara herself, imaginativley aged by thirty years.

The *roman à clef* aspect of *Some Tame Gazelle*'s characterisation might have been inhibiting if superimposed on three decades of her friends' post-Oxford careers. From her youthful perspective, however, Pym was free to imagine histories for her characters which in several cases came remarkably close to the truth. Robert Liddell, the Nicholas Parnell figure of the novel and called 'Jock' in Pym's diaries, remained a close friend, correspondent, and trusted critic. He says of *Some Tame Gazelle*:

> No doubt she wrote better later on, but this book seems more than any other to contain her essence. It is set in a small village inhabited or visited by many of us, her friends, but nearly forty years on. This is a brave and unusual idea for a novel . . . . For after a brief wartime marriage Hilary was always at her side, and in this way the *Tame Gazelle* was prophetic. Other people have not fulfilled her prophecies. Her great love, 'Lorenzo' did not become an Archdeacon, and rector of the parish where the two sisters lived – a gloriously comic character, given to extraordinary literary sermons, and still devotedly loved by Belinda; while Harriet spent her emotions easily on a series of curates. John Barnicot was not accidentally shot in Prague, 'looking on at a revolution'; I never became Bodley's Librarian.[13]

Strangely, since most of the characters are drawn from her Oxford circle of friends, *Some Tame Gazelle* is the Pym novel least tinted by realism. It has a pastoral setting, a broadness of characterisation approaching caricature, and a near fairy tale structure.

The village of the sisters Bede remains unnamed and its location unspecified, a brief train ride away from Oxford. As R. E. Long notes, it is 'not only small but also gives the impression of being sealed off hermetically from the outside world.'[14] Instead of the pastoral tradition that Long suggests it approximates, however, it is ripe ground for the novel of manners. A friendly, familiar, almost Utopian island floating in untroubled country waters, the village is difficult to place in a time frame. No clues exist to mark it as the 1950s or the 1930s or, indeed, even a half century earlier, so an element of timelessness pervades, and as in most closely knit communities, the closeness can generate both sympathy and claustrophobia. Pym writes several 'village' novels where these qualities combine, most notably *Jane and Prudence*, and *A Few Green Leaves*, but none as singly innocent, intimate, or feminine as *Some Tame Gazelle*.

For this is a community of women. The Archdeacon, the curate of the moment, and Harriet's perennial suitor Count Ricardo comprise the only significant male inhabitants. A parade of unattractive visitors marches through – a librarian and his assistant, a bishop, a wan curate or two – but it is the female characters who anchor the society. As in Mrs Gaskell's *Cranford*, although the ladies know 'all each other's proceedings, they are exceedingly indifferent to each other's opinions. Indeed, as each has her own individuality, not to say eccentricity, pretty strongly developed, nothing is so easy as verbal retaliation; but somehow good-will reigns among them to a considerable degree.'[15] Despite the subtle sexual competition, the occasional jealousy, and the awareness of social class that sometimes separates them, the women of this community are free to enjoy each other's company, with a lightheartedness that the men never share. At an impromptu tea party they overindulge in potato cakes, Belgian buns, and gossip:

> At tea they were all very gay, in the way that happy unmarried ladies of middle age often are . . . When they had finished . . . Edith suddenly began doing a Balkan folk dance which encouraged Harriet to give a very ludicrous imitation of Mr Mold's proposal. (STG, 169)

This spontaneous celebration among women who enjoy each other's company and share the small pleasures of their circumscribed lives typifies the atmosphere of *Some Tame Gazelle*.

At the center of the novel are the two sisters, as contrasting yet complementary as any comic duo. Belinda, tall and timid, given to fussing over small issues of propriety, is quietly devoted to the first love of her life, who married another. Harriet, jolly and plump, vivacious and impulsive, flirtatiously mother-hens the young curates who rotate through the parish. Edith Liversidge and Connie Aspinall, 'a kind of relation', serve as comic doubles for the sisters. Connie plays the harp and dreams of past glory and status as a companion to a lady in Belgrave Square; Edith, brusque and efficient, has an embarrassing habit of discussing her war work in mixed company: 'Work of rather an unpleasant nature too, something to do with sanitation' (STG, 15). On the upper end of the social scale the archdeacon's wife, the formidable Agatha, plays the role of the grande dame, and on the lower end is an assortment of dressmakers, shopkeepers, and Sunday school teachers.

Although it purports to present middle-aged versions of personalities familiar to Pym, the characters are curiously without pasts. Beyond a few very brief mentions of the friends' interaction at Oxford – books exchanged, sherry parties, a pair of crimson socks purchased on holiday in Venice – Pym seems to have consciously revised the novel to keep reminiscence at bay, removing several backward glances. In the first version, Mr Mold, the assistant librarian, recalls an unflattering image of the Barbara/Belinda of their Oxford days, 'a tall girl inclined to be fat, smart in an untidy sort of way, with a perpetual grin on her face and something of a roving eye' (MS Pym 2/2, fol. 327). The removal of many such personal references tightens the final version of the novel, but also severs the continuity of the characters' lives. Without the details of the thirty year imaginative leap, Belinda and Harriet seem static, unchanging, perpetually middle-aged, without other family, jobs, or connections outside the community. A single reference to 'their dear mother' seems jarring, the likelihood of a childhood remote. Only the immediate rituals and traditions built into the life of the village – garden fêtes, musicals, seasonal domestic duties – define them, not a real past of family, generational links to the land, or evidence of outside social engagement. Belinda Bede reflects, 'There was something frightening and at the same time comforting about the sameness of it all' (STG, 16).

There is comfort too in the plot symmetries and ironic pairings of the novel. The book spans a calendar year, ending as it began with the welcoming of a new curate to the parish. In between fall

two marriage proposals and two refusals for the Bede sisters, and
the novel concludes with two weddings, more than satisfying the
dictates of the fairy tale that all live happily ever after.

In her work on Pym, Jane Nardin likens *Some Tame Gazelle* to a
Jane Austen novel 'stood on its head.'

> The plot situation that Austen uses in every one of her novels
> except *Northanger Abbey* is this: a group of young unmarried
> women, some of them sisters, are living peacefully in the country,
> when their peace is disturbed by the entrance of disruptive
> individuals into the previously quiet life of their village. The
> young women and their families must, through a process of
> difficult, yet ultimately beneficial change, adjust to the novelties
> of thought, feeling, manners, and morals that the disruptive
> characters have introduced. Whether these characters and the
> ideas they represent are absorbed, expelled, or changed, the
> process of dealing with them alters the world of the novel and
> helps the young characters to make their most significant decision
> – the choice of a marriage partner – properly. Hence the novels
> always end comically, with celebratory marriages that prove that
> significant lessons have indeed been learned.[16]

Here, however, she sees an ironic reversal of the Austen marriage
plot, since both Belinda and Harriet refuse their respective suitors,
choosing instead the familiar pattern of their peaceful cohabitation.
At the climactic wedding ceremony which gathers all of the established community in celebration of the future, Belinda rejoices in the
preservation of the past, suddenly realizing that 'she was happier
than she had been for a long time. For now everything would be
as it had been before those two disturbing characters Mr Mold and
Bishop Grote appeared in the village . . . . Dr Johnson had been so
right when he had said that all change is of itself an evil' (STG,
250–1). Like virginal princesses cloistered from unwelcome suitors,
they narrowly escape marriage to the wrong men, choosing instead
lives dedicated to comfortable routine and to what Nardin calls
'passionate celibacy'.[17]

Since the novel of manners deals so often with the ramifications
of proper or, more likely, improper social behavior, the boundaries
of propriety must be clearly established. Belinda Bede's careful
measurement of acceptability, usually most strictly applied to herself, sets the tone for the moral code of the village. Nice people,

for instance, do not not mention toilet facilities or exhibit their underwear, even inadvertently:

> The new curate seemed quite a nice young man, but what a pity it was that his combinations showed, tucked carelessly into his socks, when he sat down. (STG, 7)

They do not patronise public houses before noon:

> One must be careful not to judge people too hardly and I dare say that in a town there is really no harm in a man going into a public house for a pint of beer in the morning, but these things *are* regarded rather differently in a village and I should have thought he would have realised that. (STG, 100–1)

Even casual visits to each others' homes must conform to unspoken standards of decorum. Belinda, discounting her own feelings, will not allow herself to linger indiscreetly at the Archdeacon's when his wife is absent, and when Edith and Connie drop in unexpectedly and are invited to stay for supper, certain rules apply:

> Oh, please don't trouble to make any difference for us,' said Connie. 'Bread and cheese or whatever you're having will do for us, won't it, Edith?'
> Edith gave a short bark of laughter. 'Well, I must say that I should like to feel an effort was being made, even if only a small one,' she said in a jocular tone. 'I think we all like to feel that.'
>
> (STG, 90)

Each person must be allowed her measure of dignity, even when that is defined by the luncheon arrangements for the visiting seamstress:

> The trouble was that Miss Prior wasn't entirely the meek person one expected a little sewing woman to be. Belinda had two feelings about her – Pity and Fear, like Aristotle's *Poetics*, she thought confusedly. She was so very nearly a gentlewoman in some ways that one felt that she might even turn out to be related to a clergyman or something like that. She could never have her

meals with Emily in the kitchen, nor would she presume to take
them with Belinda and Harriet. They must be taken in to her on
a tray. She was so touchy, so conscious of her position, so quick
to detect the slightest suspicion of patronage. One had to be *very*
careful with Miss Prior. (STG, 46)

Minor as these social strictures may seem, they define deeper, less
comic, issues that given free rein would prohibit the coherence of the
community: aberrant behavior, grossness of language or of bodily
function, denial of individual worth, interference between husband
and wife. Nardin notes that although the transgressions of propriety
about which Belinda worries are often 'so tiny or remote that the
reader cannot take them very seriously, her concern is generally
based on a laudable desire to spare embarrassment and consider
others' rights'.[18] Slights, intentional or imagined, especially when
seeming to undercut an individual's dignity, rate near the top of
the list of taboos. When Bishop Grote ignores Harriet outstretched
welcoming hand, ungraciously handing her instead a box of travel
slides for his evening lecture, Belinda is indignant: 'How rude and
casual of him! she thought. How like a bishop!' (STG, 175). As
usual, though, she quickly tempers her disapproval by 'realizing
the injustice of this generalisation', revealing more about her own
social tolerance than the Bishop's *faux pas*.

Almost as much as by issues of behavior the novel of manners is
defined by detail, and strict attention paid to food and clothing is
a hallmark of Pym's style. Later novels continue the practice to a
greater or lesser degree but *Some Tame Gazelle* uses these mainstays
of human existence as delineators of character and as definers of
plot. E. M. Forster could not have imagined Pym's technique when
he wrote:

Food in fiction is mainly social. It draws characters together, but
they seldom require it physiologically, seldom enjoy it, and never
digest it unless specially asked to do so. They hunger for each
other, as we do in life, but our equally constant longing for
breakfast and lunch does not get reflected.[19]

Especially in the early novels of Barbara Pym, the planning, purchasing, preparing, preserving, and consuming of food is of para-
mount importance. Food becomes not just subsistence, but a communal activity, a measure of character, a metaphor for love, and

therapy for what ails you. Mistakes in its preparation, such as the discovery of a long greyish caterpillar found floating in a cauliflower cheese, require profuse apologies ('perhaps you would like a poached egg, or two poached eggs?') and the services of 'a modern poet to put . . . into words. Eliot, perhaps' (STG, 51). Generosity of spirit can be discovered in the Bedes' spontaneous offerings to guests; its opposite, a psychological parsimony, characterises Agatha Hoccleve and her table, 'An old dried-up scrap of cheese or a bit of cottage pie, *no* sweet, sometimes' (STG, 52). The unexpected addition of a curate to a previously all-female dinner party results in a menu instantly upgraded from the planned macaroni cheese.

> They would all benefit from Mr Donne's presence, [Edith] knew, and noted with sardonic approval that there was a large bowl of fruit salad on the table and a jug of cream as well as a choice of cold meats. (STG, 92)

Sometimes Pym uses food imagery as a comic mirror for plot developments. Struggling with a particulary uncooperative batch of paste for ravioli, 'sticky, full of little lumps, and greyish looking', Belinda is interrupted by Theodore Mbawawa, Bishop Grote, come to offer the most pathetically comic proposal of marriage since *Pride and Prejudice*. Quoting ungraciously that she 'is not fair to outward view' and, worse, mis-attributing the quote to Wordsworth, the complacent suitor assures Belinda that she is 'equal to being the wife of a bishop'. Rebuffing these lukewarm advances, Belinda sends him on his way and returns to the kitchen to discover 'joyfully' that the much toiled-over ravioli paste has achieved a state of perfection when left on its own.

As with food, Pym's accurate attention to clothing, both her own and that of her fictional characters, unmistakably characterises her style. The diaries inventory her wardrobe for each college term, record her own favorite outfits and those of her friends, linger over the tailoring of her Wren's uniform, and plan acquisitions and reconstructions. Always thorough in recording minute detail, she lists each item of clothing worn for a memorable event like a first date, even to the lingerie underneath: 'Blue Celanese trollies – pink suspender belt – pink kestos – white vest' (AVPE, 21). During the war, rationing controlled her consumption if not her concern for fashion:

We now have to give coupons for clothes, as you know, so it is no good buying something that won't be useful afterwards – but it needs great ingenuity to plan everything. We shall get shabbier and shabbier but who cares. (AVPE, 110)

As able a seamstress as a literary craftsman, she filled her closets and her home with her handiwork as well as her bookshelves with her books. Hazel Holt describes Pym's home with Hilary as 'one of those Virginia Woolf-like places with skirts hanging on the backs of doors' awaiting alteration, and Barn Cottage is filled with the sisters' needlework.

Beginning with *Some Tame Gazelle* and consistently throughout her work, Pym uses clothing to introduce and define character. In the hands of the novelist of manners, what a character wears, the image he presents to the world, is the first and often the most significant measure of his personality, class, and social role. Writer-critic Alison Lurie acknowledges the existence in both literature and life of an unavoidable 'language of clothes' through which humans reveal 'important information (or misinformation) as to their occupation, origin, personality, opinions, tastes, sexual desires and current mood'.[20] Relying on this language, Pym uses a character's clothing as often as her dialogue to reveal personality.

This first novel opens with Belinda and Harriet preparing to entertain the new curate at dinner, their expectations established by the dresses they choose: Belinda in her 'rather dim' second-best, 'quite good enough for the curate', and Harriet 'radiant in flowered voile' with tropical flowers 'of an unknown species' rioting over her plump body (STG, 10–11). Pym fills the novels with a variety of social occasions all demanding an extensive and lovingly detailed description of the participants' attire. Even speculating on costume choices can be a pleasurable occupation, as when Belinda whiles away an hour of sewing, imagining the scene at an upcoming garden party:

Agatha Hoccleve would of course wear a nice suitable dress, but nothing extreme or daring . . . . Then there was Edith Liversidge, who would look odd in the familiar old-fashioned grey costume, whose unfashionably narrow shoulders combined with Edith's broad hips made her look rather like a lighthouse. Her relation, Miss Aspinall, would wear a fluttering blue or grey dress with a great many scarves and draperies, and she would, as always, carry that mysterious little beaded bag without which she was never seen anywhere. Undoubtedly the most magnificent person there would be Lady Clara Boulding, who was to perform the opening ceremony. (STG, 20)

Edith, solid as a lighthouse, Connie a fluttering lightweight – their clothing matches their personalities; for Lady Boulding and Agatha it is an indicator of public position (actual or aspired to) and social role.

Self-image especially beomes sartorially expressed, at least among the females. Men in Pym's fiction, tend to worry less about the public statements made by their appearance and consequently make more errors of taste. Even the clergy's clothes come under scrutiny, some being more 'well-cut' than others.

Sometimes a character's statements on another's dress are doubly revealing: 'It isn't right, thought Belinda indignantly, for a clergyman's wife to get her clothes from the best houses. She ought to be a comfortable, shabby sort of person, in an old tweed coat and skirt or a sagging stockinette jumper suit. Her hats should be shapeless and of no particular style and colour' (STG, 49). Belinda's formula for acceptable dress reveals both Agatha's pretensions and social aspirations and Belinda's envy of her.

Worn for warmth, modesty, protection, or occasionally enjoyment, clothes express our feelings about ourselves and our position in the world. The making or altering of clothes or the knitting of a sweater becomes an expression of creativity, satisfies a domestic urge, fills a practical need, and can also be a measure of caring or a metaphor for enduring love. Belinda daydreams about knitting the archdeacon a sweater, something in a 'lovely clerical grey' but the act is fraught with emotional risk: 'When we grow older we lack the fine courage of youth, and even an ordinary task like making a pullover for somebody we love or used to love seems too dangerous to be undertaken' (STG, 83). It might not fit. Agatha might detect a mistake. She will knit something 'suitable' for herself instead. Later discovering that Agatha has assumed just such a risk and has knit a pair of ill-fitting socks for Bishop Grote, Belinda is overwhelmed and sympathetic, 'The pullover that she might have made . . . lacked the pathos of the socks not quite long enough in the foot' (STG, 226).

Rarely in Pym do clothes assume outrightly sensual properties. Elegance is admired over ostentation, and although women dress to please men and occasionally apply cosmetics sparingly, discretion dictates that clothing enhance but not allure. Underwear, the making, wearing, and hiding of, becomes a leitmotif in *Some Tame Gazelle*: these practical necessities are best discreetly hidden from general view, like many of our deepest opinions. The visiting missionaries congratulate themselves on the shapeless clothing they have imposed upon their African converts 'in keeping with the Christian ideas of morality', but Belinda wonders 'were they not happier in their leaves and flowers?' (STG,178). Sensuality lurks in the consciousness if not the closet of a Pym character, sometimes breaking out in unexpected ways. Mildred Lathbury will timidly shop for a lipstick shade named Hawaiian Fire; Jessie Morrow will vamp in a velvet gown; Belinda displays new sensibilties when she orders a new 'closely fitted' dress for the wedding with a 'timid and carefully phrased request for something a little less shapeless than usual' (STG, 242). Close attention to the actualities and attitudes about dress is essential for the Pym reader.

From the title of *Some Tame Gazelle*, to its characters' fondness for quotation, to its abundance of literary allusion, both straightforward and sub rosa, Pym's fondness for English literature is never more apparent than in this first novel. Pym admitted that her Oxford studies contributed to the development of her style, in fact, 'It was probably my study of English literature that turned me toward a different style of writing' (MS Pym 98, fols 74–5). Later in her career the tendency toward quotation would be tempered, but in the earliest novels scarcely a page goes by without a character alluding to a line from a favorite hymn, enumerating the titles in a bookcase, remembering passages of poetry, or evoking the names of the greater and lesser figures of British literary history. As she much later wrote to an inquiring critic about *Some Tame Gazelle*, 'And of course the almost excessive number of obscure quotations shows that the author must have been a young woman just down from reading English at Oxford!' (MS Pym 98, fol. 123). The range of references in this and other novels spans centuries and genres, from the most familiar to the esoteric and includes most notable British authors from Shakespeare to Betjeman. A complete study of Pym's use of quotation and allusion should take into account the catalogue of her personal library (MS Pym 175), a list of her university courses, a survey of the book-lined shelves of Barn Cottage, and a recent article, "Some Small Smattering of Culture': Literary Allusions in the Novels' which provides an encyclopedic overview.[21]

Most often a Pym allusion functions comically or ironically to set up a dichotomy between the high-brow reference and the low comedy it is affixed to. Selections may be purposely misquoted, incorrectly attributed, inappropriately applied, or unsuitable for the occasion, thereby characterizing the speaker or the listener as an aspiring, if not entirely successful, intellectual. Usually the characters glibly recall extended bits of poetry, and the narrative voice presumes the audience's recognition of unattributed allusion, commanding the reader's intelligent participation. The shared knowledge provides comfort, community, and a link to the past, even when comically or ironically applied.

Sometimes a quotation springs forth unconsciously, causing a character like Belinda to question its appropriateness: 'Perhaps it was hardly suitable, really, and she was a little ashamed of having quoted it, but these little remembered scraps of culture had a way of coming out unexpectedly' (STG, 59). Conjoining the two adjectives 'little remembered', Pym doubles the pleasure: the snippets dislodged from memory are indeed brief, as well as often forgotten. The source or reason for Belinda's vast knowledge is never explained except that she 'often wasted her time reading things that nobody else would dream of reading' (STG, 55). She takes pleasure in the bittersweet memories this reading evokes, 'How much more one appreciated our great literature if one loved, thought Belinda, especially if the love were unrequited!' (STG, 89) but she is practical enough to choose a 'light novel' over the weightier *Oxford Book of Victorian Verse* for her sick-bed reading.

The frequent, sometimes excessive, use of literary references in *Some Tame Gazelle* and in the next novel, *Crampton Hodnet*, show that Pym was still seeking the support of her literary heritage at this early point in her career. She was, as one critic calls her, an 'extraordinarily accomplished mimic',[22] capable of adopting another's style or tone with apparent ease. Although these derivative voices never appear in the finished novels, her letters and journals show how easily she could absorb and reuse identifiable stylistic quirks. In several letters to Henry Harvey and his wife she presents herself with the ironic mockery of Stevie Smith's *Novel on Yellow Paper*: 'And you will be asking now who is this Miss Pym, and I will tell you she is a spinster lady who was thought to have been disappointed in love, and so now you know who is this Miss Pym' (AVPE, 67). Some letters and short stories reflect the haltingly precise language of Ivy Compton-Burnett, of whose effect she said, 'I couldn't help being

influenced by her dialogue, that precise, formal, conversation' (MS
Pym 95, fol. 8). The diaries mention that Virginia Woolf's techniques
attracted her too, and in later years she listed those writers to whom
she owed particular debt:

> Writing influences. Surely nobody would dare to say they've
> been influenced by Jane Austen? But if you admire a writer you
> probably sub-consciously do try to write in the way they do. I can
> remember when I first discovered the novels of Ivy Compton-
> Burnett, trying to write dialogue in her style – then I greatly
> admired those novels of the twenties and thirties by 'Elizabeth'
> – *The Pastor's Wife, The Enchanted April*, (once married to Bertram
> Russell's brother?) And Aldous Huxley's *Crome Yellow* which I
> read when I was sixteen. Then I like very much the novels of
> Charlotte M. Yonge – to name one living author -- Anthony
> Powell. *The Golden Bowl* – Henry James greatly admired – but
> so complex one could spend years on a desert island studying
> it. (MS Pym 98, fol. 32)

As in her personal life, when she discovered a favorite she was
intensely loyal, reading and rereading the canon, making literary
pilgrimages, copying long quotations into her notebooks. The author
Denton Welch preoccupied her for a time, 'When the winter comes
we can read Denton again. October-March – his months' (MS Pym
46, fol. 29). She visits his street in Greenwich, sits in the rain gazing
at his house and sketching its façade into her pocket journal. Two
notebooks have quotations from him copied onto their first pages,
as a combination of goal, good luck talisman, and consolation:

> 'I do not think that people want love most, they need the settled
> reverie, the calm testing and tasting of their past and the world's
> past.' D. W. Journals p. 201, 12 May 1946 (MS Pym 47, fol. 1)

Despite the delight she herself found in this kind of shared literary
glory, most often when she creates a character like the Archdeacon
Hoccleve, given to interminable quotation, it is to emphasise the
pompous pretension the practice implies. The melange of quoted
material, indiscriminatly selected, marks him, not as a discriminat-
ing intellectual gourmet, but a gluttonous gourmand of language.
If a particularly apt allusion goes unduly unappreciated, he will
inflict it on the next passerby. The Archdeacon makes Belinda feel

she should also be reminded of something 'out of self-defence', and he cautions a young curate 'Never waste your erudite quotations on [the evening congregation], they don't appreciate or understand them' (STG, 69).

Sometimes Pym uses literary parody to initiate comic reverberations, creating a unifying running gag from a single reference. When the archdeacon waylays Harriet in the street quoting Johnson's praise of Gray's *Elegy*, 'Sentiments to which every bosom returns an echo', Harriet confounds him with a returning parlay about 'the Apes of Brazil'. Troubled because he cannot identify the reference, 'it seemed somehow Elizabethan', he must wait several chapters before she enlightens him on the source, culled from party small-talk on natural history:

> It's quite simple really, she said. 'When the Apes of Brazil beat their chests with their hands or paws, or whatever apes have, you can hear the sound two miles away . . . . You said something about sentiments to which every bosom returns an echo, so I naturally thought of the Apes of Brazil.' (STG, 78)

Belinda attempts to smoothe the tension between the two by suggesting that 'the minds of the metaphysical poets must have worked something like that', but Harriet emerges the winner in this game of one-upsmanship. She will delight in reminding him of the incident several more times in the course of the novel, and Pym gains much comic mileage on the deflating effect of the literary mistake.

In 1936, after finishing *Some Tame Gazelle*, Pym worked briefly on a second village novel, *Civil To Strangers*, with a beautiful young heroine married to another selfish Henry Harvey character. Originally titled *Adam and Cassandra*, the work shows Pym again creating fiction out of the might-have-beens of her Oxford affair, but this time adding an international flavor, inspired by a 1935 visit to Budapest. Hazel Holt edited this 362 page manuscript (MS Pym 5) into a work half that size, and in 1987 released it, along with four stories, a radio interview, and three other 'reduced' novels, as the fourth posthumous Pym publication.

The three unpolished novels written between 1937 and 1941 make up most of the second half of this volume: one set in Finland, one with a wartime home front setting, and one an overplotted spy novel – all mildly unsatisfactory for the reader who expects to discover the familiar Pym conventions. The editor admits that all three manuscripts were 'in a fairly "raw" state', but that 'very few people read Barbara for her plots . . . it is the characters, the incidents, the set-pieces and even the single observations that one remembers and cherishes' (CTS, 3). In these elements the three short works succeed, although they are not the writings to which a first-time reader should turn.

The first, 'Gervase and Flora' (MS Pym 7), grew out of a series of letters between Pym and Henry Harvey, written when he left Oxford for Helsinki and his new position as a university lecturer. Pym devoured books on Finnish language and culture, and included many details from Harvey's letters, but the foreign setting of 'Gervase and Flora' seems like a roughly painted backdrop behind an English village novel. The expatriate community in Finland, centering around the home of Miss Emily Moberley (whose name becomes foreverafter in the Pym world a generic term for any elderly female autocrat), is remarkably like any small group Pym might gather in Shropshire. Even the few Finns portrayed conform to the social niceties of teatime and Ovaltine.

What Holt has entitled the 'Home Front Novel' (MS Pym 8–9), Pym never finished. In 1939 the Pym family took six evacuees from Birkenhead into their Oswestry home, and with the increase in cooking, housekeeping, and volunteer work, leisure time for writing was at a premium. 'October 10th. Cross with the children – they were all running about like Bears in the kitchen. Too tired to write my novel' (CTS, 217). The experience did have its positive side, 'I am gradually learning to pick up a baby with a nonchalant air' (AVPE, 96), as well as providing timely comic scenes of wartime life on the homefront. The novel shows Red Cross bandaging practice in the Canon's drawing room, blackout curtains made from canonical robes, the simultaneous billetting of children and headlice, and bridge parties justified on the grounds that their winnings go 'for the comfort of the troops'.

In this work Pym occasionally attempts to mingle the genuine trauma of war with her usual comic proceedings, but the effect is seldom successful. The wife of the local member of Parliament and her maid listen together to the news of Germany's invasion of Poland:

> They sat quietly listening, Mandy in her smart dress of black crêpe-de-chine printed with small cerise flowers and Rogers very stiff and starched in her uniform. As Mr Chamberlain

spoke, Mandy felt the tears welling up in her eyes and Rogers had turned her head away, so that Mandy would not see her weeping. (CTS, 235)

The mingling of clothing description, class boundaries, and hidden emotion is typical of Pym, but the mature writer would never tie this scene to such a momentous historical event as Britain entering the war. Later in her career, in search of something publishable in the 1960s, she took a second look at this novel, rejecting it again in favor of beginning fresh on *The Sweet Dove Died*. Holt wonders 'what she might have made of it if she had worked over the carefully observed wartime detail (supplemented by very full diary entries for the period) at the height of her mature powers' (CTS, 218).

Wartime inspired her as well to attempt a spy novel, 'So Very Secret' (MS Pym 12/ 1-4), also included in *Civil To Strangers*. Reminiscient of her more heavily plotted short stories, and overloaded with characters, the story is, is one reviewer's term, simply 'muddled'.[23] While at work on this piece, Pym confided to her diary, 'It is getting rather involved and I don't quite know what I'm driving at – that's the worst of a plot' (CTS, 271). The story has too many coincidences and mistaken identities, an unlikely escape by bicycle, and its villain apprehended by a stray bomb from an enemy plane.

That said, the novel is not without its charm, and the idea of a narrating innocent bystander caught in international espionage is a time-honored technique. Cassandra (again) Swan, a sixtyish spinster, demonstrates imagination and a plucky courage, even enduring chloroform without giving up the goods. She is a more than plausible heroine, as Hazel Holt suggests:

The idea of an Excellent Woman as the heroine of a thriller is not as incongruous as it might appear; the Excellent Woman, after all, always copes when those around her (especially Men) are failing to do so. (CTS, 272)

It is, however, the title piece *Civil To Strangers*, Pym's second full-length novel, which anchors the volume. Its genesis may have been the novels of 'Elizabeth' [von Arnim], especially *Elizabeth and her German Garden* and *The Enchanted April*, since on several occasions Pym admits to enjoying 'their wit and delicate irony, and the dry unsentimental treatment of the relationship betwen men and women' (MS Pym 95, fol. 6). These may, says Holt, have been 'the springboard' for this book:

> There are several parallels: the selfish, uncaring husband, the apparently submissive wife who, nevertheless, observes life with an ironic eye, and the transformation of a difficult husband by the Romance of Abroad. The style has something of the same cadence – formal, light, elegant, slightly sardonic. (CTS, 4)

Pym presents her usual cast of characters settled comfortably in the country: the village rector, his wife, and their as yet unmarried daughter, a gawky curate, a professor's widow engaged in courtship with an elderly dyspeptic bachelor, a desperately aggressive spinster, and a heroine ready for some change, however small, to enter her life.

The plot details the arrival of a smiling handsome Hungarian into the Shropshire village of Up Callow and his effect upon the all-too-settled marriage of Cassandra and Adam Marsh-Gibbon. Stefan Tilos 'had about him all the glamour of Budapest, against a background of medieval castles, *tzigane* bands and vampires. Above all, he was a single man, so far as anyone knew.' The mysterious stranger sets village tongues awagging by falling enthusiastically in 'love at first sight', not with one of the town's two eligible women, but with Cassandra, at the time mildly disenchanted by her husband's self-absorbed distraction. The foreigner's open courtship of a respectable young matron brings an air of romance and impropriety to Up Callow and provides the villagers with months of speculation on the nature of the relationship. With arms full of lilies and bottles of Tokay he pursues her, undaunted by her reluctance and by her married state. The village scenes of the first half of the novel follow these romantic manipulations (underscored by two other pairs of reluctant lovers) until midpoint, when unbeknown to each other, both Tilos and Cassandra depart for Budapest on the same train.

Once the confines of the village are left behind, this novel of manners begins to fragment. The selfish husband does an abrupt about face. Cassandra's problem is resolved in her own mind before the train pulls into Budapest. A new and underdeveloped group of characters are introduced: first, a gaggle of British tourists on the train, then four Hungarian relatives of Tilos. The international flavor of 'gay, sunny, Budapest' feels like a cardboard mock- up in front of which the conventions of English society are played out; even the natives are familiar: 'To Cassandra's surprise Mr Tilos's aunt was exactly like her own Aunt Beatrice, who lived in Tunbridge Wells and was a typical English spinster of gentle birth' (CTS, 160). The plot is resolved with the reconciliation of the Marsh-Gibbons and the marriage of Tilos to his Hungarian fiancee, but for the reader the return to Up Callow comes too late.

Most unusual in *Civil to Strangers* is the denouement. The return to England brings not only a resolution of the conflict but also the announcement of the forthcoming birth of a child. For Pym, children are not usually a factor in her characters' marriages, indeed conspicuous by their absence. Only Caro of *An Academic Question* is the mother of a young child, and Kate is kept conveniently off stage by her *au pair*. Several characters are parents of older children, but the trials and triumphs of child-rearing play almost no part in Pym's world. Most characters would seem to side with Adam Marsh-Gibbon:

> Adam and Cassandra had no children, at least not yet, Cassandra used to tell herself, because she was always hoping that he would see her point of view about it before it was too late. He thought they would interfere with his work, and said that it would make him so old to see a creature growing up in his own likeness. He did not seem to realise that the child might quite easily grow up in the likeness of Cassandra . . . . at the back of her mind there was always the hope that Science might one day prove weaker than Nature. (CTS, 26)

The veiled reference to birth control is vintage Pym; the closing announcement of its failure, singular.

Pym's posthumously published *Crampton Hodnet*, begun in 1939 between versions of *Some Tame Gazelle*, is, like that first work, heavy with quotation. It continues the characteristic interest in food and clothing, but the alter ego character, here named Barbara Bird, is more Pym's own age and style than Belinda Bede. This novel breaks no new ground, as many of the early novels do not, but displays a view of the Oxford community that Pym loved and the value she placed on the experience gained there.

Although Pym initially thought the novel had ' . . . some bits as good as anything I ever did' and hoped the novel 'might be a comfort to somebody', when she readdressed the work after the war it seemed, according to Hazel Holt, 'too dated to be publishable'

(CH, vi). Editing the novel for publication in 1985, Hazel Holt admits *Crampton Hodnet* has flaws: 'Occasional over-writing and over-emphasis led to repetition which, in preparing the manuscript for press, I have tried to eliminate' (CH, vi). Holt calls this book 'more purely funny than any of her later novels', despite its several weaknesses.

The 'dated' quality of this novel of north Oxford manners results from Pym's careful evocation of place and period, detailing a comic view of university life in the 1930s. Critic A. N. Wilson cites Pym's reconstruction of the era as a placid antidote to contemporary life:

> Bedside lamps are thought a luxury. Spaghetti comes out of a tin . . . Young dandies wear 'suede shoes, pin-stripe flannels, teddy-bear coats and check caps' and every motor journey starts with oil on the fingers before pressing the self-starter . . . . The charm of *Crampton Hodnet* for our generation is that we have all, as it were, been wearing daffodil yellow and coral pink since the Sixties, so that it seems most refreshing to come across the drab greys and browns in art.[24]

After the future fantasy of *Some Tame Gazelle*, an academic novel must have seemed a more natural progression from the school-girl confessionals of Pym's Oxford diaries. The one-to-one correspondence of the first novel's autobiographical characterisation is not so apparent in *Crampton Hodnet*, but its potpourri of Oxford types – dons and dilettantes, Socialists and spinsters – were drawn from familiar personalities. Set almost entirely in Oxford, the scene shifts only when the would-be lovers arrange unsatisfactory trysts. Less idealised than the village of *Some Tame Gazelle*, the university town and its stuffy suburbs are only slightly more realistic, but do provide a more densely populated world, with several circles of society occasionally intersecting.

How little they touch may be one of this novel's weaknesses: the several plot lines spin independently, linked only by the forward progress of unsuccessful romances. The first plot follows the tentative and continuously thwarted love affair between Francis Cleveland, a middle-aged don, and his adoring if sexually skittish pupil, Barbara Bird. The second revolves around the household of Cleveland's tyrannical aunt, Maude Doggett, her companion Jessie Morrow, and their handsome new lodger, the Reverend Mr Stephen Latimer.

Pym's methods for dovetailing the blunt edges of parallel plotting in *Crampton Hodnet* show an early, rougher, version of the seamless construction of the later more polished novels. She writes here in short staccato chapters usually no more than seven or eight pages long and, as in none of her other novels, titles these chapters in the manner of Dickens: 'Mr Latimer Gets an Idea'; 'Love in the British Museum'; 'An Unexpected Outcome.' As the novel moves from October to October through an academic calendar year, an early sentence in each chapter announces the month and the weather: 'It was a wet Sunday afternoon in North Oxford at the beginning of October' (CH, 1); '"Well, this is a cosy sight," said Francis Cleveland, coming into the drawing-room on a cold December afternoon' (CH, 48); 'The next day it was raining heavily, as it often does in the middle of an English summer' (CH, 193). This somewhat inelegant glue provides cohesion, but the repetition serves to heighten the stop-and-go effect of these brief scenes. The lack of transition, notes one critic, becomes an identifying characteristic of Pym's style:

> She cuts from scene to scene in the manner of a film editor, breaking directly into the next vignette, avoiding a ponderous explanation of the process of moving characters physically from one place to another: they simply appear – at the train station, the tea-table or the office. She describes journeys when they serve best to show her characters meditating . . . . Pym's usual method of transporting character is to begin a new paragraph or sentence abruptly at the new location.[25]

In later novels Pym will continue this blackout technique, but usually after providing longer, more developed comic scenes.

Sometimes an abrupt shift will be linked to a previous scene by overlapping the narrative slightly with location or character. An early chapter begins, 'At the exact moment when Miss Doggett was walking up the drive to her nephew's house, Anthea Cleveland, his daughter, was being kissed in the library' (CH, 12). Similarly the juxtaposition of fantasy and reality will allow another overlap later in this chapter when, retiring for the night, Anthea blows kisses from her window in the direction of the young man's college. Simon, we quickly learn, 'was not thinking about her. He was lying happily awake . . . going over a speech he hoped to make at the Union debate on Thursday. Of course he adored Anthea, but "Man's love is of man's life a thing apart", especially when he is only twenty and has the ambition to become Prime Minister' (CH, 28). The none-too-subtle dig at Julian Amery notwithstanding, the passage is typical of Pym's method of shifting gears rapidly for comic effect.

Beyond a talent for rapid scene handling, the heart of Pym's comedy often lies at the basic level of sentence construction. She frequently adds a surprise trailing clause which may heighten or undercut a previous statement. She may rely on the piling up of unvoiced rhetorical questions or the dramatic withholding of a periodic sentence, or she may combine all of these techniques in a single paragraph. Jessie Morrow watches from the sidelines as each woman at a church sale seeks Stephen Latimer's compliment for her homemade cake, pot of jam, or new dress:

> Miss Morrow would never have dreamed of asking a man such a question, she had for so long now worn the sort of clothes about which nobody could possibly say anything complimentary without telling lies. Her clothes were no more than drab coverings for her body. How do you like this grey jumper suit Mr Latimer, with its sagging cardigan and dowdy-length skirt? How do you like this felt hat of the sort of grey-beige which goes with everything and nothing? How do you like this blouse which I bought in Elliston's Sale two years ago because it was, and still is, that shade of green which even the prettiest girl can't get away with? (CH, 30–1).

Both the fierce pride and the wry self-appraisal of a woman sliding into spinsterhood, are coupled in the comic presentation of this interior monologue.

The episodic nature of *Crampton Hodnet*, heightened by the rapid and abrupt scene changes, results in a novel more farcical than any of Pym's others. The pace is breakneck and the obstacles to love's completion include cactus plants and capsized canoes. No single narrative voice anchors the novel, so the comic perspective shifts from character to character, providing multiple opportunities for comic encounters and kaleidoscopic impressions.

While Pym devotees have welcomed any new addition to the oeuvre, critical reception for *Crampton Hodnet* as a late and edited addition to the canon has been mixed. Some complain of its 'weakness in structure and plot'[26] or its author's 'apparent inability to suggest the possibility of strong emotion.'[27] Most recognise the marks of inexperience in the repetition of jokes or in an 'excessive eagerness to establish the looks, habits and clothes of each character as soon as his or her name is introduced'.[28] Pym herself must have abandoned the novel as unworkable, leaving it untouched even when she was most anxious to see a new work in print. She cannibalized it several times, lifting both characters and situations for other efforts. Anthea, Miss Doggett and Jessie Morrow appear in only slightly altered form in the short story 'So, Some Tempestuous Morn' and the latter two are again reincarnated for *Jane and Prudence*. Barbara Bird, who drops abruptly out of *Crampton Hodnet* after her flight from Francis and the Dover hotel, reappears briefly in *Jane and Prudence* as a middle-aged novelist reeking of cigarette smoke; Nicholas and Jane Cleveland of that novel share only a last name with Francis and Margaret Cleveland. Many of Pym's favorite quotations from *Crampton Hodnet* get recycled, including Christina Rosetti's lines, 'Better by far you should forget and smile/Than that you should remember and be sad' which nearly become a refrain in the next published novel, *Excellent Women*. This 'salvaging technique', as Hazel Holt calls it, shows Pym reusing favorite material from what she felt was an unpublishable work.

However, the strengths of *Crampton Hodnet* lie in its finely sketched characterisation and masterful handling of dialogue. Pym offers a trio of weak but attractive men as romantic possibilites for the altogether more capable women, but no male is as fully developed as the plot demands. The memorable characters, as always, are female. Miss Maude Doggett, the arbiter of taste and decorum, sets the standards for the community: no rumor must go unrepeated, no whiff of scandal unexplored. As she is the first to assert, 'There are some things that one cannot let pass without comment. It is a duty one has to other people, not always a pleasant or an easy duty, but one which must be performed' (CH, 54). Pretentious about her social position, connections, and past, she never misses an opportunity for deflating the ego of others. The novel of manners will often depend upon a character like Miss Doggett to filter information: she sees or hears all, considers herself an authority, and actually understands little.

The two younger women, Jessie Morrow and Barbara Bird, provide contrasting perspectives on life's possibilities: the one unassuming yet perceptive, the other enamored of romance, but sexually naive. Pym develops these two characters in her ususal

fashion, describing the clothing, domestic habits, and social awk-
wardness of each, but deepens their psychological makeup by
offering their numerous internal conversations. Barbara Bird imagi-
natively rewrites her flight from Francis until it satisfies her need
to cast herself as romantic heroine. In ever-escalating diction she
rationalises:

> I'm free, she thought; there won't be any going to Paris. There
> won't be any more love, or at least not *that* kind of love. I've
> run away from Francis. Not *run* away, I've left him, I've given
> him up. I've *renounced* him. There was nothing shameful about
> renunciation; on the contrary, it was noble. (CH, 190)

In a similar vein, Pym will borrow from Jane Austen and others
the trick of turning a character's own language on himself. Simon
Beddoes' letter to Anthea unwittingly reveals his insincerity, his
talent for political doublespeak, and his grammatical (and therefore
intellectual) weakness. Miss Morrow analyzes for us:

> The sprawling, childish writing and curious parliamentary
> phraseology seemed to her infinitely pathetic. 'It has been
> evident for some time . . . it is not unlikely that . . . ' Miss
> Morrow jumped forward thirty years and saw Simon as the
> Secretery of State for Something, answering questions in the
> House. But then, she thought, with cynicism unsuitable in one
> who was not a woman of the world, he would avoid the truth
> at all costs. And he would probably have a secretary who knew
> where to put the apostrophe in 'haven't'. (CH, 201)

Pym overuses her tendency to italicize or capitalise for emphasis
in *Crampton Hodnet*, but is sometimes justified in terms of the
characterisation. Her young women, especially, talk in titles, as
when Anthea imagines marriage to Simon: 'She had a sudden
depressing vision of their married life together, he so young and
gay and ambitious and she trying desperately to Keep His Love, as
they said in the magazines' (CH, 138–9). In her later novels, Pym
will use many of these same methods for developing character
through dialogue, and with a gentler hand.

The closings of both *Crampton Hodnet* and *Some Tame Gazelle*
celebrate the status quo. Belinda and Harriet choose singleness,
not marriage; Francis returns to the comfortable haven of his

home, abandoning romantic illusion; Leamington Lodge prepares for another Sunday gathering. 'I suppose it will never change,' notes Anthea, 'There will always be North Oxford tea parties as long as there's any University left' (CH, 213). The satire is sunny, equilibrium is restored, and harmony and comfort rule.

4

Something
'Very Barbara Pym'

Pym thought of *Excellent Women* as her 'first adult novel' (MS Pym 98, fol. 75). Leaving behind the familiar settings of country village or university town, she moves this next work to the city, to the London suburb of Pimlico where she herself settled after demobilisation, the death of her mother, and her father's remarriage. Although living at home had been a pleasant necessity before the war, Pym's move to London gave the opportunity for a widened comic perspective and brought several new populations under her scrutiny. Some restlessness and dissatisfaction with the predictability of the few years as the unmarried daughter at home appear in her short story 'They Never Write' (MS Pym 94, fols 218–29) whose heroine is conscious of her mother's attempt to arrange for her a match with the new curate:

> Quite a sensible idea, thought Abigail detachedly. She was twenty-three years old and had already been down from Oxford two years. Many people in the town must think that her expensive education had been a waste of money, as here she was at home, apparently quite idle, and not even getting married. (MS Pym 94, fol. 224)

On the recommendation of a friend from the WRNS, Pym was hired as a research assistant for the journal *Africa*, published from the offices of the International African Institute (IAI) in London. She and Hilary adopted a comfortable social routine, 'efficient and resourceful' despite post-war rationing: 'We do quite a lot of entertaining in a mild way – hardly any drink and mostly foreign dishes like moussaka and ravioli, owing to the scarcity of meat!' (AVPE, 179). One historian notes that during this period 'the women most likely to become novelists – from the upper-middle and middle classes – were just those likely after the war to be most preoccupied with loss of status and the dreariness of austerity'.[1] But for Pym, the move to London provided an enlarged rather than a diminished world.

Not that Pym chose the cosmopolitan capital for its addition of spice and sophistication to her fiction. Indeed, in *Excellent Women*, her first urban novel, she settles her heroine in a 'shabby part of London, so very much the 'wrong side of Victoria Station', so definitely *not* Belgravia' (EW, 7). The isolated parish of St. Mary's, modeled after the church Pym attended in Pimlico, St. Gabriel's, Warwick Sq. (AVPE, 206) provides the necessary narrow community for the novel of manners, little touched by the outside world. 'But then so many parts of London have a peculiarly village or parochial atmosphere that perhaps it is only a question of choosing one's parish and fitting into it' (EW, 11).

Despite one critic's complaint that *Excellent Women* is 'dated but of too recent a vintage for nostalgic charm',[2] it successfully evokes its small corner of London's postwar years. Services in a nearby parish are held in the only undamaged aisle of the sanctuary. An anonymous donation is received to repair a bombed-out window of the church. A housing shortage prompts the letting of the vicar's top-floor room. Meager Sunday suppers of uniform texture and color include macaroni and cheese, boiled potatoes, and blanc-mange. Teatime etiquette in the time of rationing means visitors bring along their own portion of jam.

At work on *Excellent Women* even before Jonathan Cape accepted *Some Tame Gazelle*, Pym here leaves behind most of the auto-biographical underpinnings of her previous worlds and creates, therefore, a denser and more complex community. 'The most generally popular' of her novels says Hazel Holt (AVPE, 184), *Excellent Women* was chosen as a Book Society monthly selection, and serialised as a radio play for the BBC's 'Woman's Hour'.

The literary notebooks for this period (1948–50) contain several notations that find their way immediately into *Excellent Women*. She records spotting 'a worn-looking woman of 37 in Woolworth's asking for a lipstick called "Hawaiian Fire"' (MS Pym 41, fol. 7) and, after a visit to a coldly modern abbey, surmises 'Not there would one be sentimentally converted to Rome' (MS Pym 40, fol. 4). The early genesis for the novel may have been the short work 'Poor Mildred' (MS Pym 94, fols 58–75) in which an unmarried vicar lives with his older sister, unquestioning of his chosen celibacy, until an attractive widow arrives. But in that story the sister is cast as villain, attempting to thwart the course of true love with a false tale of a Brontëesque mad wife, hidden away in a distant asylum. By the first draft of *Excellent Women* (MS Pym 13) the basic characterisation is complete: the widow becomes a predatory figure, the sister a comic neutral who keeps house for her brother 'with more enthusiasm than skill', and Mildred, the Barbara Pym character, the spinster narrator.

In 1952 *Excellent Women* enjoyed a mildly successful critical reception, with most reviewers echoing the *Times Literary Supplement*'s appraisal: 'Miss Pym wears her religion without much self-consciousness, and the book shows a definite advance on her first novel, *Some Tame Gazelle*.'[3] When reissued in 1977, *Excellent Women* garnered much more attention, including what Pym called 'super American reviews' (AVPE, 324), although the verdict was not unanimous. One reviewer complained that aside from Mildred's insightful emotional awakening, the novel presents 'colorless' other characters and 'the gray uneventfulness of the life portrayed infects the style'.[4] Another suggested that unlike other of her works, this one was 'less accessible to a broad audience, more of a special treat for lovers of the high, wry style'.[5]

More perceptive critics, however, recognised the expert presentation of loneliness lurking in the folds of the comedy's fabric. In a 1964 letter to Pym, Philip Larkin writes after re-reading Mildred's story, 'EW seemed better than I remembered it, full of a harsh kind of suffering very far from the others. It's a study of the pain of being single, the unconscious hurt the world regards as this state's natural clothing' (MS Pym 151, fol. 22). By the time of the reissue in 1977 other critics agreed. The *Times Literary Supplement* reviewer Anne Duchêne, in her article 'Brave are the Lonely', calls Pym an 'expert on loneliness' in this her most 'felicitous' novel.[6] Karl Miller in *The New York Review of Books* aptly entitles his review 'Ladies in Distress'[7] and John Updike, coupling Pym with the writer Stanislaw Lem, sums up in singsong the 'atomic loneliness' he finds in each:

> Pym and Lem,
>   Lem and Pym –
> There's little love
>   In her or him.
> Out on a limb

> With Pym and Lem
> One hugs oneself
> Instead of them.[8]

Pym recognised that somber elements played a part in her work but never found them overshadowing the comedy. In a letter to Robert Smith, she comments on a new friend's response to *Excellent Women*: 'Richard has been reading some of my books . . . E. W. he found terribly sad, but witty – why is it that men find my books so sad? Women don't particularly. Perhaps they (men) have a slight guilt feeling that this is what they do to us, and yet really it isn't as bad as all that' (AVPE, 223).

In Mildred Lathbury, Pym creates her strongest and most complex heroine to date, the prototypal 'excellent woman', perhaps best defined as:

> Ready to clean up if necessary, to lend a sympathetic ear, willing to wait for the neighbor's moving van, to serve tea during crisis, to fill in a foursome, excellent women prove pleasant unthreatening company. Friends value their willingness to be inconvenienced; the church counts on them for selfless work; new acquaintances forget their names or fail to recall having met them. Nor do they deserve such treatment, for excellent women are often intelligent, educated, sensitive, loyal, eminently capable of controlling life's vagaries with but one exception: their relationships with men. Despite positive qualities aplenty, myriad personal and domestic talents, despite wit and spirited independence, despite cooking and housekeeping skill, excellent women are not sought as wives. Outsiders, they are the observers, characters incidental to love and marriage.[9]

The Bede sisters were early versions of these capable, churchy types, and *Crampton Hodnet*'s Mrs Cleveland added the virtue of generous unflappability to the type. Asked later about her recurring use of 'The Excellent Women theme', Pym responded:

> I'd probably noticed that unmarried women seemed to be expected to do all kinds of things that nobody else was willing to do and of course having got the idea I exaggerated it a little, after all art must improve on life – fiction must be a bit more

interesting and amusing than things that happen every day. (MS Pym 98, fol. 32)

Mildred, like most of Pym's excellent women, is modest and apologetic, tolerant to a fault, hiding underneath her outwardly malleable exterior a steady head and a sense of irony often aimed at herself. With no remaining family and only a few friends, she stands poised on the edge of change (or fossilisation) when the novel opens. Discontent she would never admit, but already she has initiated a few changes in previously all-too-familiar patterns:

> I had chosen St. Mary's rather than All Soul's not only because it was nearer, but because it was 'High'. I am afraid my poor father and mother would not have approved at all and I could imagine my mother, her lips pursed, shaking her head and breathing in a frightened whisper, '*Incense.*' (EW, 11)

The novel begins with Mildred, who inherits her sense of propriety from Belinda Bede, caught peeking as a moving van unloads furniture into the flat downstairs from her own. The fact that the two flats share a single bathroom embarrasses her with its implications of unchosen intimacy, as does meeting the new neighbor over dustbins instead of china teacups. Self-effacing to a fault, Mildred immediately measures herself unfavorably – 'mousy and rather plain' – against the fair-haired newcomer. A spunky pride has her quickly amend: 'Let me hasten to add that I am not at all like Jane Eyre, who must have given hope to so many plain women who tell their stories in the first person, nor have I ever thought of myself as being like her' (EW, 7). The denial serves mostly to confirm Mildred's hope that her Mr Rochester may still appear.

The plot, briefly, concerns the upheavals in Mildred's world instigated by the arrivals of two sets of outsiders. First the Napiers, the naval attache Rockingham and his anthropologist wife Helena, move into the flat below bringing a mixture of glamour, romance, and untidiness. Next, the domestic routine of the Mallorys, Rector Julian and his sister Winifred, is upset by their new tenant, the predatory widow, Allegra Gray. Mildred's role as intermediary, confidante, and peacekeeper for each group moves her in and among the comic conflicts and permits her presence for most of the action, a presence essential in this novel which she herself narrates. Telling her story in retrospect, she admits, 'I did not then know to the extent I do now that practically anything may be the business of an unattached woman with no troubles of her own, who takes a kindly interest in those of her friends' (EW, 47).

Pym's choice of the first person narrator for *Excellent Women* may seem a new narrative technique for her, but it grows logically out of her journal-keeping habits and the practice is evident in most of Pym's early drafts. Often, when working out plot and characterisation for a new novel, Pym casts herself as the heroine, relying on the personal pronoun 'I' or 'me', until she decides on the narrative perspective. Halfway through an early draft of *Excellent Women* (MS Pym 13) Pym decides to separate the plot lines and not to marry Everard Bone to Allegra Gray: 'No – Everard to propose to *me!*' (MS Pym 13, fol. 8). Later, while working on *Quartet in Autumn*, she will ask in a similar way, 'Am I a widow? I am 60 or thereabouts – on the point of retirement and going to live in the country . . . the office party and presentation' (MS Pym 53, fol. 5). The technique allows Pym a vicarious participation in the lives of her characters and may account for some of the autobiographical overtones in even those characters who seem least to resemble her.

Usually by the final draft she has moved away from the first person voice, settling instead upon a worldly, slightly satiric, third person omniscience to provide an overview of the action and characters. Physically and psychologically less constricting, the novel presented by an all-seeing narrator can move smoothly in and out of multiple consciousnesses, accommodating the episodic structure Pym usually favors. The social stratification of the novel of manners seems to be best defined by a variety of viewpoints and consequently the single narrating voice is not common. Only in this novel, in *A Glass of Blessings*, and in the posthumous (and less successful) *An Academic Question*, does Pym choose to retain the limited point of view initiated in her early drafts.

In *Excellent Women*, however, the filtered story of Mildred's dealings with the forces of change necessitates the level-headed consistency of a single voice. It adds a perceptive psychological depth to the story of a strong, solitary woman. In his review of this novel John Updike recognises Mildred's place in an elite sorority:

> Mildred Lathbury is one of the last (I would imagine) of the great narrating English virgins, and though she tells us she is 'not at all like Jane Eyre', her tale has some of the power of, say, the portion of *Bleak House* narrated by Esther Summerson – the power, that is,

of virtue, with its artistic complement of perfect moral pitch and crystalline discriminations.[10]

Elsewhere in his criticism he recognises that 'the first person voice shelters us from the kind of confrontation with massive, inexorable reality that the great third-person novels provide. A first person narrator is a survivor, or he wouldn't be there on the page.'[11] Mildred Lathbury is, above all, a survivor, hurdling life's larger stumbling blocks,

> I did part-time work at an organisation which helped impoverished gentlewomen, a cause very near to my own heart, as I felt that I was just the kind of person who might one day become one. (EW, 12)

tripping on its sidewalk cracks,

> The burden of keeping three people in toilet paper seemed to me rather a heavy one. (EW, 10)

Her field of vision, though narrowed by her own limited experience, is steady and consistent.

Counter-balancing Mildred's steadiness are a circus of eccentric minor characters and two contrasting romantic possibilities, Rocky Napier and Everard Bone. Although the latter is unmarried, a regular church-goer, and suitably stuffy and standoffish, it is the former who initially intrigues Mildred. For her, the exoticism of his foreign service indicates risk and sexuality; his name alone is like 'a precious jewel in the dustbin'. Anticipating his entrance, 'He might arrive with a parrot in a cage', Mildred conjures up images of a swashbuckling roué, a connoisseur of Victoriana, a gourmet cook. Even before their first encounter her suppressed sexuality is so aroused that she contemplates purchasing a new dressing gown, 'something long and warm in a rich colour' for venturing toward their shared bathroom.

As her information about Rocky accrues, Mildred becomes more cautious, the image of a trail of Wren officers succumbing to his flattery never far from her mind. Good looks notwithstanding, he proves himself glib and shallow, cavalier in his treatment of women, and niggling about the division of marital property during a temporary separation from his wife. Upon the Napiers' reconciliation, in part engineered by herself, Mildred has a last poignant vision of the power and evanescence of his charm:

> Once more, perhaps for the last time, I saw the Wren officers huddled together in an awkward little group on the terrace of the Admiral's villa. Rocky's kindness must surely have meant a great deal to them at that moment and perhaps some of them would never forget it as long as they lived. (EW, 225)

After Rocky Napier, the dashing hero gets little play in Pym's novels, most of her men being decidedly inferior to the women they encounter. Later she would be amused to find how many men of her past recognised themselves in this one charming cad:

> I sometimes think that my service in the Wrens provided me with the only one of my male characters at all resembling a romantic hero – I mean Rocky Napier in *Excellent Women*. When that novel was published, it amused me to find that several men I knew identified themselves with Rocky! Of course, he was really a composite figure of at least three people. I wonder if one's friends are as eager to claim identity with a comic or ridiculous character?! (MS Pym 98, fol. 75)

Through Rocky and Helena Napier, Mildred meets the second, and more suitable, romantic lead – the churlish anthropologist, Everard Bone. Like Mildred, he shares little of Rocky's glamorous aura. Prickly and fiercely independent, he too has a limited circle of friends and little family and seeks his solace in the church. Although Pym leaves the outcome of their relationship deliberately ambiguous at this story's end, we later learn in three separate novels (JP, LTA, and AUA) that Mildred has indeed married Bone, assisted his anthropological career, and learned to type. He too reappears, characteristically complaining about his own inconvenience when she suffers the flu. Their 'full life' together is a predictable combination of his ego and her subservience – indexing, proof-reading, peeling potatoes – and lacks the spark she felt for Rockingham Napier.

With the character of Everard Bone and his circle of anthropologists Pym takes a first glance at the world of professional academia (a world which she would later flesh out in *Less Than Angels*), but the primary comic focus in *Excellent Women* is the institution of the Anglican church. For Pym the correspondence between these two worlds is close; she sees in each the same intentional demarcation between insiders and outsiders; she relishes the special language and traditions each treasures; she satirises the inability of each to laugh at its own conventions. Only in *Less Than Angels, The Sweet Dove Died*, and *An Academic Question* does Pym not center the community on the church, and in those novels she intentionally moves the focus away from the constricted cosiness of a local parish.

In *Excellent Women*, the Church of England, its clergy, customs, and collections of oddball hangers-on come in for minute scrutiny, in this case at its most benign. In her subsequent novels *Jane and Prudence* and *A Glass of Blessings* the satire will sharpen, but here the church community provides a spiritually satisfying hub around which the plot revolves, providing 'a feeling of intimacy with each other and separateness from the rest of the world' (EW, 49).

The novel offer two parishes: primarily St. Mary's, Pimlico with its appropriately virginal parishioners; and, to a lesser extent, the bombed shell of St. Ermin's where, in a symbolic image rare for Pym, Mildred sees, 'incongruous in the middle of so much desolation . . . a little grey woman heating a saucepan of coffee on a Primus stove' (EW, 49). Here too she re-encounters Everard Bone, a disturbing interloper into her devotional thoughts.

> The preacher was forceful and interesting. His words seemed to knit us together, so that we really were like the early Christians, having all things in common. I tried to banish the feeling that I should prefer not to have all things in common with Everard Bone but it would keep coming back, almost as if he was to be in some way my Lenten penance. (EW, 51)

In the midst of the physical decay, some critics see Pym presenting a desiccated Church, 'hampered by three language-related problems: a stock of pious words that has been devitalised, outmoded devotional forms that often do not appeal to the modern sensibility, and a clergy that has difficulty communicating the ancient faith to its contemporary flock'.[12] But this analysis misses the comic possibilities that Pym, like contemporary novelist David Lodge, finds in the language and practices of the Church. Her loving looks at the foibles of the institution contain no malice or crusading correctives, only a comically accurate portrayal of contemporary social behavior.

She recognises in each parish microcosm its own internal stratification: 'Strictly speaking, she was socially inferior to Miss Enders and Miss Statham, it was only her participation in parish activities that gave her a temporary equality' (EW, 63). Diana Benet, studying Pym's use of Christianity in the novels notes,

> Membership in the Church or close association with the clergy is a convenient and reliable way of 'placing' people socially. A church affiliation is akin to belonging to a club; it is a guarantee of a certain social standard and common background that is reassuring to everyone concerned.[13]

The delegation of work and the rewarding of labor are socially agreed upon, continuing unvaryingly in time-honored patterns. The church bazaar has always been held two Saturdays before Christmas; the flowers decorating the high altar for Whit-Sunday have always been lilies; any suggestion for change is suspect. The rhythms of the church year dictate patterns in the outside world too: Mildred cuts out a new dress pattern and begins to clean cupboards because she 'always did these tidyings on Easter and Whit-Monday, but somehow not at any other time' (EW, 121). Any religious fervor, passionate conviction, or evangelical proselytizing is an embarrassment in this world of undemonstrative Anglicanism. Confronted with the question 'You are a Christian lady?' from an ebullient hymn-singing Nigerian, Letty Crowe of *Quartet in Autumn* describes her own quiet Christianity as, 'a grey formal, respectable thing of measured observances and mild general undemanding kindness to all' (QIA, 66).

Any elaborate show of faith, especially if linked to the Roman Catholic tradition, strikes a note of fear and disapproval with most of the characters, especially those with little education or sophistication. The vicar's biretta, the smell of incense in the church, and the expectation of 'Catholic privileges' upset Mrs Morris, Mildred's 'woman' who comes twice a week, but she recoils in special horror at the thought of 'kissing the Pope's toe'. A line of priests from a Roman Catholic seminary waiting at a bus-stop cause one staunch Anglican to whisper, 'Like a lot of beetles . . . I bet they'll try and push in front of us' (EW, 194). But Mildred, like a fictional forerunner in Pym's story 'English Ladies', can be openly disappointed when an Abbey visit provides little in the way of mystery and appeal, 'for there was no warm rosy darkness to hide in, no comfortable confusion of doctrines and dogma' (EW, 196). No matter how the chapel versus church discussion is presented in Pym's novels, the gradations of social behavior in the various British religious institutions, ranging from the most ascetic to the most elaborate, provide a wealth of detail for a novelist of manners.

Since we have seen that good humor and the novel of manners usually go hand in hand, it is not inappropriate for Pym to parody that which she holds most dear. She acknowledges that 'when you make a close study of something or some body you do tend to become fond of it. In the same way that I joke about the Anglican church and I'm very fond of that' (MS Pym 98, fol. 32). She shows a fine appreciation for the traditions and formalities of the system, all the while recognizing the possibilities for amusement when they are too rigidly applied: 'Lent – is whale meat a fish?' (MS Pym 40, fol. 6). 'Religion in the summer is rather a bore – all those Sundays after Trinity' (MS Pym 40, fol. 13). 'Writing to a clergyman in Lent. Ought one to use purple ink?' (MS Pym 46, fol. 3). Any absurdity or nonsequitur amuses her, as does the close conjunction of the spiritual and the practical. A single journal page contains three entries:

> Refreshment Sunday (4th in Lent). George Herbert's lovely hymn (93 in English Hymnal) and the vicar in sardonic mood. 'If there are any men in the congregation who are interested in music perhaps they would help to move the grand piano after the service. I want 6 volunteers.'
>
> Prayers are difficult when choir practice interrupts – the organist making jokes.
>
> We pray for streets – 'Warwick Square', says the vicar, his tone seeming to gain in fullness. (MS Pym 98, fol. 35)

The diaries are filled with these observations or questions on religious decorum, many culled from the Church of England's monthly newspaper *The Church Times*. This publication itself becomes an occasional target, one hostess offering its pages in lieu of absent toilet paper.

Perhaps the clearest statement of Pym's religious faith comes not in any of her dozen novels but in an interview she provided for a radio series entitled 'Desert Island Disks' in which celebrities discussed their choices of entertainment for the proverbial isle: Pym chose Henry James's *The Golden Bowl*, a potpourri of classical music, and a case of white wine. In this 'musical autobiography' she expresses a fondness for Chopin, Schubert, Mozart, and Verdi for the 'special pleasure' they give, but first in her 'musical heart' is Bach.

> For more than any other composer's, almost more than any other artist of any kind, his music expresses what I feel to be the profoundest truth about human life, namely that it is only to be understood in religious terms. On earth our experience is always imperfect. Beauty fades, joy passes, our greatest hopes are liable to be disappointed. And we mind this because spiritually we are not completely at home on this earth, we are natives of another world, the Divine world, perfect and unchanging, for which our souls are always yearning. Art, and especially music can give us an image of this world; and no music does it like that of Bach. In the words of Sir Thomas Browne, the 17th century writer: 'It is an echo of that harmony which ever sounds intellectually in the ears of God.' (MS Pym 148, fols 25–6)

Since Pym believes human life is only to be 'understood in religious terms', her lighthearted treatment of the Anglican church throughout her work cannot be discounted. Imperfect as she finds the declining contemporary institution, comic as she recognises its all-too-human foibles to be, it nevertheless provides comfort, community, and tradition. For despite the fond irreverence and the poking of fun at the quirks of Anglican life, Pym's belief in the consolations of faith was evident even to her friends. In his appraisal of the early novels Robert Smith acknowledges that for Pym's characters religion involves 'no anguish of conscience ("social" or personal), no dark night of the soul, but discussions about what vestments should be worn on Mid-Lent Sunday, what shall be served for luncheon on Fridays in the clergy house'.[14] The closest a character comes to a declaration of faith is when the elegant Wilmet Forsyth bows her head to pray.

> One or two people were kneeling in the church, and I knelt down too and began to say one of those indefinite prayers which come to us if we are at all used to praying, and which can impose

themselves above our other thought, so often totally unconnected with spiritual matters. (AGOB, 25)

Outside Pym's novels too her religious faith played an important role, sustaining her throughout her life. Robert Liddell would write after her death, 'Barbara had all the cosy domestic virtues, as well as stoicism, and she was firmly and sincerely religious; her natural courage was supported to the end by faith and resignation.'[15]

In her next novels, however, it is neither faith nor resignation but dissatisfaction and disillusion which propel the works. *Jane and Prudence* (1953) and *A Glass of Blessings* (1958), although on the surface among the most comic of Pym's works, carry underlying fissures of discontent.

Even though *Jane and Prudence* received generally favorable reviews at its first publishing in 1953 and at reissues in 1978 and 1981, at least one critic complained:

> Some incidents occur; they are not easy to recall after one has closed the book. A former Oxford don, Jane is highly literate, as indeed her creator evidently is. For Miss Pym writes well, and this chronicle of her heroine's doings is really very small beer indeed to have come from a brewery in which Oxford, a taste for Jane Austen, and an observant eye have all played their parts.[16]

Outside of Britain, where Pym gathered her usual devoted followers, an international audience seemed unlikely. The lukewarm reception for her latest novels dismayed her, as she wrote Robert Smith:

> I had a letter from Jock recently. He liked *Jane and Prudence* very much. But the Americans and Continentals most definitely don't and now I am feeling a little bruised! In answer to my enquiries Cape tells me that 8 Americans and 10 Continental publishers saw and 'declined' (that seems to be the word) *Excellent Women* and they are still plodding on with *J and P*. So humble yourself Miss Pym, and do not give yourself airs. (AVPE, 191)

Time seems to have increased reviewers' tolerance for these versions of 'small beer'. The novelist Joyce Carol Oates, a Pym devotee, rates *Jane and Prudence* along with *A Glass of Blessings* as her favorites,[17] and Pym herself calls their heroines, Prudence and Wilmet, 'my own favorites' (AVPE, 223). Both of these novels rely chiefly on a parish setting, but unlike *Excellent Women*, each reveals the possibility for tension and ill-will among the community. Each contains some of Pym's most sustained criticism of men and their treatment of women, together with themes of narcissism and disillusionment.

Pym patterns *Jane and Prudence* on a principle of alternation, building its comedy after the shape of the familiar tale of the city mouse and the country mouse. Her story opens yet again in Oxford at a reunion of the college where two decades before Jane and Prudence had been tutor and pupil. After the nostalgia wanes, each returns to her separate milieu: Jane and her clergyman husband to a new parish assignment; Prudence to London and her numbing job editing unspecified scholarly manuscripts. The novel moves between the two settings, detailing in each a range of minor characters, business, church, and social occasions, and the alternating visits of Jane to the city and Prudence to the country. The experiences of each woman on the other's turf provide the basis of most of the comedy, and perhaps the purest example of Pym's novels of manners.

As well as in their rural/urban milieux, the two women oppose each other in their physical appearances. Jane is fifteen years the senior and casual to the point of sloppiness in her dress, given to drooping undergarments and old tweed coats, 'the kind of coat one might have used for feeding the chickens in' (JP, 49), 'the kind of coat a woman could wear only in her husband's presence' (JP, 53). Pru, fastidious, but usually overdressed for any occasion, wears eye shadow 'startlingly and embarrassingly green' and French perfume that she hesitates to name because 'her French accent was not good and the name was of an amorous kind that sounded a little ridiculous when said out loud' (JP, 78).

Jane cheerfully anticipates her new position as the wife of a rural vicar, hoping to transform herself from a slapdash housewife into a character from Trollope, 'gallant', and 'cheerful', or the efficient head of a 'large Victorian family like those in the novels of Miss Charlotte M. Yonge' (JP, 8). But she is an incompetent housekeeper and a mediocre and unenthusiastic cook, given in uncomfortable social situations to quoting obscure and often inappropriate poetry. The excellent women of the parish polish the brasses and decorate the church without her. When it becomes apparent that the transformation will not occur and that she will remain the Jane Cleveland of old – haphazard in domestic skills, master of the social gaffe, and mother only of the eighteen-year-old Flora – 'she was again conscious of failure'.

Jane recognises that although hers is basically a sound marriage it lacks the romance and fulfillment she had dreamed of as a young woman. Her marriage to Nicholas, her college sweetheart with the 'delphinium-blue eyes', is now blurred by 'mild kindly looks and spectacles'. Husbands, she has come to learn, although welcome 'to tell one's silly jokes to, to carry suitcases, and do the tipping at hotels' (JP, 10–11), 'expect women to do quite everything for them' (JP, 189). Her unvoiced assessment of men in general is more condemning:

> . . . it was splendid the things women were doing for men all the time . . . Making them feel, perhaps sometimes by no more than a casual glance, that they were loved and admired and desired when they were worthy of none of these things – enabling them to preen themselves and puff out their plumage like birds and bask in the sunshine of love, real or imagined, it didn't matter which. (JP, 75)

The lack of fulfillment of her romantic fantasies is tempered by Jane's natural buoyancy. She has noticed that women 'are getting so much bigger and taller and men are getting smaller' and while she considers herself a failure in the role of a clergyman's wife, actually does quite well at assessing social situations, 'I notice the things one shouldn't', soothing ruffled feathers, and exhibiting compassion and charity. Two diary notes from this period confirm Pym's admiration for her capabilities: 'Jane herself perhaps not such a failure as she thinks' (MS Pym 43, fol. 7) and 'Jane has not been really successful but a happy marriage and a child, people might say rather reproachfully wasn't that something?' (MS Pym 43, fol. 2). The double title notwithstanding this is ultimately Jane's book; she is, as Anatole Broyard dubs her, 'The Woman Who Overflows Her Situation', filling this narrative with her presence:

> This woman, this archetype, this unsung heroine of the ordinary life, is always reaching for a further reference, always trying, in

E. M. Forster's sense, to connect the low and the high, the near and the far, the everyday and the eternal.[18]

She looks around herself and finds 'all this richness' (JP, 21).

For Prudence Bates, as for Wilmet of *A Glass of Blessings*, the idea of romance is more appealing than its actuality. Since their college days Prudence has continued unmarried, exchanging, like Pym herself, one illusory and inappropriate infatuation for another. The stiff formality of her romantic visions is reflected in the Regency elegance of her furniture (which not so coincidentally mirrors that at the home of her latest romantic challenge, Fabian Driver), 'very Vogue and all that' complains one visitor. She dislikes 'being called "Miss Bates"; if she resembled any character in fiction, it was certainly not poor silly Miss Bates' (JP, 36), but the comparison is troublesome to her because it aligns them in spinsterhood, though not in garrulity.

Three alternatives to the principal women characters are presented in the novel. Flora, the Clevelands' only child, excels at all the domestic skills at which her mother fails, but chooses the same kind of colorless, non-threatening man. Her presence makes Prudence uncomfortable, a reminder of her own aging: 'It was awkward when one's friends' children suddenly became grown-up people . . . She was glad when Jane made some joking remark about not liking Flora to use nail varnish, thus turning her into a child again' (JP, 85). Prudence's college friend, a spinster ironically named Eleanor Hitchens, presents a picture of the manless life awaiting Prudence if she abandons her infatuations: 'weekend golf, concerts and theatres with women friends, in the best seats and with a good supper afterwards . . . . One had to settle down sooner or later into the comfortable spinster or the contented or bored wife' (JP, 200).

Jessie Morrow, the third and more complex foil, begins as 'a thing without personality of her own, as neutral as her clothes' (JP, 56) but quickly metamorphoses into a man-eater. The Jessie Morrow of *Crampton Hodnet* was a gentle, smart, self-effacing realist, who never ruled out the possibility of love's finding her but no longer expected it. In *Jane and Prudence* she is redrawn as calculating and ambitious, stealing oyster cakes from an afternoon tea and a velvet dress from a dead woman's closet, and capable of using sex to entrap her prey. Although Pym never confirms a sexual encounter, there is an undercurrent of sexuality in all the Jessie-Fabian scenes which fades discreetly to a blackout at the chapter's end.

More sexual freedom is available to the men. Both Arthur Grampion her boss and Geoffrey Manifold her co-worker approach Prudence openly although the first is married and the second probably not her social equal. Fabian Driver's reputation as 'more interested in other women' than in his wife, only adds to his cachet.

Pym patterned the Fabian Driver character after BBC broadcaster Gordon Glover, with whom she had a brief love affair in the early 1940s. At the time he was separated but not yet divorced from Pym's friend Honor Wyatt, and was as unreliable in his affection for Pym as Henry Harvey before him.

> Gordon Glover/Fabian. A Gordonish character in the village. His wife, to whom he had been consistently unfaithful, died – his outraged surprise and confusion of sentimental symbols. (AVPE, 187)

Glover ended their affair by requesting a year's separation, a means of escape for him, a period of pain for Pym. Of this separation she wrote:

> Even if we ever did get together again he wouldn't really want the same things as I do and surely would fail me again . . . . It's somebody else I've got to look for. Some fantastic dream lover. (MS Pym 109, fols 74–5)

The Glover affair ended painfully for Pym, and at its demise she described herself as 'drearily splendid' in coping with another rejection. Its fictional transformation, however, presents a supreme comic egoist: one who would place on his wife's grave not a conventional headstone, but his own photograph, carefully framed.

Incorporating some of Glover's cruelty, Pym makes Fabian Driver both insensitive and unfaithful, capable before his wife's death of inviting his lover of the moment for a week-end visit. The act lacks malice, we are given to understand, because of his limited intelligence: he can neither sustain a literary conversation nor read a complete book, always a measure of a man's acceptability for Pym. Although the infidelity of a man like Driver is taken for granted, there are ground rules in a parochial village: 'It seems suitable that things like that should go on in London . . . It is in better taste somehow that a man should be unfaithful to his wife away from home' (JP, 70). Even he must conform to certain behavioral codes, however, recognizing 'that one did not play fast and loose with the friend of one's vicar's wife' (JP, 103), and while avoiding Prudence he falls into the grasp of Jessie Morrow. She, we feel sure, will tolerate none of the mistreatment endured by his first wife.

Here, as in the earliest novels, Pym uses food – its preparation, consumption, and clean-up – to underscore the abyss separating the sexes. In *Excellent Women* meals were a shared responsibility. For Mildred Lathbury the mere thought of Everard Bone's invitation to cook his dinner provokes a back ache; when she does agree to a repeated invitation, she is pleasantly surprised to find that he has arranged for his housekeeper to perform the preparation: she need only serve the meal. In *Jane and Prudence*, too, men expect service – 'typing a . . . thesis, correcting proofs, putting sheets sides-to-middle, bringing up children, balancing the housekeeping budget.' Women use food as a palliative: Jane lingers over a display of *foie gras* instead of shopping for Confirmation presents; Prudence consoles herself after hearing of Fabian's engagement with,

> the kind of food she deserved . . . . a dry Martini and then a little smoked salmon . . . a slice of the breast [of chicken] and a very few vegetables. No sweet, of course, unless there was some fresh fruit, a really ripe yellow-fleshed peach, perhaps? And afterwards the blackest of black coffee. (JP, 198)

The exquisite precision of her choices mirrors her personality: carefully arranged, aesthetically pleasing, narcissistic.

The men are also measured at mealtime. Fabian and Prudence lunching together reveal their similarities in vanity and self-love while simply ordering food. Prudence chooses 'perhaps more carefully than a woman truly in love would have done'; Fabian's choice was 'equally deliberate and not quite the same as hers' (JP, 102). Even as they settle into romantic chit-chat, food, sexuality, and narcissism combine, as Prudence is unable to concentrate solely on her would-be lover:

> The chicken will have that wonderful sauce with it, thought Prudence, looking into Fabian's eyes. She had ordered smoked salmon to begin with, and afterwards perhaps she would have some Brie, all creamy and delicious. (JP, 102)

Pym recognised that food could be an indicator of social status, with women usually shortchanged, as a diary entry from this period notes: 'Lunch with Barbara Evean at Simpsons – gorgeous roast beef. Men eating meat – and never is a woman given as much as a man' (MS Pym 47, fols 1–2).

Pym differentiates Jane and Prudence by such broad- brushed strokes as their marital states, their milieux, and their temperaments, but she develops their personalities by delineating the minor details of dress, food, or social behavior. Lamenting her failure as an ideal wife for a clergyman, Jane claims her only advantage is that she does not drink. When the company suggests that the stereotype is invalid anyway, she takes a glass of sherry, cautioned by her husband, 'It seems a pity to waste it.' For Prudence, however, alcohol is a familiar comfort: 'She was wondering whether there would be a glass of sherry or a drop of gin waiting; she was so used to that little comfort at the end of a day's work and one seemed to need it even more in strange surroundings' (JP, 80). A country gathering for Bridge proceeds as dryly as Prudence expected, 'like being at a cocktail party without anything to drink' (JP, 93) until Fabian invites her to escape with him to a local pub; Prudence orders not a lady-like light ale, but a strong fortifying whiskey, 'with no false modesty or beating about the bush' (JP, 94).

In *Jane and Prudence*, Pym has the City Mouse twice define her favorite bedside reading material: she professes to enjoy novels 'well-written and tortuous, with a good dash of culture and the inevitable unhappy or indefinite ending, which was so like life' (JP, 156), novels remarkably like Pym's own. Earlier in the novel, however, she takes to bed steamier escapist fare: 'not a very nice book . . . but it described a love affair in the fullest sense of the word and sparing no detail' (JP, 46).

Whatever 'well written' means for Prudence, the disarming simplicity of Pym's style cloaks the complexity of her work, with much of the success of her modest plots residing in her strict attention to language. Always conscious of the crafting of language, she could complain to a friend of romance novelist Barbara Cartland's style, 'I was tempted to point out that her novel is easy to read because no paragraph has more than one sentence, but she is a much more popular and successful writer than I am so it would probably be sour grapes' (MS Pym 158, fol. 207).

Her own sentence structure is deceptively simple, relying as she does on dialogue and interior musings. The literary notebooks show a tendency, probably due to their informality, to rely on dashes instead of punctuation and on static nouns with few verbs.

> Her memories of him were associated with delicious meals – (as mine of Julian Amery) – is that how it turns out as one grows older. Interesting study – or does it depend on the people. Some with tears others with chocolate mousse in Balliol – (MS Pym 40, fol. 21)

The result is a series of still moments minus action, a technique which reproduces itself on a larger scale in the novels. Especially in the early works she relies too heavily on rhetorical questions, underlining, and italics to carry meaning: 'Really, Jane, what an extraordinary question – you are a funny old thing! Am I Fabian's *mistress*? Is there anything *wrong* between us? I couldn't imagine what you meant!' (JP, 123). Occasionally she errs and an awkward phrase or clumsy repetition slips in: [emphasis added]

> After the mousse they had cheese and a bottle of her father's port, which Dulcie had found in the cellar and *decanted into one of the decanters* which had stood empty on the sideboard since his death. (NFRL, 126)

One critic complains she sometimes directs the reader's response too firmly, 'noting, for example, that Belinda spoke "loyally" or "irrelevantly";[19] another that 'occasionally there are lapses into the idiom of the Woman's Page (there are too many cozy "It so happened that" 's), and references to foreign literature, philosophy and other esoteric matter are sometimes awkward.'[20] Her own peculiarities of language may be attributable to the age. In his study of British culture in the twentieth century, sociologist Daniel Snowman talks about self-restraint, control of aggression, and insularity as identifying characteristics of the period. He finds these manifested in the fondness of the British idiom for 'understatement, the double negative, the qualifying phrase, the ability to try to keep calm under fire'[21] – all qualities evident in Pym's style. Since the characteristic irony that identifies a Pym novel resides not usually in situation, but in her characters' dialogues or internal observations, the astute reader must observe in addition to total scenes, the impact of single sentences, even single words.

The chief identifying characteristic of Pym prose may well be its use of qualifying words, those which limit, modify or restrict the meaning of an outright assertion. Words like 'rather', 'almost', 'such', 'perhaps', 'not quite', 'something like', or 'just' signal the modification of statement to include the possibility of error on the speaker's part. The practice admits room for outside opinion, adds an air of graciousness and tolerance to a bald pronouncement, and identifies the speaker as a reasonable presence, willing at least to consider an alternative position. This show of good manners is altogether appropriate in a genre so dependent on measurement of behavior, and Pym uses such qualifying language both straightforwardly and ironically. In the opening scene of this novel, for instance, Jane and Prudence silently evaluate each other across a room crowded with their peers, in a passage loaded, by virtue of its qualifiers, with simultaneous admiration, criticism, and self-revelation. [emphasis added]

> She wished Jane wouldn't say these things in her *rather* bright, loud voice, the voice of one used to addressing parish meetings. And why couldn't she have made *some* effort to change for dinner instead of appearing in the baggy-skirted grey flannel suit she had arrived in? Jane was *really quite* nice-looking, with her large eyes and short, rough, curly hair, but her clothes were terrible. One could *hardly* blame people for classing all university women as frumps, thought Prudence, looking down the table at the odd garments and odder wearers of them, the eager unpainted faces, the wispy hair, the dowdy clothes; and *yet* most of them had married – that was the strange and disconcerting thing.
>
> Prudence looks lovely this evening thought Jane, like somebody in a woman's magazine . . . . It was odd, *really*, that she should not *yet* have married. One wondered if it was *really* better to have loved and lost than never to have loved at all, when poor Prudence *seemed* to have lost so many times. For *although* she had been, and still was, very much admired, she had got into the way of preferring unsatisfactory love affairs to any others, so that it was becoming *almost* a bad habit. (JP, 9)

In addition to the reliance on qualifiers, Pym creates much of her humor, especially that which relies on irony, out of the quick juxtaposition of seemingly incongruous pairs. She notes that 'Pilgrimage by luxury coach seems a contradiction in terms' (MS Pym

44, fol. 20), and has a morose heroine sip her cup of smoky, bitter tea 'as if she were putting an end to herself with Lysol' (JP, 203). The comedy rides on the whiplash effect of the language.

She has a personal collection of words that carry specialised meaning, identifiable by the faithful reader. Critic Rosemary Dinnage notices that '"splendid" which might mean something quite different, to her means being stoical in dreary circumstances'.[22] 'Suitable', another favorite approbation, connotes much more than mere propriety for the occasion, falling just short of 'excellent.'

By frequently invoking familiar landmarks, Pym lends authenticity to her work, even while specific settings remain unnamed and unlocated on the map of England. Neighborhoods like Pimlico or Queen's Park, recognisable streets of London or Oxford, even specific department stores or cafeteria chains create familiarity in a fictional context. Her reader must be sensitive to the differences implied when she sends a character to shop at Gamages, Marks and Spenser, or Harrod's, or to consume her afternoon tea at Claridge's, a Kardomah, or the Lyons Corner House. Also characteristic of Pym's style, nurtured in the postwar 1950s, is the use of brand names of familiar products to add realism: Dulcie Mainwaring offers 'Rennies' for what she perceives as Viola's indigestion; and most heroines know that 'life's problems are eased by hot milky drinks', like Horlick's, Ovaltine, or Earl Grey.

Pym's admirers often cite her manipulation of dialogue as an identifying characteristic of her style. Characters define or condemn themselves through their conversations with an efficiency and concentration that belies the artistry involved. Pym realised that the pitfalls of character delineation through dialogue are many, and that,

> . . . generally dialogue needs very careful editing and stylizing. Jane Austen was, of course, a brilliant writer of dialogue and how well a character like Miss Bates, in *Emma*, comes out through her conversation. But she is more amusing than such a person would be in everyday life. (MS Pym 98, fol. 68)

To create mindless boring chatter for a vapid minor character, while never boring the reader, requires a delicate touch. Actual conversations, transcribed into fiction are 'unusable', Pym notes, because,

> most 'real' dialogue . . . is far too rambling and incoherent, and it very seldom, as dialogue in a book must, does anything towards

furthering the plot . . . [It] must show character and it must help the story along though sometimes even the novelist must be allowed a few banal sentences – somebody must offer the heroine another cup of tea and she must be allowed to accept or refuse it. (MS Pym 98, fol. 67)

Her ear is attuned to the inherent comedy in dialogue repetition. She can characterise affectation (and poke gentle fun at Henry Harvey, whose favorite it was) by having the pompous archdeacon Hoccleve overuse the phrase 'remarkably fine'. In *Jane and Prudence* Miss Doggett continually repeats that 'Men only want one thing', revealing in the multiple assertions that if Miss Doggett ever knew what the one thing was, she has long since forgotten it. Aylwin Forbes of *No Fond Return of Love* can never remember the heroine's first name until another suitor uses it to bid her goodnight. Not to be outdone, he responds in kind. In his mind she becomes always 'that nice Dulcie Mainwaring', the parroting of the phrase evidence of his shallow imagination. Henry James recognised that 'stylistic disorders are an indication of moral and psychological ones',[23] and Pym similarly denotes character by speech affectations. A turgid, pompous sermon bespeaks a vain, self-centered cleric. She mocks academic or professional jargon for the exclusivity it pretends to, with special barbs for sociological or anthropological lingo: 'kinship tables', 'matrilineal lines', or any language indicating 'that the dead hand of the sociologist had been at work . . . words [like] "interaction", "in-depth" and "grass-roots"' (AAQ, 77).

Jane and Prudence, along with *A Glass of Blessings, No Fond Return of Love,* and *An Unsuitable Attachment* can be considered Pym's 'marriage novels', the ones in which she gives the closest consideration to the advantages and disadvantages of the married life, so often the province of the novelist of manners. Pym's own attitude to marriage, both in her life and in her fiction, is ambivalent. On one hand marriage seems the ultimate goal, as she writes in parodic Austen style:

It is known that every women wants the love of a husband, but it is also known that some women have to be content with other kinds of love. (AVPE, 84)

or

Prudence Bates was twenty-nine, an age that is often rather desperate for a woman who has not yet married. (JP, 7)

At the same time she can record a fictional conversation between a character named Mrs Pym and her daughter Barbara:

> Mrs Minshall seems to want us all to be either dead or married', said Mrs Pym . . .
> 'Well, I do not see what else we can be, said Barbara in a thoughtful tone. 'I suppose we all come to one state or the other eventually. I do not know which I would rather be in.'
> (AVPE, 80)

Jane Cleveland (said by Hilary to be patterned on their mother) may be the most happily married of Pym's heroines, despite her comments on the inadequacy of men, and she clearly relishes her role as matchmaker:

> She began to plan lunches and dinners for [Fabian and Prudence]. Really, she was almost like Pandarus, she told herself, only it was to be a courtship and marriage according to the most decorous conventions . . . . No, when she thought it over, Jane decided that she was really much more like Emma Woodhouse. (JP, 96)

For an ex-Oxford don Jane remembers little of Emma's missteps as a matchmaker, and although unsuccessful with this couple, as the novel ends she is 'full of a wonderful new idea' for her friend and the local MP, Edward Lyall. In the final pages, with three men seeking her company, the still single Prudence is 'suddenly overwhelmed by the richness of her life', while Jane, with her husband's arm around her shoulders, apologises disappointedly:

> We can only go blundering along in that state of life unto which it shall please God to call us . . . . I was going to be such a splendid clergyman's wife when I married you, but somehow it hasn't turned out like *The Daisy Chain* or *The Last Chronicle of Barset*. (JP, 212)

The mixed message on marriage gets fuller attention in *A Glass of Blessings*. Resembling *Jane and Prudence*, it considers similar questions of family, marriage, and life within the church community. It, too, has a married heroine for its protagonist, Wilmet Forsyth who, like Mildred Lathbury, narrates her own tale of moral and emotional growth.

Manuscript evidence suggests that *A Glass of Blessings* was longer in its genesis than many of Pym's other novels, but the finished work contains no indication that the creative process was troublesome. Notebooks and journals reveal more than the usual number of plots conceived and characters considered, but Pym writes enthusiastically across the top of one page listing a long catalogue of potential characters, 'Oh, but I love a crowded canvas' (MS Pym 17, fol. 34). An early draft entitled 'The Lime Tree Bower' (MS Pym 17) employs the third person for its narrative voice before the final version settles on a story self-told by the heroine. This narration is appropriate, notes one critic, 'because Wilmet Forsyth, the heroine-narrator . . . is snobbish, spoiled, and somewhat foolish, she must tell her own story in order to gain our sympathy and understanding in spite of her faults'.[24] *A Glass of Blessings* also marks the first time Pym shared a novel in progress with her co-worker Hazel Holt, thus beginning a long and successful literary relationship.

A dust-jacket blurb from a paperback edition of this novel describes it as 'an intricate drama of romantic errors', a 'netherworld of human feeling where the unspoken is tangible, where just the hint of an illicit relationship can change the direction of a life'.[25] The titillating suggestion of marital misconduct is misleading, for the novel is not a bodice-ripper but a Bildungsroman of the moral consciousness, the story of a woman's psychological journey from I to We, in terms of her marriage, her friendships, her church, and her community. Wilmet must learn the difference between love and romantic fantasy, always a difficult task for a Pym heroine, along with the difference between moral worth and matters of taste.

The portrayal of the most intimate of social contracts, the institution of marriage and the subsequent generation of family, gets curiously ambivalent treatment in *A Glass of Blessings* and indeed in most of Pym's novels. The Bede sisters reject two marriage proposals; within the confines of her novel Mildred Lathbury is non-committal about the chances of conjugal bliss with Everard Bone; and Prudence Bates prefers 'more negative relationships.' Only three heroines, Jane Cleveland, Wilmet Forsyth, and Caro Grimstone, begin their stories married, and only two, Dulcie Mainwaring and Ianthe Broome, actively seek this conventional resolution for their love affairs. Yet for most of Pym's single females, marriage is the assumed goal, and the already married play matchmaker to swell their ranks. A married woman claims the admiration of her single friends, even when the marriage is generally regarded as a failure. A widowed character in *Less Than Angels* holds a slight and inexplicable social advantage over her unmarried sister, reminding her callously of the incompleteness of the spinster's life, 'You don't know what it is to lose somebody you love' (LTA, 238). The assumed inferiority attached to the single state occasionally extends even to the males. Piers Longridge is 'vaguely unsatisfactory' both because he has not fulfilled early expectations of brilliance and because 'It was also held against him that he had not yet married' (AGOB, 6).

The assessment is often ironic because, for most Pym heroines, marriage constricts the world. Jane Cleveland must abandon her literary career; Prudence Bates knows 'husbands took friends away'; Dulcie Mainwaring recognises a married sister's discontent:

> It was rather sad . . . that an apparently happily married woman should confess to a secret hankering for such a life. And yet, stealing a glance at her brother-in-law . . . she could appreciate that perhaps a desire for escape was not so surprising. Many wives must experience it from time to time, she thought, especially those whose husbands smoked old pipes that made peculiar noises, and were so preoccupied with their harmless hobbies that they would hardly have noticed if their wives had been there or not. (NFRL, 109–10)

Catherine Oliphant of *Less Than Angels* mourns the lack of 'rapture' with her live-in companion Tom Mallow: 'we're just like an old married couple . . . in the worst sense, where dullness rather than cosiness seemed to be the keynote of the relationship' (LTA, 69).

As a young woman Pym seems to have assumed that she would marry and the early diaries speculate on the idea of marriage with the particular man of the moment. No passionless union for the sake of convenience, no sterile meeting of the minds would ever have been acceptable, she suggests, while commenting on the break-up of her sister's marriage:

> Hilary is happier without her husband – who was nice but much too cold and intellectual and logical to live with. They were not really madly in love when they married but it seemed a good thing, and of course lots of marriages of that kind turn out very well. But personally I would prefer the other thing, even if it wore off, as I am told it does. Maybe I shall be able to keep

my illusions as it doesn't look as if I shall ever get married.
(AVPE, 180)

Although she was never to know personally whether 'the other
thing' wore off or not, the positives and negatives of the married
state figure prominently in her fictional world, perhaps never more
so than in *A Glass of Blessings*. Henry James notes, 'One's attitude
toward marriage is . . . the most characteristic part doubtless of
one's general attitude toward life . . . . If I were to marry I should
be guilty in my own eyes of inconsistency – I should pretend
to think quite a little better of life than I really do.'[26] Minus
James's misanthropy, Pym and most of her characters take marriage
ambivalently: the golden ring is always sought but not necessarily
enjoyed. Pym explores the nuances of the institution from a variety
of stances in this novel: the lukewarm marriage of Wilmet and
Rodney, the late-life courtship and marriage of Sybil and Professor
Root, the homosexual arrangement of Piers and Keith, and the final
celebratory union of Mary Beamish and Marius Ransome.

A corollary to the discussion of marriage in this and other of
Pym's novels concerns the value of the extended family. Children,
we have seen, do not enhance a heroine's life. Wilmet, almost
certainly by choice, is childless, and Rowena promises not to 'inflict'
her own children on Wilmet at breakfast time. But, a relationship
with an older adult – parental figure, sibling, or even distant cousin
– is often seen as beneficial. Her mother-in-law Sybil is a warm and
stabilizing presence for Wilmet, who has no other family but her
husband's. In *Less Than Angels*, Catherine, another adult orphan,
envies Tom his family, and seeks the suburban 'safety and comfort'
of the Swan household when bad news arrives. Harriet and Belinda
Bede prefer each other's company above all others.

The protective cocoon of the family can smother as well as nur-
ture, however, depending upon the inner resources of the dependent member. Only the death of Mrs Beamish can free the dutiful
Mary from her bullying parent. After basking for two weeks in
the ministrations of two surrogate mothers, Catherine 'begins to
feel restless, like a trapped bird who might be safe and happy in
a cage but must go out into the cruel world because it is the natural
thing' (LTA, 248). Watching a friend duty-bound for home, Dulcie
Mainwaring knows 'At Christmas . . . people seemed to lose their
status as individuals in their own right and become, as it were,
diminished in stature, mere units in families, when for the rest of

the year they were bold and original and often the kind of people it is impossible to imagine having such ordinary everyday things as parents' (NFRL, 109). Measuring the demands of family against the vulnerability of independence, a Pym heroine will not usually compromise her own individuality.

The young matron Wilmet, named for a character from the Charlotte M. Yonge novel *The Pillars of the House* (MS Pym 17, fol. 12), begins her story shallow and vain, incapable of understanding the events or people around her. Her marriage to Rodney Forsyth, a civil servant 'going bald in a rather distinguished way', has lost its early spontaneity and romance, signalled by his annual birthday present, a transfer of money from his account to hers. Hints of their wartime courtship in Italy suggest a lost period of youth and frivolity, carefree romanticism, and the formation of lifetime friendships. There, young Wren officers Wilmet and Rowena had met their future husbands, then 'rather dashing army majors', and Wilmet, standing on Harry Talbot's shoulders, had romantically written her name 'on the ceiling of an officers' mess somewhere near Naples' (AGOB, 37). Her attraction to Rodney lay in his 'peculiarly English qualities', the very qualities which seem to stifle Wilmet as the novel opens.

The plot unfolds like a detective story, but with the heroine cast as a slightly inept investigator, discovering truths only after the reader does. Seeking to counteract her feelings of uselessness – no children, no job, and no social causes to care for – Wilmet seeks a relationship with Rowena's brother, the charming, slightly seedy Piers Longridge. Ostensibly on a campaign to bring Piers to social respectability, she in fact spends much of the novel trying to create a romance between them. Simultaneously, for the second plot line, Pym develops a complex community of clergy and communicants in whose lives Wilmet becomes increasingly involved. In the course of the novel's year, Wilmet learns to look for truth beyond surface appearances. She must discover that love takes many satisfactory shapes beyond the simply romantic or aesthetic. Finally she comes to agree with the Bishop's closing sermon, as he reminds his congregation that 'we must not think that beauty was everything. It was not *nothing* – he certainly would not go so far as to say that – but it was not so very much, not nearly so important as people had imagined' (AGOB, 252).

Initially Wilmet's ego manifests itself in every area of her life. Even while engaged in the most mundane of activities, like meeting a friend at a bus stop, her eye is always squarely focused on herself: 'I thought we must have made quite a pleasing picture – two tall tweedy young Englishwomen embracing on a Surrey roadside' (AGOB, 33). She misinterprets much of what goes on around her, evaluating events only in terms of their effect upon herself, sure, like Emma Woodhouse, that her assessments are correct. Her obsession with Piers prohibits her from recognizing the truth of a proposition from her friend's husband, helps her to ignore Mary Beamish's offer of friendship, and propels her insistence upon visiting Piers's flat and meeting his 'colleague'. Blinded by her equation of beauty and love, she cannot see the three less-than-aesthetically-perfect pairs of lovers before her: Sybil and Arnold lack her youth; Marius chooses Mary who lacks her beauty and style; Piers prefers the socially unacceptable Keith. Even her husband's infidelity escapes Wilmet.

A bored, married, and childless heroine expends much effort on herself, and the portrayal of Wilmet allows Pym to include many scenes of a wealthy woman filling her leisure time; indeed, critic Edmund Fuller calls her story a comic *Hedda Gabler*.[27] Since her husband prefers that she not work, she spends her days at the traditional activities of women of her class: shopping, tea parties, and some genteel volunteer work. She dabbles in languages, enrolling in an evening class more for the instructor's appeal than for a knowledge of Portuguese. She plans dinner parties for her husband's business associates or for old friends where the ladies' conventional departure and the mens' post-prandial port is strictly, if amusedly, observed. Her talents include arranging flowers to appear an oxymoronic 'artistically natural' and imagining romantic interludes that never come to sexual fruition. Kate Heberlein notes that Wilmet is an atypical heroine for Pym:

> . . . married, she is affluent, she is vain of her appearance; she seriously considers having an extramarital affair (adultery is present in fact or in fantasy in every Pym novel, but rarely with the protagonist as one of the principals) . . . . Most Pym heroines lead blameless lives.[28]

Relentlessly overestimating Piers's need for her, Wilmet plans a dalliance that is safely asexual and unusually above-board. She never suggests an intimate encounter or imagines her own response to one, limiting her fantasizing about Piers to his workplace and neighborhood, instead of his body or bed. She forthrightly informs either Sybil or Rodney about her meetings with Piers, thereby conducting the most proper of marital indiscretions.

All these scenes of a woman with too much time on her hands enable Pym to develop Wilmet's character through a series of vignettes which move her across a wider spectrum of the world than her class or experience would seem to allow. Evening class, giving blood, visiting a Settlement house, a trendy coffee bar in London, or a pretentious antique shop in the country – all allow the kind of detailed background that a novelist of manners requires to establish mood and develop character. The details Pym selects for *A Glass of Blessings* provide a realistic look at a traditional and conservative Britain on the brink of change. Apart from its nostalgic value, Pym recognised that such detail must work aesthetically as well:

> Many modern novels set in a contemporary framework . . . are so contemporary and contain so much detail that they will probably very soon become dated because of that . . . It is very difficult for the novelist to know just what to put in and what to leave out. For posterity may very likely want to know these things. I suppose the answer is that details should come in naturally and not appear to be dragged in to give a sense of period, as they sometimes are in bad historical novels. (MS Pym 98, fols 56–69)

The evening class at the university, which Sybil and Wilmet attend throughout the fall and winter, provides an opportunity to add this detail by the introduction of fourteen minor characters, a panorama of 1950s adult-ed humanity:

> Miss Wetherby and Miss Cane, two elderly spinsters who planned to hitchhike round Portugal and write a book about it; Miss James and Miss Honey, young and pretty girls, who seemed to be learning the language for personal and romantic reasons, and always giggled a good deal when it came to explaining the different ways of saying 'like' and 'love'; Miss Childe, whose reasons for learning were never clear to me; and Mrs Marble, who seemed to have a passion for evening classes in themselves, and had done Spanish last year and Italian the year before that. The men – Messrs Potts, Bridewell, Stanniforth and Jones – were all engaged in commerce and were struggling to read letters from Pernambuco, Sao Paulo and Rio de Janeiro,

but Dr McEntee wanted to be able to decipher contemporary documents about the Lisbon earthquake. Sybil and I, with our unashamed admission that all we wanted was to learn enough to get about on a holiday, seemed to have a less noble aim than the others, for even the two young girls hoped eventually to acquire husbands. (AGOB, 65)

The classroom provides a forum for Wilmet's pursuing of Piers, but the catalogue of students also adds a thickening agent to the novelistic soup. The texture of the novel of manners is not diluted by these additions and Pym need not develop them any more fully than she does here. When they do reappear briefly in later scenes of the language class, their characters, defined by these identifying traits, are easily recalled.

In a different fashion, Pym introduces a single minor character to highlight Wilmet's first experience at donating blood: a character who never reappears, who does not advance the plot, and whose sole function, apart from her oddity, is to serve briefly as a moral foil for Wilmet. The scene grew directly out of Pym's own experience:

4 May. I give blood in the crypt of St. Martin in the Fields . . . . I can imagine (for a novel) a little frail laden woman saying 'Oh I have given blood' and putting others to shame. (AVPE, 194)

Miss Daunt, as she becomes in the novel, undauntedly demands the special appreciation that she feels her rare Rhesus negative blood-type commands: '"*This precious blood*" . . . . that is the phrase used. And you expect me to wait here behind all these people!' Wilmet has previously viewed the experience with much the same sort of elitism, considering it 'exciting' and 'a kind of a treat', assessing her fellow donors as lacking 'nobility' with a disdain similar to Miss Daunt's: 'I came to the conclusion that while some were young, the majority were of the burden-bearing type, middle-aged and tired-looking, the sort of people who would take on yet another load in addition to all the others they already bore' (AGOB, 77). Neither as demanding nor as disheveled as the 'mad-looking' Miss Daunt, Wilmet nonetheless feels shock and embarrassment for the woman's performance because subconsciously she knows it mirrors her own.

A second more serious foil for Wilmet, Mary Beamish, fills her days with service to others: keeping house for her invalid and domineering mother, doing good works in her church and community, escaping to a nunnery to avoid her feelings for the young Father Ransome. Mary actively seeks Wilmet's friendship, accompanying her to the blood bank and soliciting her help for a shopping trip, but initially Wilmet keeps Mary at bay, refusing to acknowledge even their shared fondness for poetry.

Along with Mary, Wilmet's mother-in-law Sybil serves as a role model of charity and selflessness. Sybil is an atheist, a fact which Wilmet finds dangerously risky for one of her advanced age. But she is more generous than her daughter-in-law, leaving presents of expensive coffee and Egyptian cigarettes for a friend in 'reduced' circumstances, packing donations of clothing for the poor, and volunteering at the Settlement house. Unlike Wilmet, she is capable of domestic quietude, knitting, cooking, reading (and likewise incapable of artistically arranging flowers), and of conducting a genuine romance with a well-matched companion. If her man of choice, Professor Arnold Root, seems inappropriate to Wilmet, it is because the younger woman cannot disassociate shine from substance.

The failure of her romantic quest, the revelation of Piers's preference for his lover, Keith, and his questioning of her capacity for love, bring Wilmet to her lowest point. She confesses to Mary:

> 'Life isn't always all it's cracked up to be,' I said rather frivolously. 'And then sometimes you discover that you aren't as nice as you thought you were – that you're in fact rather a horrid person.' (AGOB, 205–6)

Mary and Piers are each responsible for Wilmet's growth, and their roles in her development exactly intersect: Piers goes out of her life on the day Mary returns from the convent to live temporarily with her. Her companionship is 'soothing' and her presence re-connects Wilmet to the life of the church, allowing her 'to enter the charmed circle of decorators' at the parish hall, where she has never before felt comfortable.

This is, as several critics have noticed, the most Christian of Pym's novels. Wilmet moves from vanity, egotism, and isolation, through doubt and error, to self-awareness, humility, regeneration, and integration into her community – the paradigmatic journey to salvation. As the book opens, Wilmet's litany of prayers begins with herself, 'I closed my eyes and prayed for myself on this my thirty-third birthday, for my husband Rodney, my mother-in-law Sybil, and a vague collection of friends who always seemed to need praying for' (AGOB, 5). Wilmet must gain humility in the course of the novel, moving away from self-satisfaction to uncertainty, as Pym imagined for her in a journal note:

> May 5. The knowledge might come to me – and I dare say it would be a shock – that one wasn't a particularly nice person (selfish, unsociable, uncharitable, malicious even) (AVPE, 194)

Passing through several stages of enlightenment, Wilmet joins the community at the novel's end in celebrating the marriage of Marius Ransome and Mary Beamish, then contentedly returning to her husband, family, and new home.

From the first entries in her journals, it is clear that Pym would center this work on the Church, and that the outcome of the novel would reflect the hope and promise of its title. Written in unusually large letters comes the first inkling that ecclesiastical imagery will once again spark her imagination:

> *What is My Next Novel to be*? It can begin with the shrilling of the telephone in Freddie Hood's church and end with the flame springing up – the new fire on Easter Sunday in the dark church. Hope and a blaze of golden forsythia round the font. But what about the middle?
>
> When starting to tell a story you have to choose exactly the point to plunge in. Perhaps on a fine Spring afternoon at the induction of a new vicar – 'We had had an early lunch . . . ' (AVPE, 194)

She settles on her first choice: not the vicar's induction, but the urgent and shrill sound of a telephone, whose ringing distracts the thoughts of a noontime worshipper. The potential anachronism of the church in the modern world consistently concerns Pym but she usually mediates the discomfort with comedy: '24th August – Saw today, after going to see Helen and Fanny at the B.M., a nun coming out of a telephone box. An early Betjeman – Mount Zion is in Touch with the Infinite' (MS Pym 46, fol. 30).

Even though it includes the usual wide range of comic types, the parish life of *A Glass of Blessings* is less satirically presented than in earlier novels. Wilmet, unlike many Pym parishioners, actually kneels in prayer at her chosen church, and in her portrayal of Mary Beamish, Pym presents the most devout and unselfish of her excellent women. The services at St Luke's are provided by a trio of clergymen who exhibit the range of ecclesiastical quirks one comes to expect from Pym's clerics, but who are less severely caricatured than many. The aesthetic Father Thames takes pride in his Dresden china and Fabergé egg, but is generously unperturbed by Wilf Bason's periodic pilfering. Marius Lovejoy Ransome, self-indulgent if not epicurean, buys a motorcycle with an inheritance too small to do 'some spectacular good with', then wins our approval by abandoning celibacy for life with the saintly Mary Beamish. The last words of the book belong to the solid and unprepossessing Father Bode, 'always so much better than the rest', who pronounces the concluding ceremony 'all very satisfactory'.

The choices for worship in the Pym world are doctrinally narrow, eliminating strict Protestantism on one hand ('none of the people one knew went to [the Methodist] chapel, unless out of amused curiosity') and the mysterious lure of Roman Catholicism on the other. Pym's Anglican church has several class levels, like her society, identifiable as High or Low Church from the level of liturgy offered, the celibacy of the clergy, the make-up of the congregation, and the appurtenances of wealth or ritual it exhibits. The appeal of the High Anglican Church of England lies in its obvious aura of elitism, layered in tradition, and its historical connection to Roman Catholicism – 'incense and good music, vestments and processions . . . going to Confession, and getting up to sing Mass at half-past six on a winter morning' (JP, 55). A low church rests solidly on its Protestant roots, less top-heavy with the demands of ritual, more broad-based in its population – 'less exotic, [but] the yoke was easier' (JP, 55). Even the most dedicated clergyman's wife, like Jane Cleveland, takes pleasure in the variety, as she explores the offerings of both ends of the spectrum in a London religious bookshop: 'Just looking round the Anglican Church, from one extreme to the other, perhaps climbing higher and higher, peeping over the top to have a look at Rome on the other side, and then quickly drawing back' (JP, 218). Wilmet's choice, St. Luke's, is, of course, suitably High, but the sound of a telephone ringing can nevertheless intrude.

Much of the comic success of *A Glass of Blessings* results from the effects of deflation of this sort. Many of the characters, Wilmet chief among them, aspire to a 'high' style in matters of appearance and social behavior, a style which is repeatedly undercut. The inspiration for the title, with its reference to George Herbert's religious poem 'The Pulley', probably came from a sign Pym noticed in a tube station: 'Seen in Charing Cross Station: How to make money – Make Taper-Lock your standard method of fixing pulleys. George Herbert's poem' (MS Pym 49, fol. 7). Frequently in Pym's work, some detail will interfere between aspiration and actuality, playing off the low against the high: her journal finds humor in a 'Union Jack hanging on the washing line (in the clergyman's garden)' (MS Pym 53, fol. 9); the Easter altar candles at St Luke's are ignited by the server's cigarette lighter; the splendid building of 'rose brown brick, with minarets almost in the Turkish style . . . decorated with carved swags of fruit and flowers' seen from a distance turns out to be a furniture depository, whose rosy façade is white with bird droppings.

Most of the minor characters and some of the major ones as well are drawn after this same principle. A journal entry notes her consciousness that this conjunction of low and high style might not always create a comic effect: 'The contrast between the worlds of Miss Pope and Miss Prideaux and Piers and his little friend – a rather frightening thing' (MS Pym 48, fol. 4). Usually the result is comic, though not strictly a matter of class or gender: the venerable Father Thames values equally a rare Fabergé egg and old photographs of himself in rowing attire; Miss Prideaux, the ex-governess of European aristocracy, dresses for tea in a jumble sale sweater once owned by Wilmet and a hat topped with rakishly pinned artificial violets. Occasionally the setting of a scene will put to use this principle of deflation: in *A Glass of Blessings* the drawing room of a London mansion 'which had been a fashionable residential area in the late eighteenth and early nineteenth centuries . . . and retained many of the pleasing elegancies of that period' is now a meeting place for a Settlement house committee meeting.

Here as always Pym continues the delineation of a finely textured background, using the human necessities of food, clothing, and shelter as tools for creating fictional worlds. Describing this desire for enlightening texture, Pym mentions two of her favorite authors, one who shared her penchant, and one less generous in delivering up detail:

But, on the other hand, when we are reading, we do want details. Denton Welch, again, writes in his Journal – 'I wish that people would mention the tiny things of their lives that give them pleasure of fear or wonder. I would like to hear the details of their houses, their meals, and their possessions.' And I think we do enjoy hearing about such things, not necessarily for social history but because they are pleasing in themselves. One wishes sometimes that Jane Austen had given us more detail about her heroines' clothes – what, for example, did Emma wear, when she went to dinner at the Coles'? (MS Pym 98, fol. 56)

Any of Pym's own novels could present myriad examples of this attention to physical detail, but *A Glass of Blessings* pays particular attention to the physical space surrounding its characters.

Home, shelter, safe haven, retreat, the grand or modest place, country house or bed-sitting room, in which one defends one's individuality from the outside world, defines character as closely as behavior in Pym's novels. Everything from the choice of neighborhood and exterior style to interior space and colors of walls, the period of the furniture, or the number of the knick-knacks, describes the kind of person who by virtue of choice or necessity lives in a particular dwelling. Economic class can be indicated by a great Georgian house (although there are few of these in Pym's solidly middle-class world and they are generally in need of repair) or by a third floor bed-sitter, 'not properly self-contained', that is, sharing a kitchen or a bathroom. Country cottages like that of the Bede sisters suggest a cosy domesticity with dampness held at bay by the warmth of the hearth. Suburban homes with postage-stamp gardens, like that which so stifles Deirdre Swan in *Less Than Angels*, gain the extra status of exclusivity and privacy if they are 'detached' or even 'semi-detached'. Post-war urban housing includes every variation from the spacious London townhouse of Sybil Forsyth to the rabbit-warrens of the waitresses and typists of *No Fond Return of Love*. Declarations of self-image as well as of wealth and class are implied in the housing assigned to a character, and Pym is faithful to the cultural changes of the 1950s and 1960s, recognizing that, as one contemporary magazine warned, 'where money is no object, good taste is often the first casualty'.[29] Garish and shoddy as the new construction rising around London seems to her, Pym's purpose is not to use her novels as vehicles for social or architectural reform. She will allow a character to regret the passing of a grander era while standing in front of a terrace of once elaborate homes now converted to flats or government offices:

... he could not help feeling that there was something depressing about seeing rows of filing cabinets in what had once been somebody's drawing room, wooden trestle tables standing on the parquet floors, wire trays and even a thick white cup glimmering faintly in the moonlight. If we lamented the decay of the great civilisations of the past, he thought, should we not also regret the dreary levelling down of our own? (LTA, 163)

She balances this view by presenting a panorama of possibilities for placing her characters in their physical worlds: some ten different domiciles in *A Glass of Blessings* alone. Wilmet describes the house she shares as 'very bleak and respectable . . . fitting for Rodney, a civil servant; but it hardly seemed to suit Sybil, my mother-in-law – who is what one calls a real character, though not in a tiresome way' (AGOB, 10). In addition, in the course of the novel Wilmet visits: the clergy house of St Luke's with its three contrasting quarters for Fr Thames, Fr Bode, and their live-in cook and housekeeper Wilf Bason; the home of Mary Beamish and her domineering mother, where the handsome Father Marius Ransome lodges temporarily; the cramped quarters of Miss Prideaux, filled with silver-framed photographs of her past life on the payrolls of aristocracy; the country home of friends Rowena and Harry Talbot, built in 1933 'in Elizabethan style', where next door is the great house 'now turned into a country club, with swimming pool and American bar, as the noticeboard proclaimed'; the pastoral retreat house where Mary tests her faith; and several houses of the Lord.

The most evocative of lodgings is kept tantalizingly from both Wilmet and the reader. Although she had often fantasised about Piers Longridge's living arrangements – 'the narrow hall with prams and bicycles and the smell of stale cooking' or, worse, 'the unmade bed – perhaps littered with galley proofs – . . . the bottle of gin, the unwashed glasses and cups, and the unemptied ashtrays' – the reality enlightens her. Newly apprised of the homosexual relationship between Piers and Keith, Wilmet accompanies them home to their crowded block of peeling stucco houses 'not even noble in their shabbiness'. The best comment she can find to make is that they are 'rather continental', all the while feeling 'a kind of deadness about this house on this fine Saturday afternoon', an atmosphere which duplicates her own sense of loss. Inside the small flat she discovers the primly fastidious decor of the homosexual housekeeper and evidence of Keith's elaborate preparations in her honor. Grudgingly abandoning her romantic fantasies about Piers, she admits 'it was quite obvious that I was going to find it impossible to dislike Keith', even after realizing that the scope of their conversation would always be limited to household hints.

For most of the novel this heroine has no home of her own. Upon hearing of Sybil's intended marriage, Wilmet assumes no changes in the status quo, 'obviously we should all live here together'. Sybil and Arnold, however, desire a more conventional marital seclusion, and Rodney and Wilmet, like Adam and Eve cast out from the garden, must make their solitary way to a new home. Their choice reflects the course of their future:

> Our search for somewhere to live seemed to have brought us closer together than we had been for years, though it had taken us a long time to decide whether it was to be a house or a flat, and in town or suburban country . . . . There had been the tempting advertisements – self-contained wings of Georgian rectories in Wiltshire or Hampshire, suburban residences in favoured positions, with tiled cloakrooms and double garages . . . In the end we had done something safe and dull, and bought the lease of a flat a stone's throw from Sybil's house and a good hundred yards nearer the clergy house than we had been before. (AGOB, 247)

The closing mood of *A Glass of Blessings* is confident and hopeful. Wilmet comes to a new appreciation of Rodney, seeks a closer relationship with her family and her church, and willingly shares Herbert's lines with Mary Beamish, now Ransome, recognising the potential for her own life to 'be a glass of blessings too. Perhaps it always had been without my realizing it' (AGOB, 256). No longer blinded by the superficiality of 'good taste' or of shallow fantasy, Wilmet has come to value her own position; like Jane Cleveland, she sees around her 'all this richness' (JP, 46; AGOB, 226).

At work on *Less Than Angels*, her fourth published novel, Pym too delighted in all the 'richness' she found surrounding her life. The mid-to late fifties brought her security in her job and a happy combination of London domesticity and publishing success, all of which contributed to the light-hearted tone of *Less Than Angels*. She says of this period:

> After the war I got a job as a kind of research assistant at the International African Institute in London. It was the sort of work

I liked doing – mostly preparing material for publication and it gave me a certain contact with the academic world. It was not well paid but I seemed quite well off in those days when there was so little to buy. London just after the war was shabby but life was free and pleasant. (MS Pym 98, fol. 80)

The International African Institute introduced her to the peculiar world of the academic anthropologist and she was quick to make fictional use of it.

As early as the rewrites of *Some Tame Gazelle*, Pym began to incorporate extended vignettes of anthropological academics or their canonical counterparts, church missionaries, into many of her plots. She reworked notes for a short story written in the 1940s (MS Pym 42, fol. 2) into a never- transmitted radio play with the same name – 'Parrots' Eggs' (MS Pym 95). The title refers to the custom of anonymously sending five parrots' eggs to inform an incompetent chief that his suicide was expected. Written sometime before *Less Than Angels*, the story similarly satirises the jealous rivalry among a group of anthropologists and the trivial nature of the work they all engage in. Although Pym never used the idea of an anonymous tribal warning in *Less Than Angels*, she originally intended to; 'You must have Parrots Eggs in somewhere' (MS Pym 45, fol. 6), she reminds herself.

Excellent Women contains Pym's first sustained look at anthropologists with the characters Helena Napier and Everard Bone, and includes a scene at a learned society much like the IAI. Anthropologists turn up for a dinner party in the quiet neighborhood of *An Unsuitable Attachment*, and the posthumously published *An Academic Question* centers on academic back-biting in the anthropology department of a redbrick university. Pym's interest in the discipline lasted even beyond her retirement from the IAI: Emma Howick, the heroine of *A Few Green Leaves* is an anthropologist by training who attempts unsuccessfully to observe her fellow villagers (and her own self) with professional detachment. But it is in *Less Than Angels* that Pym most closely scrutinises the behavior of anthropologists and analyzes the world of work for the central focus of a novel of manners.

Apart from her writing, which was a lifelong occupation, Pym's working career spanned twenty-eight years as Assistant Editor for *Africa*, the journal of the IAI. Hazel Holt remembers fondly the more than twenty years that she and Barbara shared a small office among the anthropologists, observing the observers. Pym's office work and, consequently, the working lives of many of her characters (those who work at all) both correspond to the pattern of her novels: the constricted or nondescript setting, the parade of unusual personalities, the small pleasures of food, friendships, and routine. In an essay entitled 'The Novelist in the Field: 1946–1974',[30] Hazel Holt details their working conditions, responsibilites, and amusements among the anthropologists.

In its original 'rather grand' location in Lower Regent Street, then in 'an interesting part of London' in Fetter Lane, and finally in a 'blank modern block' in High Holbern, the Institute devoted minimal floorspace to editorial duties, never more than 'eighteen feet square'. Here, at two scarred desks piled high with manuscripts, letters, proofs, and books in need of reviewers, the two friends worked, surrounded by olive-green metal cabinets for filing and map storage, and benignly supervised by their own sacrificial idol, the 'Juju':

> This was constructed from various 'magical' objects: a wooden bull-roarer (brought back from Nigeria by one of our anthropologists), a Salvation Army badge, a feather, a lock of my hair (Barbara had trimmed it for me one afternoon in the office when we were feeling bored) and the signature of the Father of anthropology, Professor Malinowski, cut from a letter in the files. Occasional 'offerings' – a pressed flower or a paper-clip – were made to the Juju if we needed a new reviewer or our proofs were late – only partly in jest.[31]

The Director of the Institute, Professor Daryll Forde was an ex-geographer and accomplished fund-raiser, who 'could always manage to coax just one more grant from UNESCO or the Ford Foundation for a new project'.[32] As a boss, he could be both exasperating and endearing, much like his fictional counterpart, Pym's Professor Felix Mainwaring of *Less Than Angels*, and Holt acknowledges there were 'moments of stress between two such opposite personalities':

> Daryll Forde, energetic, extrovert and 'do-ish', used to say 'Barbara has no sense of urgency' and 'Barbara never initiates anything'. They lived and worked at different tempos: 'Get him on the phone right *away*, my dear', he used to say briskly. Barbara would give a compliant smile and go quietly away

and write a well-turned letter instead. The results were usually the same.[33]

Pym's duties at the Institute included editing the articles chosen by Forde for each quarterly issue of *Africa* and making the preliminary selection of books for its review. She collected items for the 'Notes and News' column and compiled the journal's annual indexes. Along with Holt, she typed all correspondence for the Institute, Forde's own letters and lectures, long passages of manuscript revisions, bibliographies, and indexes. Accuracy, not speed, was her virtue: Holt admits 'We both of us typed with two fingers.'[34]

Occasionally the work had more glamour, since Pym also oversaw the advertisements for each issue of the journal: 'This was another bit of "mystique" which gave her great pleasure. When she was dealing with the agency that handled the more important advertisements for banks, airlines, and so on, she would assume a slightly dashing air, the faintest hint of Madison Avenue.'[35] She and Holt delighted in inventing personae and milieux for the anthropologists and writers they often never met or knew only slightly, and sometimes it became difficult to untangle fact and fiction. Pym writes,

> I had a card from dear John Beattie – how nice of him to write to me and so typical of the character we have invented for him.[36]

> I couldn't ask W. if his Mother was better because I couldn't remember if we'd invented her. (AVPE, 183)

Even in times of unpredictable obstacles – a tardy reviewer, a printer's strike – the quarterly issue of *Africa* always appeared on time, a matter of no small pride to both Pym and Holt. Says Holt of Pym's office demeanor, 'her general air of vagueness and tentativeness hid a formidable professionalism. She never seemed to hurry; there was always time for a chat – indeed we had the reputation of never seeming to do any work; but, somehow the work was always done. And done well, and on time.'[37]

Lunch breaks were long, 'to make up for the meagerness of our salaries . . . usually an hour and a half', and most of their lunching spots found their way into Pym's novels: the favorites being the Lyons Corner House, and the chain of Kardomah cafeterias with their trademark mosaic peacocks.

There was also the ABC teashop, later the Lite Bite (AGOB, AUA and NFRL), the health-food Oodles in Fetter Lane (TSDD), Hills in Fleet Street (where Digby and Mark once memorably took Esther Clovis and Gertrude Lydgate) and the Rendezvous in High Holborn (where the protagonists in *Quartet in Autumn* used Edwin's luncheon vouchers).[38]

Often Pym ate alone in these spots, reading or simply observing the sea of London humanity around her. Occasionally she shopped in the nearby book and department stores, browsing more often than buying. Sometimes during the unpublished years, she would use the time frugally to hand-deliver a manuscript to a potential publisher.

Returning to the office, she might quickly jot into her journal any oddities witnessed during lunch, or, occasionally, steal a few moments to work on her own writing. Tea breaks were precious, as were time-outs for cigarettes. Although both later conquered the habit when health demanded, Holt remembers that in the early days they smoked 'endlessly'.[39] Pym wrote to Philip Larkin that this fact even affected plans for their office redecoration: 'I am to have a new carpet – speckled black and white that won't show the cigarette ash' (AVPE, 237). Blue smoke and ash notwithstanding they maintained a selective tidiness at the office:

> The cleaning at the Institute was always rather sketchy and we both kept dusters in our desk drawers. Once in a fit of exasperation at the grit and grime in the curtains (London was being rebuilt around us in the 1950s and 1960s), Barbara took them home and washed them herself.[40]

Pym successfully kept her two professions separate. The continent of Africa held little interest for her; although some of her characters visit and return, she herself never traveled there, nor used it for the setting of a novel. She allows one character to define the profession in the most pedestrian of terms: '[Anthropologists] went out to remote places and studied the customs and languages of the people living there. Then they came back and wrote books and articles about what they had observed and taught others how to do the same thing' (LTA, 15). Outside the office she saw little of its documenters, and life at the Institute itself was never all engrossing: 'It ought to be enough for anybody to be the Assistant Editor of *Africa*, especially when the Editor is away lecturing for six months at Harvard, but I find it isn't quite' (AVPE, 217).

She published six novels during her tenure at the IAI but, with the exception of Holt, few of her colleagues were aware of the novelist among them. Holt notes that Professor Forde 'read one, found it, I suspect, largely incomprehensible, and read no more'.[41] Another colleague admits that it was 'a good three years beyond its publication' that he encountered his first Pym novel, *Less Than Angels*, and only then thanks to the suggestion of an American friend.[42] Visitors to her office usually remember little of their contact with the reticent assistant editor. Even when offering their warm appreciation in an obituary tribute, the anthropologists proved how little they knew Barbara Pym the novelist:

> When in 1961 her publisher turned down her seventh [novel], Barbara Pym was so dejected that she vowed she would never write another. For the next fifteen years she held to her resolve, directing her literary talents into her careful and conscientious editorship of *Africa*. It was not until after her retirement from the Institute . . . that Barbara gave in to the dictates of the writer's creative urge, and started to work on another novel. Even now, she had no intention of publishing again.[43]

Only an anthropologist could be so obtuse. She was more perceptive of them, however, recording their behavior as carefully as any field worker studying a strange tribe.

Quick to appreciate the conjunction between the two fields, the novelist often spoke of the similarities between constructing fictional worlds and documenting foreign ones. The same qualifications were required: detachment, observation, analysis, synthesis, presentation. Pym notes their similar methodology: 'I learned how it was possible and even essential to cultivate an attitude of detachment towards life and people and how the novelist could do fieldwork as the anthropologist did' (MS Pym 96, fol. 9). This detached observation was already second nature from her habit of recording in notebooks and journals the comic, sad, or unusual behavior and beliefs that she witnessed around her. Like the anthropologists, she recognised that social ritual was a measure of private beliefs and she preserved and presented her observations with meticulous detail.

The greatest difference she found between her own field work and that of the social scientist was the latter's unwillingness to incorporate imagination or humor into his work.

> For many years I worked with anthropologists . . . and I occasionally regretted that more of them did not turn their undoubted talents to the writing of fiction. Their work often showed many of the qualities that makes a novelist, accurate observation, detachment, even sympathy. It only needed a little more imagination, plus the leavening of irony and humour to turn their accounts into novels.[44]

She copies into her notebook, with certain irony, the following anthropological caveat which reminds the stranger to control his provincial responses to the unfamiliar:

> It is important that not even the slightest expression of amusement or disapproval should ever be displayed at the description of ridiculous, impossible or disgusting features in custom, cult or legend. (from *Notes and Queries in Anthropology*) (AVPE, 189)

The self-imposed strictures on an anthropologist studying in the field reveal more about the cultural values of the observer than about the tribe observed. The novelist admits no such restraints.

A letter to Pym from historian and critic Lord David Cecil offers the compliment, 'No other living novelist writes books that amuse me as yours do; they enlarge my imagination so, by introducing me to new worlds' (MS Pym 148, fol. 3). When she chooses to document the anthropologists' world for the basis of *Less Than Angels*, she opens the novel with a party held in the library of an academic organisation remarkably like the IAI, with a cast of characters remarkably like the ones she knew there. Her diary notes cryptically on October 15, 1955, '*Less Than Angels* out on Monday. Rather dreaded' (MS Pym 47, fol. 4) and the *roman à clef* aspect of the novel may have troubled her. The anthropologists it pictures, though, are fondly mocked; so much so that a contemporary reviewer of the novel suggested that 'some well-directed malice would have served to pull it together more effectively'.[45] What it lacks in malice it makes up in scope, examining in comic close-up a wide range of anthropological personalities, as various as the tribes they study, and as similar as any such inbred community, with a built-in social hierarchy. Benefactors, administrators, seasoned anthropologists returned from the field, a harried staff, young students anxious for their chance to impress – Pym presents a great chain of anthropological being, troubled with the same dissatisfaction as the humans of Alexander Pope's poem:

> What would this Man? Now upward will he soar,
> And little less than angel, would be more;
> Now looking downward, just as grieved appears
> To want the strength of bulls, the fur of bears.

Attempts to resolve this dissatisfaction drive the two plots and the numerous characters of this novel. The 'communal' plot involves the professional rivalry that surrounds the awarding of a research grant; the 'romantic' plot considers the competition among several young women, primarily Catherine Oliphant and Deirdre Swan, for a confused young graduate student, Tom Mallow. Ironically, there are no winners in either contest.

Not surprisingly, the Pym novels most touched by anthropology both in subject matter and style, *Less Than Angels, An Academic Question*, and *A Few Green Leaves*, present the largest casts of characters. Unlike the latter two, this novel operates without a central consciousness, indeed minus a single hero or heroine. Without resorting to a collection of eccentrics, Pym creates, as she did in *A Glass of Blessings*, 'the crowded canvas' she prefers, this time with three interlocking circles: the London scene of young people shaping their worlds; the suburban cocoon of family and established traditions; and the over-ripe softness of decaying aristocracy. Although this work is less contained in its settings than most of the early novels it still shares much with this group: the view of a select community, the esoteric language they adopt, the rituals and customs they continue; the presentation of detail to affirm underlying truths; and, finally, the relationship between the haves and have nots, between employers and employees, professors and students, clergy and laymen (to a lesser degree here), and, especially, between men and women.

With the anthropological institute providing much of its usual function, the church plays a more diminished role in *Less Than Angels* than in most of the early novels. Attendance is more a matter of competition than comfort for the two sisters, Rhoda Welcome and Mable Swan, and young Deirdre includes church-going as merely another of the stifling suburban conventions she wishes to avoid.

When a curious French anthropologist visits a Sunday service, he immediately commits a *faux pas*, occupying a pew that unspoken tradition has assigned to others:

> There are few things more disconcerting or even upsetting for a regular worshipper at a church which is not normally very full than to find his usual seat occupied by somebody else. Perhaps such a thing had never happened to the Dulkes in all their forty years at the church. There was indeed an empty pew in front and another behind, but that was not quite the same thing. (LTA, 81)

When the seating arrangements are settled and the service proceeds, the narrator admits it 'was beautifully conducted and there was perhaps nobody who did not feel in some way the better for having been present at it', but parish life does not engulf these characters as it does in earlier novels.

The London scenes are even more ambiguous about the consolations of religious faith. Catherine's visit to a Roman Catholic church occurs on impulse and provides her little satisfaction. On the night Tom leaves her for Deirdre she wishes for a book that would 'take her out of herself', but finds little of comfort on her nightstand: 'The only real book of devotion she had . . . told her that we are strangers and pilgrims here and must endure the heart's banishment, and she felt that she knew that anyway' (LTA,138). Pym sometimes distorts religious practice for comic effect, usually by linking it to anthropology. In Catherine's kitchen, the meat grinder with its sharp iron teeth reminds her of a fierce little African god. She wonders why the 'worshippers' in the self-service cafeteria do not make offerings of buns, poached eggs, and salads, before the mosaic peacocks decorating the walls: 'Obviously the cult of peacock worship, if it had ever existed, had fallen into disuse' (LTA, 7).

Catherine, thirtyish and unmarried, thinks of herself 'with a certain amount of complacency, as looking like Jane Eyre' (LTA, 7) and shares with that heroine both her impulsiveness and her independence. Catherine, who at first seems the most autobiographical of Pym's young heroines, supports herself by writing romantic stories for women's magazines. Like Pym, she 'draws her inspiration from everyday life, though life itself was sometimes too strong and raw and must be made palatable by fancy, as tough meat may be made tender by mincing' (LTA, 7). Surprisingly, Pym never comments on the similarity between Catherine and herself, even insisting to Philip Larkin that, 'Catherine used to be quite a favourite heroine of mine but she now seems less real to me' (AVPE, 223). Like her creator, Catherine lives on the fringes of the academic world, linked to it by her live-in lover, Tom Mallow, and the other anthropology students for whom she provides practical wisdom and the occasional home-cooked meal.

As always with Pym, names in *Less Than Angels* carry either irony (The Foresight Center for Anthropological Research), playfulness (Primrose Cutbush), literary reference (Catherine Oliphant) or implied social standing (Prof. Mainwaring admires Mrs Foresight's money but not her undistinguished Christian name: 'it was difficult to think of her as Minnie which was surely an unworthy name.') Even the lowest graduate students are conscious of the political and social signifiers carried in their professors' forms of address:

> 'Dear Boy! My *dear* Felix, my *dear* Gervase,' said Mark scornfully. 'All this bandying about of Christian names disgusts me.'
> 'We haven't yet acquired the status of being known by ours,' said Digby more mildly. 'It's an interesting study, when you come to consider it. The lower you are in status, the more formal the type of address used, unless you're a servant, perhaps.'
> 'Still, Fairfax does *know* our names, which is something.'
> 'But does he know which of us is which?'
>
> (LTA, 21)

Pym had worked at the IAI ten years when she wrote *Less Than Angels*, and the young anthropology students she observed from her desk added a new dimension to her own Oxford experiences of student life. Although she struck no lasting friendships among them, the patterns of their lives intrigued her, especially those of the Americans, and for a time she read 'all the novels she could find about American academic life'.[46]

Professors of Anthropology, Grace and Alfred Harris, were young, married, American graduate students on a year's study program at Oxford in 1949–50. Unlike Mark and Digby's student poverty, they remember living 'quite well' on their combined stipends of £12 per week.[47] They share Pym's impression that life was inexpensive in Oxford and London after the war; they had no need of a car, relying on bicycles for transportation in Oxford, and they made weekly field trips to London for tutoring in Swahili. On several occasions they visited the IAI, but suggest other names than their own as models for Pym's young graduate students. The best anthropologist authorities on Pym's career at the Institute, says Alfred Harris, are deceased, but the acquaintances and observations she made there live on in composite form in her fictional versions.

Nearly everyone in this novel is an anthropologist of sorts. Beyond the social scientists' formal observations of foreign cultures, the students constantly measure each other, their professors, and the staff. In suburbia, the neighbors gather information from behind half-drawn curtains or over garden hedges because 'how much more comfortable it sometimes was to observe . . . from a distance, to look down from an upper window, as it were, as the anthropologists did' (LTA, 256). A young French anthropology student studies the strange tribe of Englishmen he lives among, attempting to assume their cultural standards: 'I believe it is not correct to stay till the end . . . so I must be going. I like to do the correct thing where possible' (LTA, 23). Like most of these observers, however, his vision is skewed because he cannot go beyond his presupposed assumptions. The natives tolerate his questions about English suburban life because he poses them 'so charmingly that nobody could possibly have taken offense', but he, and by implication all the observers in *Less Than Angels*, miss more than they comprehend about their subjects. Empirical documentation can never be complete: 'Curiosity has its pains as well as its pleasures and the bitterest of its pains must surely be the inability to follow up everything to its conclusion' (LTA, 9). Only the artist, Catherine, can construct complete worlds, and even she must learn to include the bitter as well as the sweet. In the course of the novel Catherine moves from producing saccharine women's stories with predictable romantic endings to writing her own story of a woman betrayed. Ironically, after she documents the truth in fiction, two characters from *A Glass of Blessings* will read her story at the hairdresser's and brand it 'far-fetched'.

In addition to reflecting reality inadequately, anthropology is portrayed as a trap from which to escape: trivial, petrifying, isolating. Its very language suffocates thought, Catherine recognises, as she reads from Tom's dissertation.

She turned a page at random. *'It would, however, be dangerous at this stage to embark on any extensive analysis . . . '* she read. 'Oh what cowards scholars are! When you think how poets and novelists rush in with *their* analyses of the human heart and mind and soul of which they often have far less knowledge than darling Tom has of his tribe. And why do they find it so difficult to begin or start anything – they must always *commence* – have you noticed? (LTA, 167)

Felix Mainwaring in retirement has given away his anthropology books in favor of Shakespeare and the Bible; Mark Penfold leaves his studies, first for a debutante's ball and finally for a position in her father's firm; Deirdre abandons scholarship for love; Tom retreats to Africa to meet an absurd and meaningless demise.

Death seldom intrudes into the novel of manners (unless to provide an inheritance) and it is usually executed and reported from off stage in order to affect the behavior of others rather than to affect the plot. *Less Than Angels* contains one of the rare occasions in which Pym kills off a main character, and she removes Tom Mallow with stiletto speed in a casual paragraph. Deirdre and Catherine, exchanging the uncomfortably stilted conversation that occurs between two women who have loved the same man, discuss on a warm October day the necessity of posting immediately any Christmas cards destined for Africa. Pym then undermines the sense of compressed time just established in the dialogue, smoothly switching to an all-seeing narrator who reveals the bad news the two women have yet to learn:

> Catherine did not know, indeed how could she, that before Tom could post his Christmas cards, he would be lying dead, accidentally shot in a political riot, in which he had become involved more out of curiosity than passionate conviction. (LTA, 231)

Notification of an unexpected death could upset the conventions of this novel, injecting violence, danger, and surprise, but for its minimal effect on the community. Tom's grant money will be allocated to another equally trivial anthropology project, his brother's marriage insures the ancestral line, and the women who briefly mourn him soon find other means of fulfillment.

Only by escaping from anthropology, burning the notes that bind him to the discipline, can Alaric Lydgate, the second candidate for

Catherine's affections, re-enter the world. With Catherine's direction, he anticipates the future as a participant in rather than as an observer of life: 'I shall be free to do whatever I want to . . . . I could even write a novel, I suppose' (LTA, 229). Free from anthropology's burden, these two may marry, Pym hints, although they would make 'a difficult and peculiar couple' (LTA, 256).

Sexuality makes an unusual, if discreet, appearance in *Less Than Angels*, as Pym offers a view of mid-1950s Bohemian social mores with her characteristic indirectness. A masked Alaric dances around a bonfire fueled by the notes of his ex-career, and Catherine joins him, arms laden with rhubarb, an earth mother figure for this parodic fertility rite. Catherine and Tom have previously defied the dictates of society by sharing her flat, a cohabitation growing more from Tom's need for London lodging than from overwhelming sexual attraction. Tom's aunt, who visits Catherine to request her renunciation of Tom, (they both feel like characters from *La Traviata*), declares that she personally does not think 'there should be different codes of behavior for men and women, though of course that view *was* held, and in the highest circles' (LTA, 135). Her assumption of a double standard of sexual propriety (both in terms of gender and social class) carries extra irony since there is no indication Catherine and Tom share anything more intimate than dinner or more affectionate than hand-holding. Their relationship is so casual, in fact, that Catherine wonders silently 'whether anthropologists became so absorbed in studying the ways of strange societies that they forgot what was the usual thing in their own' (LTA, 27).

Pym demonstrates in this novel that the appeal of sexuality extends to the older characters as well. Rhoda Welcome, a spinster now in her fifties, 'would perhaps have liked what she called 'the experience of marriage', a vague phrase which seemed to cover all those aspects which one didn't talk about' (LTA, 36). The narrative voice later reaffirms a theme Pym first attempted in the short story 'The German Baron': sexual attraction does not dissipate with age.

> She was as yet too young to have learned that women of her aunt's age could still be interested in men; she would have many years to go before the rather dreadful suspicion came to her that one probably never does cease to be interested. (LTA, 150)

Overt sexuality is rarely an issue in these early novels, limited to some vague longings, unrequited passions, and the occasional lukewarm embrace. The curtain rings down on any scene threatening to exceed unstated boundaries of acceptabilty.

Probably because it connects so closely to her own working life, *Less Than Angels* gives Pym's most sustained look at the world of work. Later, in *Quartet in Autumn*, she presents a more poignant view of the subject, but here the absurdities of routine, of unorthodox schedules, of petty jealousies among co-workers, take on comic dimensions. Usually Pym's men, if they are not students, clerics, or anemic academics, toil at unspecified jobs in civil service or business. Her women, if married like Jane Cleveland or Wilmet Forsyth, are supported by their husbands; if not, like Mildred Lathbury, they exist comfortably if not luxuriously on the remainders of family inheritances. Most occupy themselves with church and volunteer work; the married with matchmaking, the single with waiting for the right man to appear. Daily toil, if pictured at all, usually consists of the mind-numbing routine of Prudence Bates's office job or the undemanding typing/filing/indexing of the academic helpmate.

Less Than Angels presents the first woman who supports herself with creative, ultimately satisfying work. Although Catherine Oliphant initially discounts her stories as 'unbearably trite and removed from life', she publishes regularly and maintains a 'detached and unsentimental' tone valued by her editor. As with Pym, Catherine's work provides refuge and release from personal problems, a position envied by at least one other woman character. Evoking Austen's *Persuasion*, Pym contrasts Catherine's rather hopeful future after Tom's desertion with that of his first love, Elaine.

> The circumstances of [Elaine's] daily life, less usual now than fifty or a hundred years ago were not conducive to an easy forgetting. While Delia and Felicity had been trained for careers, Elaine had been the one to stay at home. She might, if she had come upon them, have copied out Anne Elliott's words, especially as she was the same age as Miss Austen's heroine: 'We certainly do not forget you so soon as you forget us. It is, perhaps, our fate rather than our merit. We cannot help ourselves. We live at home, quiet, confined, and our feelings prey upon us. You are forced on exertion. You have always business of some sort or other to take you back into the world immediately, and continual occupation and change soon weaken impressions.' (LTA, 186)

The consolation of Catherine's work is unavailable to Elaine, partly by choice, partly by intellect ('Elaine was not much of a reader') and partly by her class.

Issues of class are difficult when discussing Barbara Pym, and although she considers them more fully in *An Unsuitable Attachment* and the later novels, several times in *Less Than Angels* class distinctions shape character and plot. The hierarchical rankings within the anthropological community, the kinship diagrams and categorizing they dote on, become metaphors for the equivalent stratification of British social classes. Pym presents several scenes in which subtle demarcations indicate differing levels within these groups – old family wealth, public education at the proper schools, elite military service, the aura of elegance and expected privlege are indicated (and usually undercut for comic ends) in speech patterns, preferences of dress, food, and decor. Conservative and tradition bound, Pym's few upper class families place a higher value on longevity than on beauty or utility. They wear 'good' if slightly dated clothing, live among solid if ugly antiques, manage the remnants of their estates on a combination of pride and diminished funds, marry each other, and tolerate eccentricities of behavior as a matter of course.

In previous novels Pym's landed gentry make cameo appearances, called upon to validate the local parish or to open a Christmas bazaar. With the great house empty and without such a family anchoring the village, the natives of *A Few Green Leaves* feel adrift. *Less Than Angels*, however, provides a larger than usual catalogue of this group, appropriately for an anthropological study. The formality of their manners opens wide possibilities for comic interpretation, a fact not lost on Catherine Oliphant who 'had often wondered why it was that anthropologists seemed to explore only the lower strata of their own society . . . . she was sure that the experience of a debutante dance in Belgravia would be as rewarding for them as any piece of native ceremonial' (LTA, 136).

Pym begins her exploration with the aristocratic anthropologist Felix Mainwaring, who as a young man disappointed his family by 'going to the remotest parts of the Empire not to govern, which would have been natural and proper, but to study the ways of the primitive peoples living there' (LTA, 18). Now, for a celebratory party at his research institute he serves his colleagues second-rate sherry, 'certainly good enough for the occasion', since the women, he is sure, are undiscriminating imbibers and the men 'not quite out of the top drawer'. The attitude coupled with the dated phrasing marks his privileged background, made comic by comparison with his current position: courting Minnie Foresight's money, dozing through discussions of research projects, and retiring on weekends to his country home from which all books on anthropology have been removed. Here he invites a group of grant-hungry students to determine the winner of the Foresight research money. Pym comically contrasts the clothing, appetites, and expectations of the four candidates on the home turf of their more privleged professor, and balances the lower end of the scene's social scale by including a local serving girl hired for the occasion, 'tall, awkward-looking with red hands' – teasingly named Barbara. The scenes at Professor Mainwaring's play off the social and generational differences between an anthropologist raised to Edwardian elegance and a younger group, impatient to make their reputations if not their fortunes.

A corresponding theme of the leveling down of contemporary society weaves through the novel by means of the upper class family and friends of Tom Mallow. Tom considers himself 'detribalised' from his background, moving in the course of the novel from Mallow Park, to Catherine's flat, to dingy student digs, and finally to an African hut. When he makes a brief visit home, Pym attempts, only half successfully, one of her few extended scenes of upper-class domestic life, suggesting by her selection of character and setting a landed gentry in disarray. Tom's mother, whose silhouette evokes the solidity of 'a great Henry Moore sculpture in a London park', no longer manages a huge estate but tends a vegetable garden with hands 'rough and not very clean'. His uncle, the remaining male of the older generation, sits semi-comatose before televised sporting events or programs of housekeeping hints, 'a sacrifice laid before the altar of the television set' (LTA, 181). His brother finds Tom's casual dress less than suitable, 'You must remember that many eyes will be upon you. We are still the leading family here whatever else might have changed', and equips him with a useless accoutrement, a shooting stick, 'the insignia of rank' (LTA 181).

Pym fares better when she broadens her view, juxtaposing social classes for comic or ironic purposes, as in a single scene indicating the variety of contemporary British society. A chauffeur settles the wealthy Mrs Foresight into her car, 'old-fashioned but of the best make and beautifully kept'; he carefully arranges a light blanket over her knees, but only after stuffing a Communist newspaper into his pocket. As the car pulls away with Mainwaring and the potential benefactress inside, Digby and Mark watch from the sidewalk:

> 'If he threw out a handful of coins, would you demean yourself by struggling for them in the road?' asked Digby.
> 'I don't suppose there would be an struggle,' said Mark. 'English people are embarrassed at that sort of thing. Everybody would just look the other way and hurry on. We should have the field to ourselves.'
>
> (LTA, 126)

Pym compresses into this vignette a panoramic view of the post-war British class system, but refrains from commenting directly on the distinctions she sets out. Apart from introducing the occasional MP like Edward Lyall of *Jane and Prudence* or the chauffeur with the Communist tract, she will seldom connect politics and class. Pym remains detached from the political repositionings of post-war Britain except as they affect a character's immediate surroundings, aligning her with contemporaries like Amis and Sillitoe in what sociologist Rubin Rabinovitz sees as a common apolitical approach:

> Virtually all of the novelists of the 1950s . . . are extremely concerned in their fiction with society and contemporary English social change . . . . [but] a remarkable lack of political commitment, communist or other, exists in this group.[48]

Social changes documented in Pym's 1950s fictional Britain reside in the details of middle-class housing, food, clothing, religion, jobs, leisure activities that she presents, not in staunch political views. The conservative nature of the novel of manners is complemented by the technique.

Pym would aim her focus lower when she considered the class issue again in *An Unsuitable Attachment*, presenting a romantic pair with mismatched social backgrounds. Before that ill-fated novel, however, she would turn her sights inward and create the most Pym-like of all her heroines, Dulcie Mainwaring of *No Fond Return of Love*. One critic, Jane Nardin, has incorrectly dismissed this work as the product of a 'tired imagination' and suggests that along with *An Unsuitable Attachment* it 'will not be read or taught as widely as Pym's other books' because it has 'a cumbersome and artificial plot, more like the plot of a stage comedy than like that of other Pym novels, a plot that requires the book's quiet, proper heroine to act in ways that seem . . . unconvincing and out of character.'[49] This appraisal fails to recognise both the novel's formal comic characteristics and its explication of Pym's observational style.

The plot of *No Fond Return of Love* does resemble the 'stage comedy' Nardin suggests, but in a less pejorative sense than she implies. Its multiple pairs of mismatched lovers stumbling their way to proper alignment echo any classic comedy of errors: each of the couples begins by loving inappropriately and each ends with the most suitable partner. The intrigue and machinations of all the major characters, the drawing room scenes, the whispered conferences, the information gained by eavesdropping, the congregation of all the principal characters for a climactic meeting also liken *No Fond Return of Love* to a Restoration romantic comedy, missing only the powdered wigs. Similarly, farcical elements play a larger role in this work than in almost any other of Pym's novels. The comedy is broader, the plot more hyperactive than elsewhere in her work, and the ending offers the all-but-guaranteed conventional marriage for the heroine.

Pym strays from her usual style in *No Fond Return of Love* by attempting a convoluted comic plot and basing many of the complications on a principle of tripling. Although Dulcie Mainwaring is clearly the novel's heroine, she and the two other main characters, Viola Dace and Aylwin Forbes, are introduced at a literary conference in three similar vignettes as each unpacks in cramped accommodations, uneasy about the 'prospect of strange companions at such close quarters' (NFRL, 11). The repetition of this opening scenes allows Pym to align and differentiate the women and to create both an alliance and an immediate tension between the eventual roommates. 'What does one do or wear?' asks Viola when Dulcie suggests they go down to dinner together. 'I suppose nobody really knows . . . It might be like the first night on board ship when nobody changes for dinner.' Wanting to do the correct thing and reassured that there is no precedent for proper behavior since 'it's the first time a conference of this sort' had been held in the out-of-the-way girls' boarding school in Derbyshire, they warily agree to join forces. Viola applies lipstick 'savagely, as if she were determined to make herself look as unlike somebody who worked on the dustier fringes of the academic world as possible' (NFRL, 13). The result, both 'bizarre and striking' makes Dulcie aware of her own 'careful "natural" make-up', but any companion, however suspect, is preferable to a solo entrance into the dining room.

The third bedroom scene introduces Aylwin Forbes, deftly characterised by the items he rearranges on his dresser top – yeast tablets, stomach powder, hair tonic – and by the gin he first discreetly places in the wardrobe then pragmatically removes to the small cabinet over the washbasin, risking for accessibility's sake the morning maidservant's 'quick swig'. He unpacks brushes, a fine leather stud box, the latest issue of his own literary journal, and, almost as an afterthought, the large photograph of his wife, which he is unable to place conveniently and returns to the suitcase. His egocentric preoccupation with the items of his own comfort contrast comically with Viola and Dulcie's concerns for appropriate dress and behavior.

Tripling also increases the comic potential for the three relationships that structure the romance plot: Aylwin Forbes's reluctant association with Viola Dace, inappropriate attraction to the young Laurel, and eventual pairing with Dulcie. In addition there are only three chief settings: the literary conference, Dulcie's London suburb, and the Eagle House Private Hotel, domain of Aylwin's mother, Horatia. Finally, most of the minor characters, of whom there are Pym's usual host, fall into one of three 'family' groups.

The first of the novel's three major settings opens with a Jane Austen-like introduction: 'There are various ways of mending a broken heart, but perhaps going to a learned conference is one of the most unusual.' This gathering of indexers, editors, and bibliographers, 'discussing scholarly niceties that meant nothing to most of the world' (NFRL, 11) gives Pym (and Dulcie as her alter ego) two chapters to present a new forum for the exploration of manners and morals: ' – an opportunity to meet new people and to amuse herself by observing the lives of others, even if only for a week-end and under somewhat unusual circumstances' (NFRL, 11). After the solitary bedroom scenes, we are treated to the opening dinner, the following day's dull lectures and discussions, the evening's deadly social gatherings, and the closing chapel service – a series of scenes with the contained setting, the circumscribed society, the emphasis on character and comedy that denote the novel of manners.

When considering the presentation of the several communal meals that occur during this section, Pym imagines in her journal,

At the end of the long tables the woman (or women) who happen to be sitting there serve out the soup and the portions of food. (Men very seldom do.) Often an unmarried woman does it, perhaps it satisfies some deep need, something finer than mere bossiness. (MS Pym 50, fol. 1)

Subsequently she creates in the novel the self-appointed server, who first reminds Dulcie of a 'medieval nun or friar feeding the assembled poor', but who incongruously wears a large cameo depicting the rape of Leda. When she turns out to be a renowned librarian, Dulcie has difficulty reconciling 'such eminence with this jolly woman serving out the soup'. Protocol requires that everyone end the meal by giving at least the appearance of helping; 'it seemed that nobody could leave without carrying something, even if it was only a jug of custard or an unused fork' (NFRL, 19). Forced jollity and posing characterise much of the social communication, and after dinner characters determinedly avoid each other by hiding among potted palms or slipping surreptitiously away from unwelcome conversations.

As in any country house comedy, nighttimes at the conference are for whispered conversations in hallways, taps on doors, insomnia, and speculation, but, here, all distinctly asexual. This group is given to padding about wearing flower-printed bath caps, borrowing indigestion tablets, and serving each other morning cups of lukewarm bitter tea.

The centerpiece of the conference is the morning lecture and discussion session, and Pym perfectly captures the combination of nervous tension and stifling dullness surrounding it. The room is overheated, the audience edgy, as much from boredom as anticipation, and the narrative voice reflects the mood by jumping from consciousness to consciousness. Five short paragraphs, five thinkers, five quick perspectives from which to view the scene culminate in Aylwin Forbes's fainting at the podium. As when Kingsley Amis' s Lucky Jim Dixon takes the same tumble, all is not lost, for this show of weakness allows Dulcie suddenly to appreciate Forbes's appeal: 'Why, he's beautiful . . . Like a Greek marble, or something dug up in the garden of an Italian villa, the features a little blunted, with the charm of being not quite perfect' (NFRL, 28).

The conference concludes with an undenominational service in the chapel, led by a 'grimly determined' young woman at the harmonium. Pym delights in the possibilities for comedy in the earnest practice of faith and here offers one of the more unusual of her many church scenes: a melange of worshippers brought together not by religious preference or neighborhood proximity but by vocation. The service offers a curious overlay of social consciousness onto conventional practice. When the first hymn, 'All things bright and beautiful', begins, Dulcie's indignation swells, awaiting:

> The rich man in his castle, the poor man at his gate,
> God made them high or lowly and ordered their estate.

But the offending lines suggesting social determinism have been discreetly eliminated. Robbed of her indignation she turns her attention to the layman's 'short address' (not the clergy's 'sermon'), tailored for this audience: 'He tried to show all work can be done to the Glory of God, even making an index, correcting a proof, or compiling an accurate bibliography . . . . those who do such work have perhaps less opportunity of actually doing evil than those who write novels and plays or work for films or television' (NFRL, 30). With this reminder of the nearness of Dulcie's (and Barbara's) vocation and avocation, the conference closes and the next portion of the novel centers itself around Dulcie's suburban London home, a less confined setting but one offering multiple possibilities for social interaction.

Dulcie's house, inherited from her deceased parents, is located 'in a pleasant part of London which, while it was undoubtedly a suburb, was "highly desirable" and, to continue in the estate agent's word, "took the overflow from Kensington."' Decidedly middle-class, the neighborhood borders tonier addresses, and as one neighbor crows, 'And Harrods *do* deliver' (NFRL, 32). From this haven of order and stability, Dulcie free-lances her indexing jobs and Miss Lord comes regularly to help with the housework, so neither the demands of home nor work interfere with her passion for sleuthing.

Dulcie's is a small world, her own Yoknapatawpha County notes one critic,[50] where, on any walk down a crowded London street, she expects to encounter someone familiar. Small enough that at Mrs Williton's jumble sale for the organ fund Dulcie is introduced to Rhoda Wellcome, a character from *Less Than Angels* who mentions that Deirdre and Digby Fox from that novel's collection of anthropologists have married and are expecting a child. Later at Taviscombe she tours the Forbes' ancestral castle along with a quartet of characters from *A Glass of Blessings*. These cross-over characters serve several functions for Pym, not the least of which is compressing and interlocking the fictional population.

We know the neighbors too: Mrs Beltane 'was an elegant blue-haired, stiffly-moving woman of about sixty, who imagined herself to have seen better days' since she now lets the top floor of her house to a retired Brazilian diplomat and 'of course she would never have done such a thing in "the old days"'. From his third floor window this likable foreigner, Senhor MacBride-Pereira, provides a bird's-eye perspective of the street's comings and goings, always aware of his position as outsider: '"To be a foreigner is bad enough," he would lament, "and perhaps to be an American, too, but to be a *Latin*-American – that is really terrible!"' (NFRL, 36). He speaks English well and delights in British ways and conventions, even dressing in a Scottish kilt when certain he is unobserved, to align himself with his adopted culture. Like Dulcie, he is an observer, but with a limited understanding of what he sees he must repeatedly ask himself, 'Now what have I seen . . . ?' or 'The things I see . . . Who knows what it might not be' (NFRL, 67). He glances away and misses entirely the climax of the book.

In addition to Senhor MacBride-Pereira and the vicious and pampered lapdog, Felix, (the canine counterpart of Faustina of *An Unsuitable Attachment*), Mrs Beltane also boards her two adult children, giving Pym the generational range she needs for this mini-community. The daughter, Monica, a lecturer at London University, remains palely in the background, probably because of the abundance of female minor academics in the novel. Paul, the son, works in the flower shop his mother bought for him 'just off' the trendy High Street in Kensington, and becomes the appropriate, if at first unappreciated, suitor to Dulcie's niece, Laurel.

Laurel's arrival at Dulcie's house signals the first of a series of visits by outsiders. Eighteen years old, Laurel comes up to London dreaming of 'brightly lit streets, Soho restaurants, coffee bars, and walks and talks with people her own age' (NFRL, 46). Taking up temporary residence with Dulcie, she serves as her younger foil and near rival. Laurel's shallow sensibilities, simplistic world-view, and enthusiasm for faddish culture, although presented as appropriate for her age, provide contrast with Dulcie's stability and worth, and their initial generational confrontation occurs when Laurel is not even at home.

Uncomfortable in her role as guardian, unsure of her responsibilities toward a nearly grown woman, Dulcie ventures into Laurel's room one evening when her niece stays late in town, ostensibly to deliver some flowers but actually to inspect the girl's 'private territory'. What she discovers is chaos – the bed unmade, drawers half open, clothes strewn about, 'Why the child hadn't even unpacked properly.' Her indexer's natural desire for order and neatness is offended, but immediately Pym tempers this response with a more tolerant one, as Dulcie discovers a bedside photo of 'a popular singer . . . of rock-and-roll, jive, skiffle, or whatever they called it'. Her lack of familiarity with the young idol notwithstanding, she has sympathy with the impulse to idolise, and vows to say nothing to Laurel of the unkempt quarters. This non-incident, a clash of temperament, age, and sensibilities, delineates the personality and behavior of each of the women through the details of the messy room.

Viola too will be defined almost entirely by her odd attire and careless housekeeping. Evicted from her own flat after a row with the landlady, she seeks refuge at Dulcie's house, completing the all-female family group. Before bringing them together, however, Pym distinguishes between the two women by presenting a contrasting pair of meals. For her solitary dinner, Dulcie will carefully prepare and romantically justify the simple fare:

> It would have to be one of those classically simple meals, the sort that French peasants are said to eat and that enlightened English people sometimes enjoy rather self-consciously – a crusty French loaf, cheese, and lettuce and tomatoes from the garden. Of course there should have been wine and a lovingly prepared dressing of oil and vinegar, but Dulcie drank orange squash and ate mayonnaise that came from a bottle. (NFRL, 56)

The spartan supper suits her with its combination of classic elegance and practical convenience. When her curiosity prompts her to wangle an invitation to supper at Viola's, the fastidious Dulcie is immediately struck by two impressions: 'the room was indescribably untidy, and there was no sign whatever that any kind of meal was being prepared.' Although casual to the point of carelessness, Viola has purchased for her guest a disarmingly extravagant spread of exotic salads, cold meats, and croissants. The frugality of one meal and the flamboyance of the other perfectly delineate the two characters and heighten the comic potential of future meal planning when they join forces at Dulcie's house.

Farce fills this novel. It may be only a brief undeveloped image – the stuffed eagle in the hall of The Eagle House Private Hotel, resenting the indignity of spring cleaning, inflicts a nasty scratch upon the Hoover-wielding offender. It may be a recurring joke correlating characters and their choice of footwear – Marian, the career-girl stenographer 'teetering on her stiletto heels', the dapper voyeur Senhor MacBride-Pereira 'padding softly in his orange suede shoes', the sexually-charged Viola in red canvas sneakers, or the ever-practical Dulcie with 'thin legs and sensible shoes'. Sometimes farce carries a full-blown scene, as when Aylwin's mother-in-law Mrs Williton drops by unexpectedly to determine his intentions about his marriage.

Pym sets up this scene fifty pages before it actually occurs by calling attention to the inherent ridiculousness of our language. When a minor character refers to Aylwin Forbes as a 'libertine',

> Dulcie's first impulse was to burst out laughing at the use of such an old-fashioned word, permissible, surely, only in the English synopsis of an Italian opera. The Duke in *Rigoletto* might have been so described, she thought. (NFRL, 80)

But several chapters later Aylwin's mother-in-law will think '*libertine* . . . almost out loud' when she interrupts him entertaining Laurel:

> Plying a young girl with drink . . . . It was disgusting. She had always known that her son-in-law was a man of loose moral character, but never before had she been confronted with the actual proof of his degeneracy. What might not have happened had she not chosen to arrive at that moment! And in a library, too, surrounded by great literature! (NFRL, 138)

Her discomfort heightens as she awaits Aylwin's return from seeing the young lady out, and the scene becomes more farcical on the misreading of a single vowel. Peering at the fine leather bindings and dim gilt-lettered titles on the surrounding bookshelves, Mrs Williton reads: '*The Rosciad, Night Thoughts, The Pleasures of the Imagination, The Bastard* – could it be? She peered more closely; it *looked* like "Bastard", or was it perhaps "Bustard", a kind of bird? . . . She turned away from the books shocked and confused' (NFRL, 138). This kind of word-play could seem sophomoric if it did not capture so well the shallow intellect and undaunted, if ill-advised, maternal diligence of Mrs Williton. Pym walks a thin line here, but because the interfering mother-in-law is such a familiar comic butt, the near-pun reinforces rather than offends.

The second of the novel's three family groups centers around the home of Dulcie's Aunt Hermione and Uncle Bertram, a bickering brother-and-sister team reminiscent of that in Pym's story 'Poor Mildred'. Their kitchen is ruled by the Viennese cook, Mrs Sedge, who 'had apparently retained little knowledge of her country's cuisine, if she had ever possessed it; Dulcie was always surprised at the thoroughness with which she had acquired all the worst traits of English cooking.' Pym delights in presenting the dinner Dulcie endures on her visit there: 'A dish of mince with tomato sauce spread over the top seemed to be the main dish; boiled potatoes and "greens".' Bertram dubs it 'boiled baby' recalling the institutional fare of his school days. Mrs Sedge's son, Bill, a salesman of ladies' knitwear, visits his mother and this group frequently and links the several families in the social chain by his romantic pursuit of Viola. One critic notes of Bill Sedge, 'The fact that he is an Austrian (foreigner, Not English), a salesman (bourgeois), and in the business of polyester clothing at that (synthetic material), makes him appear symbolically an ersatz husband.'[51] Though a bit shorter than Viola, Sedge 'treats her like a woman', satisfying her need for romance and companionship, and providing an altogether more suitable match than the intellectual egoist Aylwin Forbes.

We encounter the third family grouping and the third setting when Dulcie and Viola, in search of information on the Forbes family, travel to the West Country to visit Eagle House, where eccentricity and romance comically coexist. Fr Neville Forbes, Aylwin's handsome brother, has returned to mother in retreat from an amorous female parishioner. Aylwin arrives from holiday in France to spend the Easter weekend, as do his wife Marjorie and her mother, Mrs Williton. Presiding over all is the indomitable matriarch, Horatia Forbes, proprietress. These Taviscombe chapters comprise an extended set-piece examining the behavior of a small group of characters all with different motivations, removed from their usual routines, and 'on holiday' in unfamiliar surroundings.

So fond is Pym of this milieu – the slightly seedy resort hotel, with its damp beds, dearth of hot water, and Residents' Lounge where small footrests litter the floor 'like toadstools' – that she creates two such establishments, having Dulcie and Viola first register at The Anchorage, down the road from Eagle House. With double the comic possibilities Pym is able to create a greater number of minor characters, a variety of uncomfortable bedrooms, twice the opportunity for dining room non-sequiturs – 'This must be a change from Uganda, Miss Fell' – where the 'unnerving silences' are broken only by 'the sound of water being poured out into glasses – perhaps the most dismal sound heard on an English holiday'. The comedy builds on the physical and social discomforts people will endure in search of a change in routine.

Since the consumption of alcohol signifies the relaxation that a holiday implies, and since both establishments have licensing restrictions, Viola recommends purchasing a bottle of gin. Dulcie worries that it 'seems rather depraved to drink it in one's bedroom', but concedes because 'People obviously do these things all the time now' (NFRL, 173). In a journal entry from this period, Pym imagines an interchange between a clerk and an inexperienced purchaser: 'What kind of wine would you be requiring Madam? asked the young man. Oh, just something suitable for drinking in the bedroom of an unlicensed hotel' (MS Pym 49, fol. 8). Pym parlays this small exchange into a delightful comic scene of the two women buying a quarter-bottle of gin. When Dulcie inquires if they should include a corkscrew, Viola wilts with embarrassment but only corrects her friend when they are safely outside.

Their determination to behave correctly, to avoid calling attention to themselves, to remain as discreetly unnoticed as the pattern on the wallpaper, extends into all phases of the holiday. Mrs Forbes can bully them into accepting an inferior room even though the hotel is nearly empty, or at midday serve them the morning's leftover coffee reboiled. Their eagerness to please is often at the expense of their own comfort, something no man would understand, as Dulcie and Aylwin discuss:

> Yes, after breakfast is an awkward time in a hotel . . . . One has no right to exist between the hours of half past nine and twelve. So much work is going on that it makes one feel guilty.
> I suppose women – nice women – feel guilty. Men are only irritated.

> (NFRL, 221)

Only several paragraphs later, however, Dulcie will abandon her usual careful demeanor and blurt out her impatience with Aylwin's romantic missteps with Marjorie, Viola, and Laurel: 'It's time you made a *sensible* marriage.' This climactic speaking of her mind is coupled with Dulcie's realisation that she is acting out of character, more like a romantic heroine than like her usual self:

> She was by no means at her best this morning, though if it had been a romantic novel, she thought, he would have been struck by how handsome she looked when she was angry, the sea breeze having whipped some colour into her normally pale cheeks. (NFRL, 223)

More than any other Pym novel, *No Fond Return of Love* contains occasions when characters allude to themselves or each other as inhabitants of a novel. Viola is 'a disappointment . . . like a character in a book who had failed to come alive'. Mrs Williton sips a cup of tea in a railway station and the narrative voice prompts: 'It was about half past six in the evening and other solitary people sat, reviving themselves after their day or summoning up the strength to go home. Most of them looked as if they had problems worrying them – a novelist or a sociologist might have felt very near the heart of reality at that moment. But Mrs Williton was neither of these things' (NFRL, 141). Aylwin, who has been reading *Portrait of a Lady*, begins to talk in an 'odd pseudo-Henry-Jamesian way' and later justifies his rapid change of affection by recalling Edmund of *Mansfield Park*. Dulcie even wonders whether life has 'some kind of pattern . . . after all. It might be like a well-thought-out novel, where every incident had its own particular significance and was essential to the plot' (NFRL, 89).

Twice Pym closely weaves the outside world of her own literary career and this novel's interior life: once, playfully including *Some Tame Gazelle* on the bookshelf in Dulcie's guest bathroom; once by popping in herself to watch the goings-on at Eagle House:

> It was at this point that somebody came to the unoccupied table, but as she was a woman of about forty, ordinary-looking and unaccompanied, nobody took much notice of her. As it happened, she was a novelist; indeed, some of the occupants of the tables had read and enjoyed her books, but it would never have occurred to them to connect her name, even had they

ascertained it from the hotel register, with that of the author they admired. They ate their stewed plums and custard and drank their thimble-sized cups of coffee, quite unconscious that they were being observed. (NFRL, 176)

Of this scene novelist Anne Tyler asks: 'Is the novelist Barbara Pym? Has she, in her unobtrusive, quirky way, dropped in on her own story? If so, what fools those other guests are not to notice her! She is the rarest of treasures; she reminds us of the heartbreaking silliness of daily life.'[52] This technique of literary self-consciousness is appropriate when one recalls Dulcie's closeness to her creator and the attributes she shares with the novelist of manners – a sharply observant eye, a sense of detachment, a love of detail, even the recognition of occasional drawbacks: 'What is the use of noticing such details? Dulcie asked herself. It isn't as if I were a novelist or a private detective. Presumably such a faculty might be said to add to one's enjoyment of life, but so often what one observed was neither amusing nor interesting, but just upsetting' (NFRL, 60).

For the disentangling of the romantic knots after the confrontations in Taviscombe, the scene returns briefly but appropriately to Dulcie's house. Her world needs readjustment for the novel of manners to end on an ordered note. Viola and Laurel have moved and the plot seems on a melancholy downward slide with Dulcie contemplating a dimly unsatisfactory future:

But she still had her work. She was in the middle of making an index for a complicated anthropological book, and this would occupy her for some weeks. And now that she was alone she might well consider letting rooms to students – perhaps Africans, who would fill the house with gay laughter and cook yams on their gas rings. (NFRL, 252)

Reestablishing a community will be a necessity for this intrepid heroine, and it will be realised not with African students, but with the reward of an acceptable man.

The farcical and frenetic plotting, the literary playfulness, and happy ending of *No Fond Return of Love* are counterbalanced by the poignancy lurking behind the comedy. As is so often true in Pym's work, her concern for the mundane often covers real emotion or conflict, and she never allows Dulcie to avoid the somber reflection underlying much of her behavior. Remembering her broken engagement, Dulcie thinks 'perhaps it is sadder to have loved somebody "unworthy", and the end of it is the death of such a very little thing, like a child's coffin'. This heart-breakingly painful metaphor minimizing her own grief is almost a whispered aside, lost in the pacing of the novel, but as one critic aptly notes: 'The sentences that stick here and the sentences that sting, are always spoken softly.'[53] It is in Dulcie's clear-eyed assessments that the emotional depth of this novel resides: 'It was sad, she thought, how women longed to be needed and useful and how seldom most of them really were' (NFRL, 103).

Concern for others lurks painfully at the edges of her conscience as when Dulcie falls asleep thinking of her large, comfortable, and empty home:

> She would have liked the house to be full of people; it might even be possible to let rooms. There were so many lonely people in the world. Here Dulcie's thoughts took another turn and she began to think about the things that worried her in life – beggars, distressed gentlefolk, lonely African students having doors shut in their faces, people being wrongfully detained in mental homes. (NFRL, 21)

On the other hand, twice she wonders if a passing beggar is a fraud and complains why 'today such behaviour is necessary with the comforts that the Welfare state provides?' Is she naive, intolerant, or just too sensitive to others' pain? In the course of the novel Dulcie weighs and measures her own disappointment, regret, loneliness, and embarrassment as carefully as she does others'. 'Life,' she knows, 'is often cruel in small ways.' In a 1983 review of this novel Anatole Broyard calls Dulcie, 'one of those rare women who sees through people without feeling superior to them. In this she is like her creator, Miss Pym, whose irony is mixed with agape.'[54]

The sympathy she feels for the human condition and the attention to detail that defines her comic world are never more apparent than in her first eight novels. *Less Than Angels*, arguably the most lighthearted of all, *A Glass of Blessings*, and *No Fond Return of Love* mark the end of the early group of Pym's novels of manners – those dedicated to defining themselves through surfaces. Like Catherine Oliphant, Pym recognises the strength and comfort to be found in detail: 'The small things of life were often so much bigger than the great things . . . the trivial pleasures like cooking, one's home, little poems especially sad ones, solitary walks, funny things seen and overheard' (LTA, 104). The later novels with their sadder, stronger themes, will still concern themselves with surfaces, but will observe with more introspection, more ironic detachment. Issues of family, shelter, food, clothing, employment, worship, and leisure will still shape the fabric of her work, but will often be edged with black. Ten years of publishing success close with *No Fond Return of Love*.

5

Rejection, Resurrection, Valediction

Beginning with the publication of *Some Tame Gazelle*, Barbara Pym enjoyed a progression of literary successes. The London firm of Jonathan Cape produced a half dozen of her novels in thirteen years, and in 1960 she was already at work on the seventh. Although she never collected huge royalties from their sales, she did gather loyal readers, fond of her passion for detail and her evocation of quiet lives.

For *An Unsuitable Attachment*, as it came to be titled, Pym planned not to deviate from the now familiar pattern she preferred, including a contained parish setting and a broad and mostly comic collection of humanity. The opening paragraph established her familiar courtship patterns and the sorting out of affections necessary for their resolution. She structured the novel, as she had in *Crampton Hodnet*, around the festivals of the church year, and continued the anthropological interest of *Less Than Angels*. She mirrored some of the plot of *Jane and Prudence* with the creation of a matchmaking heroine, Sophia Ainger, married to a vague if well-meaning clergyman, Mark, in the mold of Nicholas Cleveland. Sophia's mission, when not ministering obsessively to her cat Faustina, was to arrange the soonest possible marriage between her younger sister Penelope and the closest, mildly-eligible male. Penelope has set her sights on the new neighbor, another Fabian Driver-type, Rupert Stonebird, an anthropologist who, almost to his dismay, had 'regained his faith'. Finally, Pym created another of those mildly restless excellent women in search of something to love, the young librarian Ianthe Broome. Nothing in the familiar genesis of this novel indicated the crisis in Pym's career it would precipitate.

She began a first draft (MS Pym 19) in 1960 and journal entries throughout the next two years (MS Pym 53 and 54) record the impressions that gave it texture. Hilary and Barbara Pym had settled into a rented flat and a new parish in northwest London the year before, and almost immediately the novelist began to transpose the new neighborhood into her fiction: 'A novel of North London might contrast rather poignantly with the elegant setting of Elizabeth Bowen's *To the North*' (MS Pym 53, fol. 10). Details of this environment, especially details which highlight class differences, find their way directly into *An Unsuitable Attachment*, like the mixture of newly gentrified small houses 'with rather self-conscious window-boxes and bay trees in tubs' and those 'too near the railway and many of the big gaunt houses . . . taken over by families of West Indians' (AUA, 16–17). Pym wrote her friend Bob Smith in December 1962 that although the new novel was well underway, she had some misgivings about its opening sections:

> My next is getting on, quite flowing now. I am at the depressed stage when I begin to type out some of the early chapters and think that not much of it will do – I can only hope that I will get through this stage, but my first four chapters always seem so dragged out, even when I rewrite the beginning. (AVPE, 208)

A month after the publication of *No Fond Return of Love*, Pym had traveled to Italy for an anthropological conference; most of the 1961 notebook devotes itself to details of this trip, details which take fictional shape when the parishioners of St. Basil's journey to Rome. She records the Eternal City, its cats, omnipresent clergy, and aura of romance inspired by ancient ruins amid exotic flowers and fruits. She travels to Amalfi, 'though so prettily situated . . . horrifyingly touristic . . . . One has a real love-hate relationship with Italy, perhaps with all "abroad"?' (MS Pym 55, fol. 9). In *A Very Private Eye*, Hazel Holt generally excised most of Pym's notebook musings on weather and local fauna, but she makes an exception for the extended Italian impressions, perhaps because their ambivalence becomes so central to *An Unsuitable Attachment*. For although Pym acknowledges her love-hate relationship with Italy, the panoramic views along the Amalfi drive inspire her:

> Acres of lemon groves all covered with matting and branches so that you don't see them until you are close to. It is for the lemon groves that one loves Italy – also for the oranges with stalks and leaves still on them and the little bundles of dried lemon leaves

which you unwrap to reveal a few delicious lemon-flavored raisins in the middle. (AVPE, 202)

These beautifully wrapped, hidden sweets carry enough metaphorical weight for Pym that she considered both *Wrapped in Lemon Leaves* (MS Pym 20, fol. 1) and *Among the Lemon Leaves* (MS Pym 20, fol. 36) as titles for this seventh work.

Departing from her usual practice of centering a novel on a single Barbara Pym-ish character, Pym here splits the role of the heroine between Sophia and Ianthe. The younger woman, a canon's daughter, is another of Pym's near-spinsters, tall, fragile-looking, dark hair touched with grey, and usually dressed in virginal blue: 'although she was not exactly smart there was a kind of elegance about her. She saw herself perhaps as an Elizabeth Bowen heroine – for one did not openly identify oneself with Jane Austen's heroines – and *To The North* was her favourite novel' (AUA, 26). The heroine of Bowen's novel, like Ianthe, is attracted to a handsome man outside her class, but the relationship ends in tragedy; Ianthe's unsuitable attachment to John Challow will end in marriage.

Confident, charming, and younger than Ianthe by five years, John joins the staff of the library where Ianthe works, and his physical presence upsets her from the first day. Previously employed as an actor, or rather as an extra, he did 'film work, actually – crowd work and that sort of thing. Dancing in a night club scene at eight o'clock in the morning – TV commercials too, sometimes' (AUA, 46). His frankness about financial matters takes her aback. 'I thought I'd better get a steady job for a bit, especially when my money ran out' (AUA, 46). The excess or absence of money is normally not a subject for polite discussion in her circles, but in John's case Ianthe finds it strangely appealing. She carefully assesses his appearance, finding no fault with 'his dark grey suit, red- patterned tie and white shirt. Only his shoes seemed to be a little too pointed – not quite what men one knew would wear' (AUA, 49). He forthrightly admits his lack of formal education, soliciting her aid with problems of pronunciation as he boldly, seductively, reads to her from Tennyson: 'Now lies the earth all Danäe to the stars / And all my heart lies open unto thee' (AUA, 50).

Although it takes both the reader and Ianthe a while to discover, the fulcrum of *An Unsuitable Attachment* is sexual attraction. Much of the novel follows Ianthe's shedding the remnants of a repressed life with her widowed mother in the shadow of Westminster Cathedral. She buys her own house, joins a new church, schedules social engagements with friends, and begins to recognise that life contains greater pleasures than parish jumble sales. Many of these pleasures, Ianthe learns, are defined by sensuality. Envisioning an elderly co-worker's life in quiet, probably lonely, retirement, Ianthe is surprised to find her circumstances less austere than imagined: Miss Grimes has a collection of fine furniture, treats herself weekly to the comforts of good wine, and ultimately marries a Polish widower she meets in the neighborhood pub. When, without warning, John kisses Ianthe goodbye at the railroad station she rushes away with a confusion of responses that includes surprise, desire, and a vision of the virginal life awaiting her if she denies his attractiveness:

> Ianthe hurried on to the escalator and began walking down. At the bottom the warm air blowing about her seemed to increase her agitation. A piece of newspaper was swirled against her legs, and she collided surprisingly, almost nightmarishly, with a nun. (AUA,135)

Her upbringing has taught her that 'one did not behave like that in a public place with a young man, suitable or otherwise, and John was so very much otherwise'. Diary entries show that Pym initially planned for Ianthe to renounce John: 'Pain, when it is removed to another setting (Italy, say), becomes remote. More remote perhaps in Africa where there is nothing to remind one . . . . Ianthe's "unsuitable attachment" might be forgotten in Italy' (MS Pym 54, fol. 7). Away from him, however, Ianthe, unlike any Pym heroine before her, is swept away by unaccountable desire, 'like a kind of illness, "giving in" to flu, conscious only of the present moment' (AUA, 147).

The Italian trip occupying the center third of the novel oozes a lushness that hints at the erotic. As she had in *Jane and Prudence*, Pym introduces the allure of Roman Catholicism, an attractive temptation for the steadfast Anglican to resist. Ianthe acknowledges the danger, ostentation, and contradictory appeal of the faith she observes abroad: simultaneously showy and secretive, disturbing and soothing, unrestrained and yet tightly controlled, it is as paradoxical and omnipresent as it is sensual. Rome is a place of no secrets where Harriet Bede worries that, 'the Jesuits have a list of every Church of England clergyman who is visiting Italy and know exactly what he is doing at every minute of the day or *night'* (AUA, 167). Unlike their more austere Anglican counterparts, priests and nuns here purchase liquor openly, are whisked by special privilege through the airport, and ride motorscooters in the streets. The relaxation of the social code extends beyond the clergy and includes hints of European decadence tempered by neither gender nor age: Sophia's elderly expatriate aunt may have bargained with the devil for the Villa Faustina, dyes her hair, and regularly entertains her Italian lover, whose striped suit reminds Ianthe of 'the skin of some wild animal.'

Unfortunately, the Italian journey does not advance the plot, serving mostly as a backdrop for Ianthe's now admitted attraction to the absent John, an attraction which might as well have been discovered on holiday in Brighton or Bath. Her fellow travelers seek out pleasures identical to those they enjoy at home: the veterinarian and his sister feed homeless cats, the women speculate on who cleans the marble at St. Peter's, they all buy postcards and take refreshment in Babbington's, the Italian version of an English tea room. Philip Larkin would later comment, 'The excursion to Rome is good and I think successful, but I hope you don't repeat the experiment too often, as I think one of your chief talents is for recording the English scene' (MS Pym 151, fols 17–18). What little action occurs could be played beside either Tiber or Thames, but the Italian setting does underscore the conflicting impressions of sexual attraction and repression.

Periodically, and usually in unpublished material, Pym had experimented with foreign settings or characters as a means of examining familiar values and behaviors. In several short stories, Pym presented themes similar to those in the Italian portion of *An Unsuitable Attachment*: along with the forbidden attraction of Roman Catholicism, the characters in these 'international stories' explore the freedom from restrictive codes of behavior and the titillating flirtation with sex, danger, and romance in a continental setting.

Uncharacteristic for its foreign setting and for its sublimated sexuality, the unpublished 'English Ladies' (MS Pym 92, fols145–55) finds Pym relying on cultural detail for contrast. Pym sets the short story in Spain and one of its heroines, like Ianthe on her Italian holiday, is confused by the attraction she feels and the danger she has been conditioned to avoid:

> As a staunch Protestant she found that there was some-
> thing disturbing and exciting about being in a Catholic coun-
> try . . . Mass that dark, sinister word that Dorothy could hardly
> bring herself to pronounce. And then there were the shops, full of
> rosaries and statues, and the churches, so dark and mysterious,
> with unintelligible services going on all the time. (MS Pym 92,
> fols 153–4)

The story begins on familiar ground, with two recognisable excellent
women, reminiscent of the Bede sisters, setting off on holiday to a
Spanish seacoast resort. Mixing the exotic setting with a pair of
friends just settling into spinsterhood, Pym creates her comic tone
with a darker than usual mood, heavy with repressed sexuality.
Hints of unsatisfied needs come early:

> Why were two middle-aged civil servants, who usually spent
> their holiday in a cottage on Exmoor, rushing through the pine
> forests of Bordeaux in the middle of the night? Then she remem-
> bered the vague feeling of dissatisfaction in the winter, the desire
> for change they had both felt.

The subplot follows Dorothy, simultaneously fascinated and
repelled by the country's flamboyant Roman Catholicism, but
the story's chief interest lies with Eleanor, 'the gentler of the two
and the better-looking', aware of life's missed opportunities. The
familiar denial of physical pleasures seems unusually constricting
abroad and admitting an alternative to their rigid Protestantism
also allows the two to chafe at long-standing sexual constraints.
Eleanor recognises the appeal of the exotic milieu. 'If we could
live primitively like peasants, how much more exciting life would
be.' Even the children seem free of the cultural baggage she carries,
'more elaborately dressed than they would be in England, the little
girls wearing gold earrings.' As the two friends seek afternoon
refreshment they regretfully bypass a cool dim bar where men sit
drinking wine and beer, and search out instead an all too familiar
looking tea room, 'with resignation now, knowing themselves to be
English women abroad, with white shoes and handbags and pale
patterned cotton dresses that did not fit tightly enough'. Their very
clothing marks their sterility in these sensual surroundings.
    After a determinedly festive luncheon ('It was difficult to remem-
ber what wines were particularly associated with the country, so

they ordered a bottle of claret'), drowsy with the heat and the wine, they retire, open the shuttered windows for air, and promptly fall asleep over their naptime reading.

> Eleanor woke first, startled and unable to remember where she was . . . Dorothy on the other bed was still asleep, breathing heavily. She had forgotten to take off her spectacles before dozing off, and the woman's magazine she had been reading lay open on her breast, showing a holiday picture, a young woman in a more scanty bathing costume than would have been allowed here, and a young man bending over her. Both were of an astonishing beauty.
>
> Well, nothing like that will happen on our holiday, Eleanor told herself sensibly and without regret. One did not expect that kind of thing any more and it made life much easier.

Awakening further, Eleanor senses someone observing her from the opposite window:

> A little boy of about five sat just inside the room on a low stool or chair. Behind him she could see heavy furniture, the corner of a table covered with a lace-edged cloth, the faint gleam of a chandelier. He was staring into their room, his dark solemn eyes fixed on her . . . . Like many unmarried women her manner with children was awkward; she was a little afraid of them, not knowing what it was that their serious disconcerting eyes saw. Then, realizing that she was in her petticoat, she reached for her dressing gown. (MS Pym 92, fol. 150)

The incident, an ironic reworking of the sleeping princess awakened by the handsome prince, contains overtones of voyeurism and sexual intrusion which the older woman is reluctant to dismiss.

> Every day, too, she looked out for the little boy at the window and he was nearly always there. Sometimes she saw him going out with his mother and she felt quite disappointed if a day passed without a sight of him. He never spoke or even smiled but his solemn silence only added to his attraction. Eleanor began to regret that she had never married and had children of her own . . . It was of course unlikely that she would marry now, but

was it not possible that she might adopt a child, some dark-eyed war orphan from a foreign country? (MS Pym 92, fol. 153)

Days later as they pack to leave, Eleanor notices the child watching from his usual spot and wishes briefly that she had bought him a present, 'but in a curious way she did not want the contact that would make him become real'.

Suddenly the romanticised view of the dark-eyed child is shattered as he prances onto his balcony with taunts of 'English ladies! English ladies!', strutting and posing in cruel imitation of them. Dorothy is indignant but Eleanor shrugs off the insult and the dream: '[He's] human and real,' said Eleanor still laughing, 'and that's what children are like, after all. How very tiring it would be to have one in the house – it would upset one's whole life.' She retreats from the experience (like many Pym heroines) with 'warm satisfaction at the thought of their comfortable orderly home'.

The lure of the unfamiliar, of experiences outside the normal pattern of a confined life, would tempt Pym as themes in these testing-ground stories. When the novelist of manners seeks foreign ground it often is to include openly the danger, intrigue, or sexual threat that remains camouflaged at home. Anything is possible when the convention's constraints are loosened, and going beyond the repression of 'English Ladies', Pym tries her hand at sex, murder, and the sensational in others of these 'international' stories.

Pym draws both on her love for travel and on her brief experience in the employ of a German family for the unpublished 'Back to St. Petersburg' (MS Pym 92, fols 51–70). This story shares with 'English Ladies' a spinster heroine who feels the threat of time passing, but in this case one who attempts to alter its course. Repression breaks through into a rare sexual encounter for a Pym heroine.

Laura Kennicote, thirty-two years old and companion to Miss Elm for the last five years, considers herself a 'capable middle-aged spinster.' Assuring herself and her employer that she 'has put all thought of youth out of her head', she nevertheless seeks a change, answering an advertisement for a governess from a German family. With the blessings of the benevolent Miss Elm, Laura leaves the safe haven of her English village in search of the excitement and passion she hopes await her abroad.

Before Laura can leave, however, Pym must introduce the Wenderbys – the vicar and his prying wife – in order to set up plot complications for the story's climax. In an awkward scene, we learn somewhat obviously that these two will be touring the Black Forest and Baden-Baden the next summer; this information forces the sardonic Laura to comment only half in jest, 'There will be no escaping you.' When the vicar compares Laura's upcoming situation to that of Jane Eyre she retorts that she is neither as plain nor as intelligent as that English governess and is 'not expecting to find a Mr Rochester in my German family.'

Once abroad, Laura finds the situation agreeable, the countryside beautiful, and the eldest son, Wilhelm, attractive and attracted. 'One evening, when the Berncastler Doktor had been flowing more freely than usual and there was a fine velvety sky and the sound of music from a cafe in the town, he had seized Laura in his arms, as they stood together on the terrace, and kissed her.' Despite the formulaic clinch and the predictable 'velvety sky', Pym presents Laura's attraction to the younger man as unsentimental and realistic in its expectations:

> Laura did not expect a proposal of marriage. Governesses are not usually considered suitable wives for German Counts of noble family five years their junior, she believed. Nor indeed are governesses usually considered as suitable mistresses, if a mistress has any special qualifications. Laura had to admit to herself that she was not in a position to know this. It seemed a great pity that there were some things no respectable woman could know. But why should she be such a woman? Her respectability concerned herself alone. She had no close relations who would grieve over her fall. Besides it was unlikely that she would ever get such another chance.

The rationalisation is unique in Pym's canon in several ways. Laura's age and lack of sexual experience justify the *carpe diem* argument. Traditional social conventions can be waived, Pym seems to argue, when the consequences of one's actions affect no one else. 'Respectability' here is only measured externally, not internally. Although conscious of their differing class and economic backgrounds, Laura can nevertheless ignore any strictures imposed on foreign soil: 'But as the days went on Laura's scruples vanished, and she gave herself up to the new experience of being a woman in love. She did this consciously, knowing that she could, if necessary, become her old self at a moment's notice.' Unlike her German mistress, whose ancestral St Petersburg is now Leningrad, Laura can go home again should she choose. The knowledge of this escape hatch, the availability of the safe haven and conformity of her previous life, makes Laura's rebellion curiously egotistical. Wilhelm's motivations remain unexplored while Laura's break with convention, we are assured, need not be permanent.

At the small resort chosen for their 'honeymoon', the lovers are of course confronted by the Wenderbys, and those arbiters of English morality are deceived by a small detail of European tradition. As a bow to conventionality Laura has adopted a plain gold wedding ring, worn in the German fashion on the right, rather than the left hand. Denied an attractive scandal, the placated tourists can only report home that Miss Kennicote was now a Countess, 'and perhaps that was enough'.

Discreetly avoiding description of Laura's sexual awakening, Pym only reveals that it 'was gratifyingly successful', and rushes the young lady back to England. When a letter from Miss Elm announces that her former position awaits should she ever need it, Laura makes a painless exit from the world of experience, returning 'soberly dressed in black, a widow sooner than had been expected'. She retains our sympathy by disarmingly informing Miss Elm of the truth, but maintains the fictional pose for the rest of society, content and satisfied that 'She had done something which had seemed as impossible as going back to St. Petersburg.'

Every foreign encounter is not so pleasurable. In an early story of international danger, 'A Painted Heart' (MS Pym 94, fols 16–30), Pym's choice of a first-person narrator forces a clumsy self-introduction by Jennifer, a disdainful beauty on holiday with a group of English students. Less likeable than Ianthe Broome or Laura Kennicote, she too is in search of foreign adventure:

> I stood a little apart from the others. I hate going about in a crowd and it was only lack of money that had driven me to visit Buda-pest in this tripperish way . . . . I, although not strictly beautiful, am attractive and nineteen years old, and can speak French, Spanish, Italian, German, Swedish, and Hungarian, imperfectly enough to be regarded as a fascinating foreigner wherever I go. (MS Pym 94, fol. 19)

With her initial attraction to their handsome Hungarian tour-guide dwindling, Jennifer spurns his next advance, much to his displeasure: 'I disliked melodrama in writing although I do not object to it in real life, but I can only describe the way in which György spoke as "hissing between his teeth".' The resort to quoted cliché unfortunately reflects more on Pym's skill than on Jennifer's, regardless of her author's intentions. Some fairly obvious foreshadowing of impending danger centered on tombs and maggoty skulls culminates when György's second choice for some romantic sightseeing is found murdered.

Pym not only falls prey to the appeals of melodramatic language, but also to some clichéd motivation to explain her heroine's narrow escape in Hungary:

> But it was different for me. I am so sensitive, so imaginative, and I knew in that moment that I have more than my full share of womanly intuition. For I realised now that something had *warned* me that it was dangerous to go with György. That was why I had given him up to Morden. Otherwise *I* might have been the one to go to the tomb and be murdered. And here I was, still tantalizingly out of reach. (MS Pym 94, fol. 29)

Jennifer will keep György's gift as a memento ('I had been kissed by a murderer, and he had given me a painted heart decorated with lovebirds'); the disdainful heroine will resurface with Leonora in *The Sweet Dove Died*; the first-person presentation will attract Pym several more times; but the melodramatic posing stops here.

In 'The German Baron' (MS Pym 92, fols 229–44) the foreign setting so affects an aging heroine that she reverses years of sexual repression to compete for the favors of the title character. Early in the story Pym introduces Harriet Moat, pointing out the 'grey woollen stockings and black glacé kid bar shoes' that identify her as a sturdy, sensible, English gentlewoman. The irony of the story plays Miss Moat's unlikely physical attractions against her need for male companionship, and, perceptively, Pym shapes this cautionary tale around the capacity of the older woman to experience desire.

Harriet wishfully interprets the continental cordiality of a fellow hotel guest as a mild flirtation. The complications accelerate when both Harriet and her traveling companion, Edith Foxe, begin a competition for the stranger's attentions. Overwrought by jealous self-pity and filled with the conflicting demands of conscience and emotional need, Harriet encourages Edith to take a foolish risk which nearly ends in a fatality.

With a kind of double denouement, the story concludes as Harriet vows a private atonement and the Baron introduces his pretty, blond, young wife. Yet another fantasy proves untenable, but Harriet's emotional needs are indefatigable. Pym ends the story by returning her full circle, with dreams of meeting an elderly Italian Count whose marital status she would, of course, immediately ascertain.

As many a Pym heroine learns, romance cultivated on foreign soil requires special caution. 'A Letter From My Love' (MS Pym 92, fols 262–77) shares with 'The Painted Heart' an authentic feel of Budapest drawn from Pym's love of travel and her fondness for Germany and the Balkan states. The story line follows a rather predictable disappointment-in-love theme and the narrative voice has an annoying adolescent coyness, but Pym's presentation of a heroine measuring her own emotions by different cultural standards rings authentic. Unhappy when her Hungarian lover discounts a wife and five children as no obstacle to their romance, the narrator is equally upset back home when her boring fiance refuses to be jealous. The richness of 'A Letter From My Love' resides in its travel poster setting, and, uncharacteristically for Pym, much of its sparkle dissipates when the scene shifts to England for the heroine's homecoming.

The reverse occurs in Pym's rejected novel. When *An Unsuitable Attachment* leaves Italy to return to England the plot stabilises, cultural mores reassume conservative, traditional forms, and events move rapidly toward one of the few marriage ceremonies in the Pym canon. Pym presents the climactic declarations of love in this novel with a compression that Jane Austen would have admired. John, suddenly remembering his un-repaid loan, rushes to Ianthe's home: 'And when the money had been handed over and refused and handed over again, there were other things to be talked about, misunderstandings to be cleared up, and – at last – mutual love to be declared and brought out into the open' (AUA, 219). The avoidance of explicit exposition of romantic scenes is not the only Austen connection in this novel. Earlier, Pym has opened a chapter with a most Austen-like lead-in, 'The day comes in the life of every single man living alone when he must give a dinner party' (AUA, 119), and the echoes do not end with the language.

Other critics have noticed the Austen influences in both the plot and characterisation of *An Unsuitable Attachment*. Robert Long cites the similarities to *Pride and Prejudice* since both involve the righting of 'misperceptions based on erroneous first impressions'.[1] Marilyn Butler, too, compares the 'cluster of courtships', likens Sophia's matchmaking skills to Emma's or Mrs Bennet's, and says Penny 'fails to get her man through too much stage-management and too much trying, rather in the style of Harriet Smith or Mary Bennet'.[2] The minor characters too, notes Butler, reflect the Austen tradition:

> Sister Dew, good hearted parish helper, is the equivalent of Mrs Jennings or Miss Bates. The mean Lady (Muriel) Selvedge, who comes to open the Church bazaar and lunches en route near Victoria for 3s 9d, might be based on the entrepreneurial Lady Denham in *Sanditon*, Ianthe's aunt, Bertha, married to the rector of a fashionable Mayfair parish, blends the hypochondria of *Sanditon*'s Diana Parker with the injudicious high living of Dr Grant in *Mansfield Park*.[3]

Pym was aware of her debt to Austen but was never willing to allow a comparison of their skills. She insisted that she never tried 'conscious' imitation, but that any writer 'must hope to acquire the tiniest scrap of her qualities if he or she writes about the same kinds of people and settings' (MS Pym 98, fol. 84).

As she was finishing the first draft of *An Unsuitable Attachment* Pym was contacted for the first time by the poet Philip Larkin suggesting that he write a review article to accompany the publication of her next novel. He had been introduced to her work by his sister[4] and hoped to help boost Pym's reputation in the literary world: 'If any one has written about your books I haven't seen it and I do think they deserve "art" recognition as well as "commercial" recognition and this it would be my earliest intention to give' (MS Pym 151, fol. 5). Later, Larkin further explained his reasons for the request:

> Barbara Pym was then in her fiftieth year. Her previous books had been well received by reviewers, and she had gained a following among library borrowers; it was time for a breakthrough that would establish her among the dozen or so novelists recognised as original voices and whose books automatically head the review lists.[5]

To his bemused surprise, Pym seemed lukewarm to the suggestion. 'She replied amiably, but was clearly in no hurry, and our
correspondence lapsed . . . for over a year.'[6] With novel number
eight already in mind, she polished *An Unsuitable Attachment* for
submission to Cape.

> Hazel and Hilary have both read it and seemed to like it, but I
> am still making a few final improvements before sending it to
> the publisher. I feel the effort of it all is so great that I shall never
> write another, yet even now vague ideas begin to turn over in my
> mind. (AVPE, 210)

In February 1963, she admitted to Larkin her misgivings that this
work might not find instant acceptance:

> I sent my novel to Cape last week but don't know yet what they
> think of it. I feel it can hardly come up to *Catch 22* or *The Passion
> Flower Hotel* for selling qualities but I hope they will realise that
> it is necessary for a good publisher's list to have something
> milder . . . . I will certainly let you have a proof copy when it
> gets to that stage but please don't think that I *expect* you to do
> anything unless you feel like it, but anything in the way of a
> review would of course be very welcome, as I don't suppose I
> shall get all that many! (AVPE, 210)

But the proof copy never materialised, and when Pym resumed
the correspondence with Larkin in May 1963, her literary world
had altered. It would be many years before Larkin could write
his review.

A notebook entry from this period shows Pym contemplating, 'a
novel about a middle-aged female novelist (like me) whose books
suddenly become fashionable'; (MS Pym 54, fol. 5) ironically, fate
would decree the opposite for her. Early 1963 was shadowed with
ill omens. Twice in four days thieves broke into the Pym flat,
the second time stealing Barbara's typewriter complete with the
letter under its platen. 'I think it was having it twice that was so
horrid . . . it gives one an insecure feeling. Yet all our friends have
had to undergo this, so why not us' (AVPE, 209). Her characteristic
buoyancy allowed her to rationalise, 'I suppose all experience
however unpleasant can be turned to good effect in fiction'; but the
thefts were only the beginning. Her editor at Cape, Daniel George,

suffered a stroke. The publisher could not provide her a copy of *A Glass of Blessings*: it had gone out of print. The worst news arrived in a letter from G. Wren Howard of Jonathan Cape with the ominous beginning, 'I feel that I must first warn you that this is a difficult letter to write' (MS Pym 164, fol. 130). She wrote to Robert Smith on March 19,

> I had a great blow from Cape, who said they didn't want to publish my novel, which they read 'not without pleasure and interest', because they feared that with the increased cost of book production &c. &c. they would not sell enough copies to make a profit! And that after six novels and thirteen years and even a small amount of prestige to the house of Cape. (MS Pym 161, fol. 28b)

Pym first records the rejection in her journal with notable depression, but also notes the surrounding detail in case she might ever wish to fictionalise the scene. The efficiently detailed list evoking the milieu of rejection could have come from any of her novels:

> 24 March 1963. To receive a bitter blow on an early Spring evening (such as that Cape don't want to publish *An Unsuitable Attachment* – but it might be that someone doesn't love you anymore) – is it worse than on an Autumn or Winter evening? Smell of bonfire (the burning of rose prunings etc), a last hyacinth in the house, forsythia about to burst, a black and white cat on the sofa, a small fire burning in the grate, books and Sunday papers and the remains of tea.

She continues immediately with a complete catalogue of her personal disappointments in the year:

> 1963 so far. A year of violence, death and blows
> The bad Winter up to the end of February without a break.
> Death of Hugh Gaitskell.
> Two burglaries.
> My typewriter stolen.
> My novel rejected by Cape.
> Dr Beeching's plan for sweeping away of railways and stations.
> Reading *The Naked Lunch*.

The Bishop of Woolwich's book *Honest to God*.
My novel rejected by Heath.
Tropic of Cancer by Henry Miller (60,000) copies sold on
    1st day of publication [4th April]).
Daniel George's stroke.

(MS Pym 57, fol. 6)

Five pages later she makes further additions to the unrelentless
parade of bad news:

Other events of 1963
Argyll divorce
June 1–2 Death of Pope John
June 5 The Profumo-Christine Keeler scandal

(MS Pym 57, fol. 11)

The sting of rejection was still smarting in May when she resumed
correspondence with Larkin:

I write this calmly enough, but really I was and am upset about
it and think they have treated me very badly, considering that I
have been with them for thirteen years and published six novels,
some of which have been fairly successful, even if the sales of
the last two were rather modest . . . . Of course it may be that
this novel is much worse than my others, though they didn't say
so, giving their reason for rejecting it as their fear that with the
present cost of book production etc, etc. they doubted whether
they could sell enough copies to make a profit. (AVPE, 216)

That *An Unsuitable Attachment* lacks the fairy tale charm of the
early *Some Tame Gazelle* or the blacker comedy of the later *Quartet in Autumn* is undeniable, but its weaknesses are not those
assigned by her publisher. After the death of Jonathan Cape, the
firm set out to collect a more contemporary cadre of authors,
'mostly men and Americans' complained Pym (AVPE, 213). When
two readers returned *An Unsuitable Attachment* with unsatisfactory
assessments, the novel was rejected with no suggestions for revision
or resubmission. Pym, understandably, felt abandoned:

Three people who have read it tell me it isn't below the standard
of my others. (I'm incapable of judging now!) I did read it over

very critically and it seemed to me that it might appear naive and unsophisticated, though it isn't really, to an unsympathetic publisher's reader hoping for that novel about negro homosexuals, young men in advertising, etc. (AVPE, 220)

To blame public taste and publishers' pocketbooks was the most palatable justification for the rejection: 'I don't think the book is much worse than the others, just not to present-day taste' (MS Pym 164, fols 152–3). She began to question each facet of the work: 'Do you think the title unsaleable? I fear the attachment is not so unsuitable as the public (reading) might wish and perhaps it is altogether too mild a book for present tastes. But then that has always been a sort of fault of mine' (AVPE, 216).

But the novel's chief weaknesses, as Pym herself recognised, were structural: 'the beginning is too vague, too many characters, and there's not enough plot. And who is the heroine?' (AVPE, 220). Tempering his criticism with a leading compliment, 'I liked the obsessional quality of Sophia's affection for [Faustina]', Philip Larkin confirms her fears: 'judged within your own canon, it may be that its effect is a little less well-organised, a little weaker in impact than, say, AGOB or EW' (MS Pym 151, fols 17–18). Much of the weakness of impact resides in the underdeveloped central conflict: the unsuitability of the attachment, notes Larkin quoting Henry James, is never 'fully done'. The class barriers that stand between Ianthe and John seem flimsy and, as a consequence, her friends' reactions to the love affair seem unmotivated. In fact, few characters explain their feelings, and their connections often seem tenuous. John Challow, if anything, is not unsuitable enough; sexual attraction is offered as the basis of his appeal but we see little of it, and Pym says she intended to make him 'worse'. Borrowing money from Ianthe is his greatest transgression of propriety, and it is nearly forgotten in the rush to conclusion.

The division of the role of the heroine between Ianthe and Sophia dilutes the reader's willing connection with either, and Sophia is particularly unlikable. Cat-obsessed, neglectful of her husband, and spiteful, she willfully manipulates the several love interests, admitting even as the wedding vows are being pronounced, 'Wasn't it dreadful, I almost hoped somebody might stand up at the back of the church and forbid the marriage – like in *Jane Eyre* – and expose John as an impostor. I wanted it to happen, and not only for Ianthe's *good*' (AUA, 254). To a friend who complains of Sophia, Pym writes that 'Sophia is not a nonentity – I must have a B Pym woman character to give my angle occasionally' (MS Pym 159/1, fol. 20). Ianthe, however, incorporates the more welcome characteristics of the 'B Pym woman' than Sophia and the division detracts from both characters.

In addition to the trip to Rome and the subsequent journey to Ravello, where little of consequence occurs and which adds a view of European decadence out of sync with the novel's English propriety, the work has other flaws. There are too many cats, at home and abroad, for even an indulgent fancier, and the abundance of cross-over characters appeals mostly to the faithful Pym reader. Philip Larkin, admitting it is a 'somewhat self-indulgent book, full of echoes', notices that Sophia and Penelope recall Jane and Prudence, or even Dulcie and Viola from *No Fond Return of Love*, that Sister Dew is Sister Blatt from *Excellent Women*, and,

> . . . that the concluding chapters . . . are a real *omnium gatherum*: Esther Clovis and Digby Fox from *Less Than Angels*, Everard Bone from *Excellent Women*, Wilf Bason from *A Glass of Blessings*, and perhaps most extravagantly of all an older but otherwise unchanged Harriet Bede (complete with curate) from *Some Tame Gazelle*. It is all rather like the finale of a musical comedy.[7]

Larkin goes on to suggest that despite its weaknesses, 'there is still much in *An Unsuitable Attachment* to cherish.' Other critics, too, heralded its posthumous appearance in 1982: one suggesting he 'can find in it no reason for the rejection so traumatic to her';[8] another calling it 'a paragon of a novel, certainly one of her best, witty, elegant, suggesting beyond its miniature exactness the vast panorama of a vanished civilisation'.[9] It contains many of the virtues of her best novels of manners, a broad but interconnected cast of major characters, a collection of eccentrics in minor roles, a well-defined social structure and a heroine in conflict with the pressures of that society and the whispered demands of her own instincts. Many of the charges against it can be countered. The vagueness of John's unsuitability may be an asset, leaving unspoken the behavioral codes of this society in post-war transition.The catalogue of persons and behaviors identified as 'suitable' or 'unsuitable', the words themselves at first annoyingly overused, becomes a measure of Ianthe's internal and external repression. The abundance of carry-over characters gives this the appearance of a sequence novel, an appropriate and favorite mode, notes one critic, with many novelists of manners like Balzac, Wharton, Proust, and Zola.[10]

The datedness about which her publisher complained may be the real strength of *An Unsuitable Attachment*. Hazel Holt, in revising the manuscript posthumously along the lines in which Pym 'intended to "improve" (her word) it', removed 'a few short passages which have dated in a way that she would have found unacceptable' (AUA, preface). But the published work remains substantially the same as Pym's final manuscript, and the world it portrays distanced by more than just the sexual revolution. The 1960s brought political assassinations, Vietnam, racial unrest, and a culture focused on the young. Larkin wrote sardonically about this year of Pym's rejection:

> Sexual intercourse began
> In nineteen sixty-three
> (Which was rather too late for me) –
> Between the end of the Chatterley ban
> And the Beatles' first LP.
>
> ('Annus Mirabilis' from *High Windows*)

In the midst of this social upheaval, a woman worried about marrying beneath her must have seemed like a refugee from Jane Austen. However, the culture which traded subtlety for excess would rebound within two decades into political conservatism and nostalgia. The absence of direct sexuality may now be a relief to readers sated by ever-escalating orgasms, and Pym's familiar social configurations, presented with simplicity of language, strong character development, and straightforward narrative returns the English novel to traditional patterns. If *An Unsuitable Attachment* is not the strongest or most original Pym novel, it did not deserve to be the reason for her literary excommunication.

How complete was this severance is detailed in Pym's letters and journals over the next fourteen years. Recognizing that 'there must be something very dogged and tenacious about writers' (MS Pym 98, fol. 32) she mailed or hand-carried this manuscript to some twenty-two publishers, occasionally submitting it under the pseudonym Tom Crampton. She contemplated a change of style or a new genre, 'could I write a more publishable sort of novel I wondered? A historical novel, or a modern romantic novel – the idea of a kind of up-dated *Jane Eyre* or *Villette* appealed to me' (MS Pym 98, fol. 77). Her journals record prescriptions for change:

> Make a strong plot – then write it keeping to and (if anything) strengthening the plot (MS Pym 57, fol. 11)

> Make much more interesting characters – no need to have anybody dull, or just mention the dull ones in passing. (MS Pym 58, fol. 7)

She never ceased writing, but recognised the importance of an audience and was fond of quoting Ivy Compton-Burnett's remark, 'I would write for a dozen people . . . but I would not write for no-one.' These dozen imaginary readers, she noted in a 1978 interview, 'spur me on, even when it seems that I'm writing for myself alone. So I try to write what pleases me and amuses me in the hope that a few others will like it too' (MS Pym 96, fol. 12). Gilbert Phelps, a novelist himself and a neighbor in the village of Finstock, remembers speculating with Pym on the effects of reputation and an appreciative audience on an author's production:

> . . . wondering what exactly it was that attracted even the most discriminating readers to some books and not to others equally good in our view; and why praise from the critics seemed so often to have little effect. We agreed that really there was nothing one could – or should – do about it: one could write only what one could write, and straining after effects that didn't come naturally, or seeking consciously to please the public or the critics, was disastrous to whatever talent one might possess . . . . But we agreed that writers, more perhaps than some other artists, needed a public no matter how small, and that the admiration of personal friends alone was not sufficient to stimulate development and growth.[11]

Hers was not a wide literary network, but her admirers like Lord David Cecil and Pamela Hansford-Johnson did try to intervene on her behalf, suggesting new avenues for publication or recommending her work to their own editors. She wrote Larkin that she would feel 'shy' about his approaching Charles Monteith on her behalf, but Larkin felt no such hesitation. He wrote caustically to this senior editor at Faber & Faber,

I feel it is a great shame if ordinary sane novels about ordinary sane things can't find a publisher these days. This is the tradition of Jane Austen and Trollope, and I refuse to believe that no one wants its successors today. Why should I have to choose between spy rubbish, science fiction rubbish, Negro-homosexual rubbish, or dope-take nervous-breakdown rubbish? I like to read about people who have done nothing spectacular, who aren't beautiful and lucky, who try to behave well in the limited field of activity they command, but who can see, in the little autumnal moments of vision, that the so called 'big' experiences of life are going to miss them; and I like to read about such things presented not with self-pity or despair or romanticism, but with realistic firmness and even humour. That is in fact what the critics call the moral tone of the book. It seems to me the kind of writing a responsible publisher ought to support (that's you Charles!)[12]

Throughout the period of rejection Pym, her self-confidence under-mined, kept her humor and her sense of irony intact, writing to Larkin about her inability to get published: 'the letter I wrote to *The Author* about not getting published was never published, which seems to be the final accolade of failure' (AVPE, 278).

This epistolary friendship with Larkin proved one of the bonuses of the wilderness years. He offered, during their nineteen year corre-spondence, friendship built on artistic admiration, encouragement, professional advice, and as Hazel Holt notes, deep indignation on her behalf: 'It seems a sad state of affairs if such tender, perceptive and intelligent work can't see the light, just because . . . some taste-less chump thinks it won't "go" in paperback.'[13] He confided to Pym his own doubts and dry spells: 'I feel somewhat in the doldrums these days . . . the notion of expressing sentiments in short lines having similar sounds at their ends seems as remote as mangoes on the moon.'[14] Pym in turn sympathised with his artistic blocks and occasionally suggested a tongue-in-cheek remedy: 'Perhaps *I* should revise your novel and *you* mine. That should have interesting results' (AVPE, 217). He looked forward to their mutual rebirth as productive, appreciated artists: 'Poetry has deserted me – I had a sonnet in the Sheffield *Morning Telegraph* last Saturday, which is how some people *start*, I suppose. Perhaps we shall kick the lids off our tombs simultaneously.'[15]

Temperamentally similar, both formal and reserved, the two writers corresponded for three years before arriving at first names.

Pym asks, 'May I say "Philip"?, if that is what people call you, or should we go through the academic convention of "Philip Larkin" and "Barbara Pym?"'; Larkin responds, 'You are welcome to use my Christian name (or forename, as librarians say austerely) – you see, I have ventured to use yours.'[16] When they finally make plans to meet for the first time after fourteen years of correspondence, Pym characteristically identifies herself by her clothing, detailing the beige tweed suit or Welsh cape by which he can identify her. Larkin responds he is not worried: the bar of the Randolph Hotel, Oxford can contain few possibilities for error. 'I'm sure we shall recognise each other by progressive elimination, i.e. eliminating all the progressives. I am tall and bald and heavily spectacled and deaf, but I can't predict what I shall have on.'[17]

The two shared more than their distrust of 'progressives'. Neither hailed from an aristocratic or literary family, nor was a part of the contemporary social or literary scene. Neither married and each lived a quiet middle-class life supporting himself at what Larkin dubbed 'toad work',[18] Pym among the anthropologists and he as librarian at Hull University. Both, eschewing current literary trends, wrote knowingly of loneliness, aging, and isolation with voices grounded in unadorned language and practical common sense. In an article calling them spiritual siblings, Joseph Epstein notes that both Larkin and Pym create art in which,

> . . . technique never overwhelms content. It is an art in which the ironic, the comic, the understated, the fearlessly honest are given full play, while the shocking and the deliberately hideous are excluded. Excitement in such an art derives from precision of language and subtlety of sentiment, not from tension.[19]

But Larkin's support could only partially mediate Pym's rejection. The fourteen-year absence from publication forms what one critic calls 'the central story of her life'[20] and reshapes her outlook and style in subsequent writings. Despite being unable to publish a new novel, Pym did not spend these years in total eclipse. *No Fond Return of Love* was serialised by the BBC radio network in 1965. For at least four years Pym served as a judge for the annual awards of the Romantic Novelist Association ('The one thing they lack is humour or irony – and of course one does miss that' (AVPE, 280)). She wrote several book reviews including one for Iris Murdoch's *The Sea, the Sea*. New Portway Reprint Series, which Philip Larkin calls 'that infallible index of what people want to read instead of what they ought to want to read',[21] reissued five of her novels during this time, and her friend Robert Smith wrote the first critical appreciation of her work, 'How Pleasant to Know Miss Pym' for the Canadian literary journal *Ariel*. Most importantly, despite the disappointments, Pym kept writing: between 1963 and 1977, she began manuscripts for *The Sweet Dove Died, An Academic Question, Quartet in Autumn*, and *A Few Green Leaves*.

The Sweet Dove Died, on which Pym worked from 1963–1968, is the bastard child of her canon and a product of the rejection of *An Unsuitable Attachment*. Although she called it 'one of the best I have ever done' (AVPE, 302) it shows a conscious abandonment of her familiar formulas and a straining for contemporaneity that sets it apart from her other work. Along with *Quartet in Autumn* and the less successful *An Academic Question, The Sweet Dove Died* heads a group of Pym novels with darker themes and bleaker realism than those written for Jonathan Cape. These are inwardly directed novels of manners, poignant and problematical, examining with more psychological depth the responsibilites of the self in society.

Not since *Some Tame Gazelle* had Pym constructed a novel from such directly autobiographical origins as she does this story of an older woman and her attraction to a beautiful, if fickle, younger man. In 1962 Pym's friend Robert Smith had introduced her to Richard Roberts, a handsome young Caribbean expatriate who owned a London antique shop, L'Atelier. Pym carefully scrutinised the world of antique dealers and auction houses as she previously had that of anthropologists and academics, visiting the narrow streets of Kensington, observing the buyers and sellers of what her heroine calls 'objets d'art et de vertu'. With Roberts as guide, she moved through shops of rare porcelain and Victorian bibelots, absorbing enough expertise to bid as his proxy at an auction of rare books. As she had studied Scandinavian languages for Henry Harvey and Baltic politics for Julian Amery, Pym learned antiques, although her interest in them was secondary to her interest in Roberts himself.

She divides his characteristics between the two male characters of *The Sweet Dove Died*, James and Humphrey Boyce; she dresses them in Roberts' clothing, they have a fondness for his trademark scent, 'L'Heure bleu', and the meals they share with Leonora echo those Pym details in her diaries. Even Roberts' mother, whom Pym never met, appears: first as a treasured photograph in *The Sweet*

Dove Died and later in *An Academic Question* as the 'exquisite' Kitty Jeffreys, mother of the homosexual Coco. Pym allots to the uncle, Humphrey, Roberts' interest in opera and luxurious possessions, and to the nephew, James, his sexual ambiguity.

What began with Roberts as a series of casual dinners and informal luncheons including Hilary and other friends, became for Pym a more serious and intimate association. Nothing in her diaries or letters indicates that Pym's relationship with Roberts, or 'Skipper' as she fondly called him, ever moved beyond the platonic, although she may have desired more.

> The memory of R. in full beauty on Tuesday night – in peacock blue shirt and smelling strangely of L'Heure Bleu – ('because you like it') is something. If only I were the man and he the girl! (MS Pym 62, fol. 1)

Certainly she wished for more of his time and devotion, and Roberts' inattentiveness caused her pain. Replicating the relationships she had nurtured with men like Henry Harvey or Gordon Glover, this association alternated between periods of neglect and subsequent happy reunions:

> Monday 5th – But it's so terribly difficult and now I begin almost to worry though I know he must be all right. What am I meant to do? Just go on and on like this? Today is so painful, I feel raw all over. This morning I almost definitely decided to call a three-months truce or silence – when he gets in touch. (MS Pym 61, fol. 4)
>
> 17th August. Summer and 'things' are good again. Happy the country that has no history! No writing in this book anyway – only to note that it is a pattern that will be repeated, the good and the bad and one must learn to live with it. (MS Pym 62, fol. 1)

His few letters to her, collected in the Bodleian papers, are brief and noncommittal, written while on buying trips abroad or on extended visits to his mother in Nassau. Pym's diary reflections show her increasingly dependent on small scraps of his affection and resorting to poetry, as she had in her earliest Oxford days, to express the frustration of unrequited love. As frontispiece to a new diary begun during this period she tapes a printed clipping of a poem, 'Symptoms of Loss' (MS Pym 63, fol. i), and later she composes her own ironic vision of isolation, opening with a fragment from Roberts' favorite popular song, 'People Who Need People':

> People who need – There are too many of us here
> And we know too much about each other
> Delving into our own and other people's childhoods
> (And) blaming it all on mother
> Yet we have no clue as to the point of it all
> Not even David Frost knows that.
>
> (MS Pym 66, fol. 12)

See-sawing between resentment and stoicism, Pym's diary entries concerning Roberts continue for several years, even after his responses trickle to vacation postcards. Now in her early fifties, Pym knew she could expect few further romantic attachments, and this sense of a last chance fills both the diaries and *The Sweet Dove Died*; it accounts for the quality which makes her friend Robert Liddell call this 'her most deeply felt novel'[22] and 'full of penetrating self-criticism'.[23]

Dedicated 'To R.', *The Sweet Dove Died* employs a smaller cast of characters and a tighter symmetry of plot than Pym had attempted before. Elegant, cool, and fastidious, the heroine, Leonora Eyre, is at least partly wish-fulfillment: Pym herself was never so detached. Although this heroine, like her predecessors, is in search of 'something to love', the issues here are power, acquisition, and control, aptly symbolised by the collecting of rare and valuable (though sometimes flawed) antiques. Jamesian metaphors abound: objects of beauty are marred by imperfections and characters themselves are items for collections.

Aware that some critics found *An Unsuitable Attachment* 'a rather mild book', she promised Larkin 'to make my next (which I have almost started) less so!' (AVPE, 217), and the versions of love Pym offers in this novel are unlike any she has previously explored. Sexual and Freudian urges prevail over romance. Leonora abjures the church and the comforts of community that it offers as well as any close friendships with women. The tony neighborhoods and elegant emporiums of Belgravia, Knightsbridge, and Mayfair provide settings far removed from Pym's comfortable milieux of village garden fêtes or parish jumble sales. When these wealthy, leisured characters venture out it is usually not by bus or train, but by private motor car to visit an estate sale in the country or an opera at Covent Garden. The one distressed gentlewoman, Miss Foxe, has ties with St Basil's parish and Sophia Aigner of *An Unsuitable Attachment*, but she is quickly dispatched from the top floor flat to make room for Leonora's newest possession, James. *The Sweet Dove Died* is Pym's most extended look at the privileged life of upper-middle-class London.

A pampered heroine like Wilmet Forsyth or a manipulating matchmaker like Sophia Ainger pose the reader some initial problems of sympathic association, but they are lovely, warm, and compassionate compared to Leonora Eyre. More like a heroine from Anita Brookner, Leonora is no excellent woman: distanced from the traditional communities of Pym's novel of manners – family, neighborhood, church, or work – she is defined by her possessions, her clothing, and her highly developed sense of the appropriate. She avoids whenever possible the two female friends whose situations uncomfortably mirror her own: one consoling herself with cats when men prove unreliable, the other fretting over a series of young homosexual companions; neither measuring up to Leonora's elegant standards. Characterised by her need to control, Leonora manipulates her environment, her acquaintances, even her own family history, to showcase herself. Retiring alone for the night, Leonora 'arranged herself for sleep':

> No Bible, no book of devotion, no alarm clock marred the worldly charm of her bedside table. Browning and Matthew Arnold – her favourite poets – took their place with her Guerlain cologne, a bottle of smelling salts, soft aquamarine tissues, a phial of brightly coloured pills to relieve stress and strain, and presiding over all these the faded photographs of a handsome man and a sweet-faced woman in late Victorian dress. Leonora had long ago decided that her grandparents were much more distinguished-looking than her father and mother whose photographs had been hidden away in a drawer. (TSDD, 17)

Physical sex, which involves a willing abdication of power, appalls her: 'Surely freedom from this sort of thing was among the compensations of advancing age and the sad decay of one's beauty; one really ought not to be having to fend people off any more' (TSDD, 92). A relationship with a younger man, who offers her nothing more passionate than a 'reverent touch on lips, cheek or brow', permits Leonora to control her world as an untouchable autocrat.

The struggle for the sweet dove James forms the central conflict of the novel, as he becomes the prize in a three-cornered power struggle among the languidly erotic (and overmatched) Phoebe, Leonora, demure and elegant, and the predatory American, Ned. Each attempts, like the speaker in Keats' poem, to weave a binding thread to tether James close:

> I had a dove, and the sweet dove died;
> > And I have thought it died of grieving.
> O, what could it grieve for? Its feet were tied
> > With a single thread of my own hand's weaving

Indeed metaphorical cages, prisons, or traps fill this novel as the characters, especially Phoebe, Leonora, and Ned, seek to collect or control those around them.

Phoebe, the least well-imagined of the combatants, is easily bested. Manuscripts show that Pym planned a larger role for her, but as Leonora's character took shape, Phoebe's importance declined, forcing Pym to note in her diary, 'Cut out all Phoebe's early cosiness' (MS Pym 65, fol. 4). The weakening of her character creates a minor imbalance in the plot which Pym explains in a letter to Philip Larkin:

> Many thanks for . . . your most interesting helpful criticisms. Nobody has ever told me what was really wrong with the book and I felt there must be something. It suffered through starting off as one thing and ending up as another, the penalty of having so little free time and energy that continuity is lost and one's ideas change in the meantime. I started not at all in sympathy with Leonora, who began by being a minor character but as the book progressed I got more interested in her and really enjoyed writing about her best in the end. (AVPE, 247)

Phoebe, who supports herself with unexceptional writing and worse poetry, is neither a good cook nor housekeeper and has suspiciously middle-class tastes in her choice of dress, food, and drink: all in contrast to her elegant opposite. Her lack of sexual inhibition and her total disassociation with the remainder of his world initially intrigue James, but she is no match for Leonora's determination.

A struggle over a small fruitwood mirror, elaborately decorated with cupids, serves as an encapsulated version of the women's struggle for James himself. Phoebe desires it as a tangible expression of her ties to its owner, 'To be involved with a man's furniture . . . adds considerably to one's prestige' (TSDD, 83). Leonora's possession of the mirror not only validates her claim to James, but also symbolises her narcissism, aesthetic romanticism, and refusal to confront reality.

> The glass had some slight flaw in it, and if she placed it in a certain light she saw looking back at her the face of a woman from another century, fascinating and ageless. It might be a good idea to use it when she made up her face, to spare herself some of the painful discoveries she had lately been making. (TSDD, 87)

Having wrested James's loaned furniture from the younger woman and installed it and him in her third floor flat (previously a nursery with protective bars on its windows), Leonora seems the winner.

Ned, however, wants none of James's possessions. While the women wrangle over mirrors, James lies in a steamy Portuguese hotel room with this 'companion he had picked up on his travels.' Away from the decorative and protective cocoon provided by his uncle and Leonora, James abroad embraces the homosexuality he had avoided in London. Twice before in the novel Pym had hinted that James transmits a confusion of sexual signals. In the background of the novel's opening scene is 'a tall man with a slightly raffish air' who tries to make eye contact with the handsome young antique dealer; James pretends to ignore him, 'not quite sure if he wanted that kind of admiration'. When the unnamed admirer tracks him to his uncle's shop several chapters later, his whispered suggestion brings 'a not unbecoming blush to James's cheek, though it was not the first time such a proposition had been put to him'. The arrival of the shop assistant precludes any further developments, but the stage has been set for Ned's entrance.

Although she treats the sexual dimension discreetly, Pym makes it clear that the source of the attraction between James and Ned is physical, and she closes their first scene together with a blackout as demure as any she had employed in earlier novels. Her Oxford friend Robert Liddell, who himself preferred life without women, says of the characterisation:

> The affair between the two young men is most delicately done, neither for nor against – and the author takes refuge in silence only after twice bringing it to a pitch following which nothing but the vulgarity of asterisks or of consummation would have been possible.[24]

Pym encountered homosexuality at Oxford and during the war, but remained generously unperturbed by the issue, allowing one of her characters to pose a possible justification: 'Women are so terrifying these days and seem to expect so much, really far more than one could possibly give' (AGOB, 9). She remained close to Liddell throughout her life, exchanging frequent letters and visiting him and his friends on several vacations to Greece. Her neighbor in Finstock, Gilbert Phelps remembers:

> She was a sincere and devout Christian, but she would have no truck with narrow-minded gossip about people's sexual frailties and peccadilloes: 'There are far worse sins than those of the flesh,' she had exclaimed with considerable passion on one occasion, 'such as greed, selfishness and cruelty.'[25]

There is nothing homophobic about her fictional presentation of male attraction except as it provides a stumbling block for her women searching for love. More often than not, she holds these relationships up for the same comic scrutiny that she does more conventional ones.

In the early novels homosexuals provide one more variation in the comic spectrum of these contained societies, but the presentation is minus any overt sexuality. Miss Doggett's favorite teatime guests, the students Michael and Gabriel, dance through *Crampton Hodnet*, bantering together in affected dialogue when they are not 'giggling at some private joke'. In *Excellent Women* the battling Napiers move from the flat below Mildred to be replaced by a more compatible duo – two retired governesses, one who wields the tea caddy, the other the hammer. Homosexuality is suggested, usually by their fussing over food, in a parade of finicky men – William Caldicott in *Excellent Women*, Mervyn Cantrell in *An Unsuitable Attachment*, and Wilf Bason in *A Glass of Blessings*. This last novel also includes a briefer version of the more fully developed affair in *The Sweet Dove Died*: a bored and aesthetically inclined woman seeks involvment with a less than enthusiastic man but cannot compete with his homosexual partner.

Ned is the most openly villainous character in Pym's fiction, not because of his sexual preferences but because he employs power ruthlessly, with all of Leonora's acquisitiveness and none of her formal scruples. Animal-like images describe him: his voice is gnat-like, his scent 'powerful and exotic', and the thrill of the hunt satisfies him more than the kill. When he invites James and Leonora to his 'pad', she is uncomfortable among the jungle-like wallpaper, dark leather furniture, and synthetic fur rugs. Confronted with the bedroom and a bed 'exceptionally wide . . . and covered in mauve velvet' Leonora can only politely inquire whether it is comfortable. Ned taunts her by suggesting, 'comfort isn't all I go for'. The cruel 'glitter' of his personality combined with James's passivity convinces them all that Ned is in control; Leonora is forced to retreat. Ned can either mock or abandon social conventions to achieve a goal, which, once obtained, loses its appeal. Although like Leonora he pretends to value the past, his appetite is fed only by the new, and his return to America is symbolically appropriate.

Pym reintroduces Ned, still fair-haired and deceptively youthful looking, as a minor character in one of her most successful short stories, 'Across A Crowded Room'.[26] Cast as dinner partner to the narrating older woman, he presents in his signature gnat-like voice a perfunctory compliment which forces the narrator into self-examination 'as it was evident from his whole demeanour [he] was interested only in women of his mother's generation' (CTS, 368). So completely imagined was Ned for *The Sweet Dove Died* that Pym has no difficulty recreating a slightly older version: he still relishes innuendo, mocking and posing throughout the evening's conversation, but his power to wound is diminished by the narrator's age and experience.

Aging, with its overlapping privileges and indignities, becomes an issue in all three of Pym's final novels, but in *The Sweet Dove Died* she studies its most public face: the loss of physical beauty. Leonora busies herself by strategically arranging her wardrobe and her environment to camouflage encroaching age, testing and re-testing her powers of attraction by engaging in minor flirtations with strangers. Wrapped scarves, dark glasses, black lace, dim lighting, and the company of a younger man disguise what the mirror refuses to hide – 'those lines where none had been before, and that softening and gradual disintegration of the flesh which was so distressing on a spring or summer morning' (TSDD, 87). Although hints of mortality occur to this heroine, she is able to brush them aside, concerning herself more with the aesthetic arrangement of her current life and 'there was no reason why one's death should not, in its own way, be as elegant as one's life' (TSDD, 18). Motifs of mortality and death that will come to the forefront in *Quartet in Autumn* are here limited to the loss of youth and beauty.

This study of a woman of an age and situation similar to her own shows Pym at her most psychologically penetrating. She balances Leonora's refusal to recognise the sterility of her life with her friend Meg's outpourings of self-analysis. In journal notes she plans a scene with Meg recounting (to Leonora's horror) the catalogue of menopausal symptoms normal 'for women of "their" age':

> Meg . . . began to talk in hushed tones about the change of life. Tentatively at first, then with growing confidence she recounted her own experiences. A sympathetic *woman* doctor who had explained so much – everything was accounted for – tears, depression, need to love a younger person, child substitute, feeling of inadequacy, wasted life, etc. (MS Pym 66, fol. 4)

When Pym comes to write the scene for the novel, however, 'the need to love a younger person', is not included, striking perhaps too close to the truth of her own situation.

She considers at least two possible conclusions for *The Sweet Dove Died*, both colored by her weakening relationship with Roberts:

> Ending No I. She gives him up (like me?) and prepares to go on with her life – the things she would do – sewing and collecting old books and walking about at lunchtime alone and proud. Ending No. II. The woman waits. He said he would call. She waits and waits and nothing comes. (MS Pym 63, fol. 13)

A more hopeful possibility occurs to her: 'Couldn't one be left with impression that in the future Leonora might fill some kind of position in James's life – speculate on what it might be' (MS Pym 67, fol. 7). Neither fiction nor reality would prove this possible. She would allow Leonora the comforts of her own delusion and the continued attentions of Humphrey, a more appropriate suitor, but for herself only 'walking about at lunchtime alone and proud'. Her time with Roberts which she called 'too long for love, too short for friendship' (MS Pym 63, fol. 14) ended, but he remained in her imagination, along with other old loves, as a bittersweet indicator of lost youth.

> Was passing through Chelesa. Rupert Gleadow's flat at 33 Cheyne Walk is demolished . . . Also L'Atelier is closed and the windows plastered with posters advertising water skiing holidays – ah, Skipper. (MS Pym 68, fol. 11)

Years later, when *The Sweet Dove Died* was received with kind reviews and popular success, an old friend asked if Roberts had seen the novel.

> Of course Richard *did* write when he had read the book . . . and I've also had an affectionate card from him from Indonesia, of all places. What did he say about the book? Well, rather wisely he didn't make much comment except to say how much he had enjoyed it. It was all such a long time ago anyway . . . Little did I think that anything as profitable as this novel would come out of it. (AVPE, 321)

While revising *The Sweet Dove Died*, Pym began two drafts (MS Pym 22–4) of what she called her 'academic novel', later edited by Hazel Holt and published in 1986 as *An Academic Question*. Holt combined Pym's two versions, choosing the first-person narrator of the original, Caroline Grimstone, the 'youngish' wife of an ambitious university lecturer. Despite her Dickensian name, Caro was, as Pym wrote Larkin, 'supposed to be a sort of Margaret Drabble effort but of course it hasn't turned out like that at all' (AAQ, note). Instead, she is an excellent-woman-in-training: nominally a wife and mother, but spinsterlike in demeanor and more concerned with pleasing than with pleasure. Despite this, *An Academic Question* is, according to Holt, 'very unlike her other books', and the least successful of the published canon. Its failure grows from Pym's abandoning the conventions of the novel of manners, straining for a new style with excesses of plot and character, tailored, she hoped, to the 1970s.

The two minor plots of *An Academic Question* add little to its cohesion: the adulterous plot is introduced only to evaporate, and the self-discovery plot leaves the heroine where she began – confused and unfulfilled. The major plot line follows an academic intrigue much like those Pym witnessed in her years at the IAI.

At the local nursing home Caro reads to a blind and bedridden missionary who hoards a trunkful of papers written during his days in Africa. This research is coveted by several factions of the academic community, chief among them Caro's husband, Alan, and his rival, Crispin Maynard. With Caro's aid, Alan steals the papers and uses the information he discovers there to attack Crispin in the pages of their professional journal. Alan leaves to Caro the job of surreptitiously returning the purloined papers to the missionary's collection, now housed in the office of the university Librarian. Just when exposure seems likely, student protesters start a fortunate fire, and the resulting water damage reduces the contents of the Librarian's office (and the evidence of the theft) to 'illegible pulp'.

The melodrama of the denouement, along with hyperactive scene shifts and underdeveloped settings, results from Pym's deliberate avoidance of previous stylistic traits. Surface descriptions are kept to a minimum with menus, wardrobes, furnishings, and social gatherings only lightly sketched. The nameless provincial university, perhaps modeled after Larkin's Hull, houses a shadowy student body who exist only peripherally: their one protest scene is observed through a restaurant window as the major characters sip coffee and liqueurs. The plot is full of coincidence, repetition, and pro forma conversations on current mores. The stuffy social gatherings of dissimilar colleagues, the depiction of which should be Pym's forte, are for the most part perfunctory, only occasionally offering the characteristic ironic detail – a dinner guest upbraiding the Grimstones for racial insensitivity while wolfing down a second helping of their casserole. This sort of finely tuned nuance is too often overshadowed by conversations on abortion, contraception, divorce, student riots, fashions of the sixties, Caribbean immigrants, or class leveling. Themes of academic and sexual competition, handled deftly in earlier novels are this time unpleasantly coupled with malice, self-pity, and pettiness, and dialogue intended as 'smart' or 'swinging' more often sounds clipped and forced.

With her time occupied by work, church, and writing, and with her social group aging, Pym had little connection to the Caros of the 1960s, and this attempt to create a heroine unique in her novels and her own experience results in a character only half imagined. Caro's emotional responses to her husband, child, and friends are controlled, like Leonora Eyre's, to the point of passivity, and instead of tough or cool she is often merely sulky or unkind. Her moral or ethical stances are blunted, probably in Pym's effort to align her with a youth-centered culture, but the effect is to trivialise her instead. She would characterise herself as unstylish, unfulfilled, and unlovable, and the reader is inclined to agree.

An Academic Question has its successes, however, mostly occuring when Pym returns to familiar territory. Caro's small rebellions against the quasi-intellectual socialism of her husband and his colleagues mirror Pym's uneasiness with the leveling-down of life she saw around her – 'There was nothing to be ashamed of in having inherited a villa from his family, and it made me glad to realise that not everyone was being whittled down to the same size'; (AAQ, 6) they also allow her to question the desirability of a homogeneous public, with homogeneous tastes. The petty wrangling over journal publications, an area of considerable expertise for Pym, rings true, and her cynical view of academia is little changed from that she presented in *Crampton Hodnet* and *Less Than Angels*.

The throwback characters, especially those drawn from her own experience, outshine the unlikely Swedish au pair or the four-year-old child. The novel's chief eccentric, the spinster Dolly, dominates each scene in which she participates. Preoccupied equally with hedgehog droppings and philosophical musings, she remembers better days: 'Kitty and I living here as young girls, going to dances and wearing flesh-coloured artificial silk stockings. Kitty used to have hers ironed to make them shiny. *Such* detail and now people wear nylon tights and we shall all soon be gone anyway' (AAQ, 37). Her rueful nostalgia for a bygone era is more believable than all of Caro's marital anguish.

Not only did she lose interest in this novel as *Quartet in Autumn* took shape, Pym cannibalised the draft extensively, as she had previously done with the unpublishable *Crampton Hodnet*. For her next two novels she transposed from it themes, individual lines, and at least one entire episode. The memorial service for Esther Clovis which Caro attends in her husband's place is likewise attended by Emma, the heroine of *A Few Green Leaves*, and a large assembly of mourners collected from earlier novels.

Discouraged by the publishing world's rejection of *An Unsuitable Attachment* and *The Sweet Dove Died*, and dissatisfied with the 'Margaret Drabble attempt', Pym opted for retrenchment. After one editor provided her a synopsis of readers' opinions mentioning her 'obsession' with detail, Pym complained to her diary, 'What is wrong with being obsessed with trivia? Some have criticised *The Sweet Dove Died* for this. What are the minds of my critics filled with?

What *nobler* and more worthwhile things?' (MS Pym 68, fol. 10). The daily notations in her pocket journal, the habit of a lifetime, could not be abandoned, but neither could she envision them becoming again the raw material for a publishable novel.

> What is the future for my kind of writing? What can my note-books contain except the usual kind of bits and pieces that can never (?) now be worked into fiction. Perhaps in retirement, and even in the year before, a quieter narrower kind of life can be worked out and adopted. Bounded by English Literature and the Anglican Church and small pleasures. (MS Pym 70, fol. 1)

While anticipating retirement she kept a close eye on the current literary scene, observing who and what were successful in the marketplace, ('Isak Dinesen (Karen Blixen) perhaps rather a tire-some person. Just imagine her with Truman Capote!' (MS Pym 71, fol. 21), but she refused to compromise her style again, awaiting the day when she could write regularly for herself.

A mastectomy in 1971 ('O little lump – almost a subject for a metaphysical poem' (MS Pym 69, fol. 3)) and a small stroke three years later prompted her to hasten these retirement plans. Letters to friends record her good humor during these illnesses: 'To have a lovely rest, to have flowers and grapes and books brought to you and to be a centre of interest is not at all unpleasant!' (AVPE, 262). The journals reveal the debilitating effects of the stroke as she struggles with shaky handwriting and misspelling, but not with fear:

> Small strope – investigation revealsed breask canser and exces of calcium thought to be from canser but bnone trace did not conferm them. Dr Burke examinned me (+ studenns!) . . . hope-fully home cerca Wednesday. Asphasia: stroke? (MS Pym 72, fol. 14)

However she rebounds quickly and within months contemplates a 'hospital novel', accelerates her already planned departure from the Institute, and offers in her diary a quiet 'deo gratias for my recovery' (MS Pym 73, fol. 18).

After her divorce from Alexander 'Sandy' Walton, Pym's sister Hilary spent her working life at BBC radio and in 1972 purchased

for Barbara and herself a small semi-detached cottage in the Oxfordshire village of Finstock. Barbara finished her last months at the IAI,
living weekdays in a rented room in London's Balcombe Street and
commuting weekends to Finstock – 'rather strange and disorienting
in a way but I feel I am getting the best of both worlds' (AVPE,
271). She began *Quartet in Autumn* 'a page a day early in the
morning'[27] during these days and always insisted it was not the
bleak study of aging that many readers and publishers saw. Later
she would admit the novel is 'less light-hearted than some of my
earlier ones . . . [but] I enjoyed the writing of it almost more than
any of the others, perhaps because I felt that I was writing for my
own pleasure with no certain hope of publication at that time' (MS
Pym 96, fol. 11). Its themes of illness, aging, and retirement, coupled
with the disappointment and rejection in this period of Pym's life,
create the darkest novel of her canon, and her masterpiece.

Unlike other Pym manuscripts in which the narrative focus,
plot lines, or major characters undergo several transfigurations,
Quartet in Autumn remained essentially unchanged from its con-
ception. Fourteen years before, she had considered a novel with
the heroine 'on the point of retirement and going to live in the
country . . . the office party and presentation' (MS Pym 52, fol. 5);
now, approaching a similar situation herself, she began again the
familiar process of fictionalizing her own experience. She knew
from scanning publishers' lists that 'the position of an unmarried
woman – unless, of course, she is somebody's mistress – is of no
interest whatsoever to the readers of modern fiction' (MS Pym 70,
fol. 5). When this diary note does become 'the beginning of a novel?'
it establishes a fictional challenge: to follow a refined if not well
educated unmarried woman (soon split into two main characters)
into retirement and obsolescence. With the additional balance of two
male characters, *Four Point Turn*, as she originally titled it, would
weave the separate stories of these four into a novel as muted and
austere as their lives.

Like *The Sweet Dove Died* before it, *Quartet in Autumn* explores
loss – of youth, love, illusion, occupation, companionship, home,
sanity, and life itself. Unlike other novels of manners it pares
discourse and social gatherings to a bare minimum and relies
more on internal monologues and austere imagery to capture the
one-note monotony of these lives. The value of polite conversation,
usually essential to establishing relationships, is undermined in the
opening pages: feigning 'apparent indifference', Letty forgoes the

chance 'to make contact' with a solitary woman sharing her silent lunch table, establishing a motif of non-communication that recurs throughout the novel.

In addition to the reduced dialogue, the novel is nearly eventless, with characters coming together only for an obligatory luncheon, a meager retirement toast, a cremation service, and the dispersal of Marcia's property. Almost as if pushing to discover how bare a novel could be stripped, Pym presents visits that never happen, conversations conducted in one imagination, physical touches that never connect. Characters are orphans or widowers, celibate or crazy, with families who no longer support and who are reduced to the caftan-clad offspring of a distant cousin. Self-sufficiency becomes a necessity in a society where the church and the medical profession are no more effective than the welfare agency in providing consolation or comfort; each individual or institution wishes to assume that another has absolved it of social responsibility. Aging means not only loss of physical beauty as it had for Leonora Eyre, but now includes all the possible horrors of isolation: loneliness, poverty, hypothermia, injury, senility, even starvation. The musical motifs indicated in the title operate for the most part ironically: although evenly balanced, the four participants never harmonise, each limited to playing his individual role with little ear for interdependence.

Pym emphasises their isolation by opening the novel with Letty, Marcia, Edwin, and Norman performing the same act individually, each visiting the local library at lunchtime. She scrupulously measures out information about them in equal portions, characterizing them first by descriptions of their dated hairstyles and unusual library habits and later by alternating their longer solo scenes. In the opening paragraph each enters unnoticed by the librarian, indistinguishable in his or her blandness, yet the omniscient narrator recognises they are 'people who belonged together in some way'. The nature of their relationship reveals itself slowly as they grapple separately and together with the problem of living purposefully into old age.

Although Pym relies upon the interweaving of their lives to provide narrative tension, the details of their pasts are sketchy. Even their surnames come slowly, as if to deny them both family connections and personal histories. Letty and Marcia are only later revealed as Miss Crowe and Miss Ivory, ironically well-defined opposing shades for two such shadowy, similar figures; Edwin does not become Mr Braithwaite until the ninth chapter, and Norman's last name we never learn. This lack of identity links them in ways that elaborate pasts could not.

Norman, the least defined of the four, is drawn like any of several familiar male characters from earlier Pym novels, except for his anger. Suspicious and snappish, he is three times referred to as an angry or 'tetchy' little dog, a telling metaphor from the cat-loving Pym. He may once have been attracted to Marcia, but has long since smothered those feelings with an engulfing misanthropy; now they share only a large jar of instant coffee, and that for the sake of economy not friendship. Pym reveals his repressed sexuality by following his lunch-hour stroll: he engages in mild voyeurism at a young girls' netball game, envies the 'semi-nudity' of the young sunbathers, and transfers his anger to nearby parked cars, whose fenders remind him of 'rumps, buttocks and bums' jutting over curbs. This hatred of automobiles distances him from his only surviving relative – a brother-in law, Ken, who runs a driving school – and confirms that Norman has been left behind by modern speed and technology. Like other Pym characters before him, Norman is eccentric but not so caricatured that he is incapable of change. When to everyone's surprise he is bequeathed Marcia's rundown house, he begins to take pleasure in the idea of home-ownership with its incumbent duties and powers.

Edwin has lived a fuller life than Norman. Once married, he still owns his own home and has a daughter and family he visits at major holidays, but he views these dutiful visits as interruptions of his greatest pleasure – attending church services. Like Norman, Edwin superficially resembles several of Pym's selfish and self-absorbed early male characters, structuring his social life around the church and its calendar but attaching himself permanently to no specific congregation. Here, however, the importance of churchgoing has shrunk, services are ill-attended, and the subsequent social activities strained: people 'only go for the light and the warmth, the coffee after the Sunday morning service and a friendly word from the vicar' (QIA, 143).

A conditioned reader of Pym expects a strong female central consciousness, but in *Quartet* it is Edwin who pushes them all toward solidarity. The more sensitive of the two males and the most capable of taking charge, he counts Father Gellibrand as a friend, takes steps to secure necessary new lodging for Letty, initiates the reunion luncheon at the Rendevouz, oversees Marcia's transferal to the hospital (where he identifies himself as her next-of-kin), and arranges her funeral service. He could be an 'excellent woman' except that he has a severely constricted emotional range and lacks the ability for clear-sighted self-appraisal.

Not surprisingly, given her penchant for female narrators, Pym creates the two women with more definition than the men and she gives to Letty Crowe most of the moral reflections of the novel. When Letty and Marcia reach retirement and leave their structured office routines, their behaviors present the counterpoint of possibilities facing the elderly woman alone. Letty, an aging combination of Harriet Bede and Mildred Lathbury, pays fastidious attention to her appearance and contains her loneliness with attention to meals, with attempts at socializing, and with biographies of lives more exciting than her own. She maintains the self-discipline ingrained over a lifetime, promising herself to abide by the 'rules': ' . . . one did not drink sherry before evening, just as one did not read a novel in the morning' (QIA, 118). Marcia, concerned with neither fashion nor food, slides slowly from eccentricity into madness when the containing routine of her office life disappears.

As has become her hallmark, Pym presents these characters' attitudes toward clothing, food, and lodging as important outward indications of their inner states of mind. Before and after her retirement Letty's attire was 'respectable and appropriate', given to pastel cardigans coordinated with discreet strings of imitation pearls, and a hairstyle 'fluffy and faded' as the prints she favored – 'an old sheep', thinks Marcia. Her snooping landlady, approving of her immaculately organised dresser drawers, is surprised only by a 'rather gaily-patterned cotton kimono which seemed not to be in character' (QIA, 82), an indication that underneath her predictable exterior Letty still preserves the possibility of a more colorful private life.

Marcia, too, has a hidden stash of nightwear. She carefully hoards new lingerie for examination days with Dr Strong, the surgeon who had performed her mastectomy and who remains in her mind as both mutilating god and fantasy lover. Pym charts Marcia's post-retirement decline in several ways, most poignantly by the omniscient recording of her tangled illogic, most comically by cataloguing her choice of rag-tag clothing.

Wiry and thin, observing the world with eyes 'alarmingly magnified behind her glasses', Marcia reminds Letty of a nocturnal animal, 'a lemur, or a potto?' and her nondescript dress and fiercely dyed hair deteriorate upon retirement as quickly as her mental health. All her energies become directed toward compulsive acts – folding and categorizing old plastic bags, hoarding well-washed milk bottles, digging for the remains of a long dead cat – and none toward self-preservation. When she reluctantly agrees to meet the others for a reunion luncheon, desiring by this time neither food nor company, her outward appearance mirrors her inner disarray:

> Marcia was thinner than ever and her light-colored summer coat hung on her emaciated body. On her feet she wore old fur-lined sheepskin boots and a pair of much darned stockings, and on her head an unsuitably jaunty straw hat from which her strangely piebald hair straggled in elflocks. (QIA, 129)

It is a tragicomic moment: the clown-like bag-lady in whose dress the out-of-season competes with the bizarre and the bedraggled, contrasting with Letty in her best tweed suit and new gloves. By summer, Marcia, spied upon by Norman, is a parodic earth mother: a white haired wraith, dressed in a pattern of overwhelmingly large pink flowers, her arms full of empty milk bottles. Days later she will be helped into one of the virginal nightgowns and sprinkled with lavender water for her final examination by Dr Strong.

Clothing descriptions decrease as the narrative eye follows Marcia's mind into chaotic justification of her aberrational behavior. What had been comic quirks of eccentricity in earlier anti-social or reclusive characters are simultaneously touching and frightening here as minor compulsions become major obsessions. As she grows weaker from self-imposed starvation and as growing impairment prevents logical connections, Marcia's thought processes gain in speed what they lack in coherence. The narrating omniscience spurts rapid fragments of detail, shards of Marcia's memories, creating a jigsaw puzzle stream-of-consciousness (or near un-consciousness in this case) unprecedented in Pym's work. The verbal barrage slows as Marcia's life ebbs, and fixated on the pattern in Dr. Strong's necktie, she slips away.

Along with clothing, the traditionally shared pleasures of food and shelter carry metaphorical weight in the novel, ironically reinforcing the isolation of the disharmonic quartet. Beginning with their separate lunch hour rituals, through solitary dinners and shared luncheons, finding new living accommodations and rediscovering old ones, the novel explores the ramifications of consuming, sharing, and ignoring basic human needs. Food for Pym has always been a social cohesive, joining partakers in pleasurable community and providing spiritual as well as physical comfort. Lodging has previously meant safe haven and independence. Here the darker possibilities emerge; mealtimes are to be endured, shelter is transitory.

A reviewer of Pym's early novels complained that she lacked Jane Austen's 'merciless grasp of the economic and social realities that shape her characters' lives',[28] a criticism never less true than in this novel. The economics of old age ground *Quartet* firmly in Mrs Thatcher's England (Edwin and Norman disagree on her personal responsibility for rising prices), as the characters grapple with pension limitations, welfare agencies, and a London landscape marked by closing grocery stores and new concrete. Pym knows this scaling down contains comic possibilities for the habits of her office workers: 'A great deal of strange food is eaten in this office because none of the older staff can afford to go out to lunch' (MS Pym 71, fol. 13). Among her papers Pym documents these times carefully with items as small as an annotated grocery receipt and as large as a sheaf of correspondence concerning her own pension application. The diaries for these years note changes in the London she had embraced so enthusiastically as a younger woman. She compares an evening's walk through the underground with a modern 'Dante's inferno' (MS Pym 65, fol. 3), notices in restaurants 'the ugly voices of young people'(MS Pym 70, fol. 2), and plans a character disenchanted with the modern city – 'The sister who tells the story can visit her sister in London and travel in the tube, noticing the sad tired faces. When did the joy begin to go from life, she wonders, was it sudden or gradual' (MS Pym 65, fol. 1).

Although urban violence has not yet impinged upon the four characters of *Quartet*, they live amidst its growing possibility. Graffiti assault each passer-by with such directives as 'KILL ASIAN SHIT.' A young derelict screams obscenities at her would-be Good Samaritan. Mild-mannered Edwin bites the heads off black jelly babies. The withdrawal from power and empire has created a Britain dense with immigrants, to the bewilderment of the unworldly Letty who shops at a grocery store now run by Uganda Asians and who unhappily seeks new lodging to avoid the sounds and smells of her ebullient Nigerian landlords. Marcia's neighbors too are emblematic of the change in traditional values of social responsibility. Superficially interested in her well-being, Nigel and Priscilla are on holiday in Spain when Marcia collapses and confess that they prefer as her replacement 'the sort of people one could invite to dinner, which [Norman], and whatever friends he might have, hardly seemed to be' (QIA, 202). Snobbery, materialism, and anonymity characterise these neghborhoods.

Anonymity also shrouds the working lives of these characters. Skillfully, Pym never reveals the nature of their vaguely clerical jobs, the make-up or hierarchy of the staff, the unspecified product or service provided, the location or configuration of the office. So marginal are these jobs that they will evaporate upon the retirement of the two men, and a computer will easily replace all four workers. The result of this ineffectuality is to distance them further from contact with each other and the outside world and to magnify the quirks of behavior they substitute for productivity.

In *Jane and Prudence* and *Less Than Angels* Pym had included comic scenes of office protocol and politics, suggesting that even the most deadening of routines could provide satisfaction, diversion, or, better, romance. *Quartet in Autumn* gives what Hazel Holt calls 'a maturer, sadder view of office life'[29] one in which romance or fulfillment seems unlikely and which culminates in the ritual of the retirement party. The comic horror of this mandatory social event, with its scale and expense pared to match the status of the honorees, unleashes the bitterest irony from the narrative voice, mocking the company's perception of its now completed responsibilities.

> Each would be given a small golden handshake, but the State would provide for their basic needs which could not be all that great. Elderly women did not need much to eat . . . and they probably had either private means or savings . . . there was no need for anyone to starve or freeze . . . There was no need to worry about Miss Crowe and Miss Ivory. (QIA, 101)

The reverberation of 'need' throughout the passage underscores the emotional deprivation of the two women who will afford basic sustenance but can nowhere purchase the human contact that would enrich their lives.

There is no indication of this bitterness in any of Pym's collected thoughts on her own retirement. The luncheon planned for her by the IAI was, according to Hazel Holt, 'a considerably more cheerful affair' than Letty and Marcia's farewell. Pym writes to Robert Smith of being consulted on the guest list, refreshments, and send-off gift:

> My retirement party went off quite well and I didn't burst into tears or anything shaming like that. There was wine and lots of nice food. John Middleton [the Director after the death of Daryll Forde] made a speech and everyone (almost) that I liked was able to come . . . . I was presented with a cheque but my real 'present', the new Oxford Dictionary, which I had chosen, rather typically hadn't arrived as it was rebinding.[30]

Life among the anthropologists, although not unpleasant, was never Pym's primary source of fulfillment. Retirement would provide more time for social, domestic, and creative pleasures, and by sharing expenses with Hilary she would face little economic hardship. Changes in the office location and personnel made leaving the Institute easier, and Pym 'was rather glad to be out of it all!' (AVPE, 280). She severed the ties to her working life slowly, however, continuing for several months to perform familiar jobs for the journal, 'the African tribal index . . . and the odd bibliography.' This period of freelance employment provided 'good discipline', and insured her a gentler easing into retirement than either Marcia or Letty enjoyed.

How one reads the presentation of retirement in *Quartet in Autumn* determines whether this is a familiar Pym comedy of manners or a darker, modern vision of social disintegration. Certainly a case can be made for the latter. Although there are moments of lightness, none of these characters is very happy: neither the state, the church, their families, nor their work can provide them support, nor do they seek it. These desiccated human relationships most resemble 'pigeons on the roof . . . picking at each other, presumably removing insects' causing Letty to wonder, 'Perhaps this is all that we as human beings can do for each other' (QIA, 9). What social activities they do engage in are inspired by habit or a sense of duty, not companionship or enjoyment. Each insists until the end upon fierce independence: Marcia starves, Norman reserves the right to sell her bequest, Edwin resumes his solitary church going, and Letty balks at realigning herself with a fickle friend. It is a bleak, cold world, one that Pym said should have been bleaker: 'I liked the British Book News review saying Quartet wasn't depressing enough – I rather agree, but perhaps I didn't quite have all that much courage' (MS Pym 165, fol. 134).

The courage needed, of course, was to overcome her usual buoyancy and the ingrained habits of a lifetime of novel construction. *Quartet in Autumn* is a comedy both for old age and for the later twentieth century, as Philip Larkin immediately recognised: 'It's so strange to find the level good-humoured tender irony of your style unchanged but dealing with the awful end of life' (MS Pym 151, fol. 114). Pym later explained she was led to write it 'because, being in that category myself, I was tired of the heavy-handed, humourless way the whole business was treated, especially by the media!' (MS Pym 165, fols 99–100) She calls upon many of the familiar patterns and comic conventions of her past successes, attention to detail, persistent characterisation quirks, repetitive routines, and diminished plot. Her characters begin by sharing little more than office space and conclude with a few tentative steps toward community. The celebratory ending of comedy, ironically reduced to a final gathering in Marcia's kitchen, is nonetheless upbeat. In place of a wedding feast, the remaining trio divides her elaborate stock of tinned food. When they discover at the back of one cupboard an unopened bottle of sherry (whose associations comically conjoin Marcia and the Queen of Sheba), they toast both the past and the future. Letty enjoys the power of choice involved in her decision where to live, and Norman delivers a credo to bring golden-agers everywhere to their feet, cheering:

> 'Don't you do anything you don't want to do, or let anybody tell you what you ought to do. Make up your own mind. It's your life, after all.' (QIA, 217)

Change, however small, will visit each of them, as signified by their unusual plans for a day's outing to meet Letty's extroverted friend, Marjorie. The potential for new relationships, even the formation of a new quartet is held out in Letty's final realisation, true for all its ironic hyperbole, that 'life still held infinite possibilities for change'.

Despite the later success she would have with this novel, Pym had no more luck placing it with a publisher than she had with the two before. One publisher's reader criticised its brevity, so she added 'twelve thousand words' (mostly the meal after the memorial service) and sent it out again (MS Pym 98, fol. 77). Another anonymous reader for the publisher Hamish Hamilton missed the comedy entirely, complaining, 'I could not help wondering, indeed, if the author was a social worker and she was simply attempting to alleviate her depression after visiting some elderly clients' (MS Pym 165, fol. 78). This response prompted Pym's friend, novelist Pamela Hansford Johnson who had recommended this publishing house, to apologize, branding Hamish Hamilton's reader 'an ass'.

Despite the help and sympathy of friends, Pym's publication problems continued. The volume of correspondence between the novelist and potential publishers generated during this period is staggering, and the careful maintenance of so many rejection slips, questionably masochistic. Several times she considered fictionalizing her own lack of success, 'Notebook for an unsuccessful novelist might be a good thing to do. I have so much material' (MS Pym 68, fol. 8). But with three completed novels still unpublished, could she write another without hope of an audience? Years later she would call the experience of rejection instructive: 'I suppose in a way it does one no harm to be humiliated and brought down, perhaps failure is better for you than success – I'm not sure about this though I do believe that no experience is entirely without its uses' (MS Pym 98, fol. 81). She was able to take pride in her past work, but the productive retirement she had anticipated now seemed an ironic impossibility.

> And when I met people I could admit that yes, I had written novels. I had published six. Jane Austen only published six novels, didn't she? But she died when she was 42. (MS Pym 98, fol. 81)

The novels that were never written during what should have been her most prolific years are the great loss of this period. Fortunately, her audience, believed by publishers to be extinct, was only hibernating.

The now familiar story of the resurrection of Barbara Pym is more fairy tale than drama. Like Sleeping Beauty or Cinderella rescued from oblivion by the attentions of a handsome prince, Pym was removed from the cold comfort of retirement to the pages of the *Times Literary Supplement*. Her champions, Larkin and Lord David Cecil, bestowing on the sleeping princess the kiss of favor, returned her to the public eye, restored her shaken confidence in her own talents, and set off a competition between publishing houses for the rights to new editions of her novels. Within a month of the *TLS* article, *Quartet In Autumn* was accepted for publication, followed soon after by a contract for *The Sweet Dove Died*.

Pym enjoyed the excitement of interviews and new contracts, but throughout maintained an equanimity that some of her supporters could not. Larkin, upon hearing news of her publishing success, celebrated in her behalf and then sat down to write:

> Super news! I am drinking (or, come to think of it, have drunk) a half-bottle of champagne in honour of your success . . . . Oh I am so pleased: I want a real Pym year . . . . Apart from the champagne, I have rung up a lady to collect some *jumble* tomorrow for some 'church players' – I've never done this before, so it's also in honour of you. (MS Pym 152)

Later in the same letter he jokingly imagines the headlines she will inspire: 'Pym Redivivius. An Early Libber. A Talent Disinterred. What fun it will all be.' The most satisfying small reward of the rediscovery was the chance to spurn Jonathan Cape's inquiries on reprinting her previous novels – ('*That*'ll be the FF ! ' [frosty Friday]) (MS Pym 76, fol. 15). The most satisfying major result included feeling 'that I am now regarded as a novelist, a good feeling after all those years of 'This is well written, *but* . . . .' (AVPE, 317). Radio and television interviews followed;[31] *Quartet* was named a candidate for the 1977 Booker Prize (losing to Paul Scott's *Staying On*); the first doctoral dissertation on her work appeared in 1978;[32] in 1979 Pym was appointed a Fellow of the Royal Society of Literature and later that year took delight in overhearing a bookstore customer inquire for her novels in paperback (MS Pym 80, fol. 17) – all indications of the renewed public and professional acclaim.

Emerging from a sixteen-year cocoon, she was quickly made aware of the increased role of publicity in the publishing world. Requests for interviews and photo sessions amused her, and although she accepted a few invitations to lecture on her work and career, her natural reticence led her to refuse most speaking engagements. She responded to one such request that 'my "rediscovery" as a novelist has not done anything for my gifts as a speaker' (MS Pym 172, fol. 1) and she declined a trip to Sweden to launch *The Sweet Dove Died*, writing to her publisher that shyness and, especially, age excused her from participating.

In fact I never do give talks or lectures and refuse such requests. I know some writers are good at it and even like doing it and I dare say I might have been one such if it hadn't been for the long gap in my literary life – it is too late to do anything unless I really want to do it! (MS Pym, fol. 52)

On the standard publicity form submitted to Macmillan she provides little more information about Miss Pym than 'Very fond of cats' and 'On the whole I prefer to stay in the background' (MS Pym 165, fols 99–100). She collected both the positive and negative reviews, articles, and interviews (a few are now saved among her papers, the rest remain in scrapbooks at Barn Cottage with Hilary), and laughed at the distorted portrait of herself that could be assembled from these reviewers' impressions: 'I sometimes think that if you put them all together you would gain a rather curious impression of me. A tall, gawky woman who wants to go to South America on [the] Concord and who reads Ovid and Vergil – a formidable combination, but only the gawky part is true, and even that was rather a surprise to me (still, it was in the *Times* . . .)' (MS Pym 98, fol. 82).

Buoyed by this wave of approbation, Pym immediately planned a new novel, one that would return to the patterns of her earliest works, away from London and isolation, back to the pastoral world of the Oxford countryside. She dedicates to Hilary and to Robert Liddell 'this story of an imaginary village' whose surface so resembles her own Finstock that the disclaimer rings only half-true. Admitting that 'When I wrote *Some Tame Gazelle* I didn't know nearly so much about village life as I do now' (MS Pym 74, fol. 4), Pym relies upon the close observations of her post-retirement home to build her final novel, *A Few Green Leaves*. She plans a densely populated scene, one that will build more on characterisation than plot: 'A novel with a village setting could learn something from *Under Milkwood*' (MS Pym 80, fol. 15). She adds to the familiar themes of her earliest novels her newly-found concerns for local history and medical care, bows consciously to the literary tradition she has always relied upon, and fills this valedictory novel with the cyclical patterns of life and death.

Pym wrote this novel well aware of her own mortality. The diaries and notebooks record with remarkable equanimity the recurrence of her earlier cancer, detailing its symptoms and attempted cures. Although she made brief notations for two future novels during this period, they both acknowledge parenthetically that her time was short:

> Idea for a new novel (if I ever write another). Women at college, perhaps two friends, one coming from a 'privileged' background and inspired to do social work. The other following a different career. This would be a chance to bring in World War II. (MS Pym 81, fol. 1)

> Went to St. Hilda's with Margaret, to lunch meeting and tea. Like the beginning of Jane and Prudence but in a different way, it might give me inspiration for another novel. (If I am spared.) (MS Pym 81, fols 16–17).

Preliminary notations for *A Few Green Leaves* alternate with reports of trips for radiation therapy and brief hospital stays where the distress of the disease is balanced by comic observations in the medical wards. She will admit after an injection 'Sunday evening – bad time. If you can survive this you can survive anything', and on the same page wonder who in the hierarchy of physicians gets the choice breast of the chicken – 'the consultants?' (MS Pym 80, fol. 22). The doctor-patient relationship she had created for Marcia Ivory continues to intrigue her, enough that in *A Few Green Leaves* she doubles the fictional possibilities with a youthful practitioner who professes an interest in geriatrics and his older partner who prefers treating the young and healthy. Underneath the irony with which she views the medical profession lies this novel's benign vision of human mortality colored, certainly, by her own knowledge of approaching death.

The plot follows the actions of a single central character, a not too young woman uneasy with her present situation, through the seasonal and liturgical events of a year in which she deals with disappointment, change, acceptance, and the possibility of an enhanced future. These terms could describe almost any one of Pym's novels, and on the surface *A Few Green Leaves* resembles them closely. The thirty-ish anthropologist Emma Howick moves to any empty cottage owned by her mother in an unnamed village, an 'almost idyllic setting of softly undulating landscape, mysterious woods and ancient stone buildings . . . to detach herself from the harsh realities of her field notes and perhaps even find inspiration for a new and different study' (AFGL, 9). She never intends to stay permanently, planning to observe the natives, write a detached report on their behavior, and retreat, but she soon becomes less objectively involved in village affairs.

Although she prefers to compare herself to Thomas Hardy's first wife, 'a person with something unsatisfactory about her', Emma more resembles, of course, the strong-willed and independent Austen heroine for whom she is named; like her predecessor, this Emma also learns after several missteps to appreciate the appropriate man. Pym's choice of her name may have arisen from an unlikely source. Two years earlier she had written her publisher questioning whether the public would accept the characterisation in *Quartet in Autumn*; he responded, 'Once upon a time, there was an author called Austen who said of one of her heroines by the name of Emma that no one but herself would much like her. Look what happened to them both!' (MS Pym 165, fol. 115). The name immediately sets off literary associations that complement the interplay of past and present underlying this work.

Austen, Eliot, Trollope – the scent of the nineteenth century novel permeates the atmosphere of *A Few Green Leaves*, ironically undercut by the intrusions of contemporary life. The English village setting leads us to expect a complex interaction of society, with character and incident tightly controlled, with family histories juxtaposed against chronological changes, with social behavior regulated by Christian moral values, and with human life closely tied to the natural world. Pym borrows much of this tradition, although she tempers it with irony and a twentieth century twist. For this is a minimalist Middlemarch, complete with two doctors of different generations; it also nods to *Emma* and to *Mansfield Park*, as well as to Trollope's Barsetshire chronicles with their interest in middle-age, marriage, and clerical life. Emma's mother, Beatrix, is a specialist in Victorian literature, a study which Emma had 'tended to despise' but which she will come in the course of the novel to appreciate and perhaps even to imitate.

Much has changed in village life since *Emma,* however, and Pym makes the opening scene emblematic of this change – a pastoral edged with plastic. The manor house which once anchored the area has 'changed hands several times and . . . the present owner made little impact on village life' (AFGL, 3). Most of the younger inhabitants have moved into a new housing development outside the village proper, leaving at its heart an aging group of hangers-on to maintain such traditions as the annual wood-gathering walk through the manor woods. But the exercise of this right is hollow: few villagers depend on gathered 'faggots' to heat their homes; Emma resents the 'Wordsworthian exuberance' of daffodils in the woods; a flash of purple on the ground proves not to be the first spring violet, but a discarded candy wrapper; what natives do appear are dressed in jeans or polyester and insulated from each other and the natural world by portable radios. The primary characters themselves are introduced as they walk, symbolically, single file through the narrow paths, one of them beating back the encroaching weeds with a stout stick. Neither warmth, beauty, nor community is discovered. So non-judgmental is this presentation, however, that the comedy is not dampened, and the outing ends with the widowed rector's small spark of interest in his new parishioner.

Anthropology and fiction merge closely in this novel, as Emma examines her new world with a sociologist's eye. Pym transposes the style of her own diaries directly into the text when Emma lists the cast of village characters for a possible anthropological project, 'Observations on the Social Patterns of a West Oxfordshire Village'. When she abandons the role of observer for that of participant, these field notes will convert into fiction as easily for Emma as they have for Pym.

The action proceeds episodically as in *Some Tame Gazelle*, as if detailing and elaborating upon Emma's appointment calendar from Easter to the New Year. Characters are brought together for such social gatherings as bring-and-buy sales, hunger lunches, and lecture meetings of the local history society, but the urban world of the 1970s intrudes upon the traditional values of this village in ways never imagined by Belinda Bede. Modern social mores recognised elsewhere (i.e. casual infidelity, homosexuality) must be accommodated; traditions still operate but under compromise. The same bareness that she employed in *Quartet* further reduces the world of this novel. Tom cannot emulate the clerical diarists he admires and wonders what society is 'failing to record now that future historians will blame us for'; his entries lack substance, he knows, but he sees no suitable subjects for profundity since 'we were all flattened out into a kind of uniform dullness these days, something to do with the welfare state and the rise of the consumer society' (AFGL, 110). The practitioners of anthropology, sociology, and medicine are mostly young and foolish, and yet for advice and consolation troubled souls seek out the doctors' examining rooms, not the parish church. Only in the cemetery do the doctor and the rector meet as equals.

The refuge and accidental meeting place for them and for several others is the church burying ground, specifically the de Tankerville mausoleum, 'an awkward anachronism in such a small and humble parish'. As well as replacing the centrality of the village square and providing a tangible link to local history, the small stone death house surrounded by late-blooming summer dahlias is the chief among many images of human mortality the novel offers. It is too close to the church for the comfort of the maintenance man who has recently lost his faith, but all agree that its upkeep is necessary, ostensibly to preserve the hallowed past, but actually in the hope the grand mausoleum will overshadow the 'execrable taste' of the more recent graves with their 'elaborate curb-stones, green marble chips and florid gilt lettering' (AFGL, 104).

The sense of aloneness extends outward from the graveyard; most of the characters live alone, often by choice, and are generally orphaned, widowed, or bypassed. The novel's collection of empty, abandoned, or too large domiciles seems to dwarf the human life that should fill them. The young doctor pompously pronounces it therapeutic for the elderly 'to have a relaxed approach to the proximity of gravestones' (AFGL, 181) and there are numerous motifs of mortality, decay, and change. The vicar's passions are not directed toward the living: he prefers to learn more about ancient requirements for burying the dead in wool and to uncover in the nearby woods the site of a deserted medieval village.

The valedictory tone of this novel extends beyond its images of mortality, as Pym calls up a host of characters from earlier works for a final curtain call. The obituary notice for Fabian Driver of *Jane and Prudence* precedes the announcement of the death of Esther Clovis, the Pym-like overseer of the fictional anthropological society. At her memorial service gather a group of elderly characters from *Less Than Angels* whose own time cannot be long. The reader familiar with the author's work cannot miss the sense of closure.

Pym emphasises the swift, unpredictable endings humans face with two contrasting incidents. A foreboding atmosphere follows Miss Vereker, a venerated symbol of better days at the manor house, on an unannounced attempt to revisit her old village. Wandering, fatigued and in some pain, she lies down, the reader is prepared to believe, to die in the woods. But she recovers. On the other hand, another elderly inhabitant, Miss Lickerish, expires without warning, so quietly and quickly that her cat is the first to know she has gone, 'Miss Lickerish's lap having become strangely chilled' (AFGL, 227). Pym's narrative technique which first establishes then denies our expectations before springing a surprise emphasizes the arbitrary and inexplicable way death comes to human life.

In 1979 Pym's earlier malignancy reappeared in the form of an ovarian tumor. Her doctors tried briefly to contain the disease with chemotherapy but soon began to discuss her wishes for living out her remaining days. Anxious to lessen the burden of her illness on Hilary, she decided to enter a hospice near Oxford. She had finished the draft of *A Few Green Leaves* only two months before and, knowing she would not live long, asked Hazel Holt 'to see it through the press'.[33] Her New York publisher, Paul de Angelis of E. P. Dutton wrote her on 9 January 1980 – a letter she did not live to see.

> You have attempted something very different . . . to have written a sort of 'study' of village life that is a very vibrant novel – this is a great achievement. *A Few Green Leaves* is not only a work worthy of your name, but in many ways the culmination of your work. (MS Pym 165, fol. 164)

She died on January 11, 1980 and is buried beside the Church of the Holy Trinity, Finstock.

For all of its grey colorations *A Few Green Leaves* ends on the the same cautiously optimistic note Pym has always preferred. The elegiac mood gives way before Emma's growing awareness that both love and fiction can enrich her life. Critic Janice Rossen has called *A Few Green Leaves* Pym's 'apologia',[34] but perhaps it is more correctly the coda, the formal close to her career. Written with the knowledge that it would be her final work, it blurs the lines between her fiction and her life only gently, especially faithful in its geography, as a trip to Finstock can prove.

As compactly as Pym constructs Emma's village, including only the briefest excursions to the outside world, so Finstock is contained. Twenty minutes outside of Oxford the visitor leaves behind traffic lights, rotaries, and paved highways, skirts Blenheim Palace, and enters the winding back roads and valleys leading toward a cluster of villages that edge the Wychwood Forest -- Fawler, Ramsden, and Finstock. Pym described these Cotswolds hamlets hidden 'off the main tourist track' in an essay entitled 'A Year in West Oxfordshire', written in the months before her death:

Few of these villages would win a prize for tidiness and elegance, and some of them even now have an air of romantic decay, dating from the depressed Thirties (when my own village, Finstock, was described by one visitor as 'a tattered hamlet', and by another as being imbued with an evil emanation from the forest). Today there is an interesting mixture of carefully restored cottages and bright new bungalows with broken dry-stone wall, corrugated iron, and nettles, and even the occasional deserted or ruined homestead.[35]

Finstock's proximity to Oxford and London has resulted in escalating real estate values since Pym's death, but little else has changed. Most of the village can be viewed from Barn Cottage, which, like Beatrix Howick's, fronts closely on the sparsely traveled main road. Should a passerby adopt Tom Dagnall's habit of peering in windows he would see there, not Emma carrying a ham mousse, but similar domestic details, the morning dishes drying on a rack or a vase of forsythia forced into bloom.

As in the novel, the past is still a vital participant in village life. The owners of a nearby manor house no longer influence village activity, but Pym's neighbors still exercise their right to an annual walk through its woods. Hilary participates in the meetings of the local historical society and avidly traces the Pym family genealogy.

The Anglican church in Finstock is neither large nor architecturally pure, having been 'improved' as in Pym's novel with regrettable 'Victorian additions to what had originally been a simple building' (AFGL, 62). On Larkin's first visit to Barn Cottage he and Pym walked to view the plaque commemorating the 1927 baptism of T. S. Eliot in this rural church; Pym notes in her diary for this day, 'So two great poets and one minor novelist came for a brief moment (as it were) together' (MS Pym 76, fol. 2). Memorial contributions solicited for Pym's own plaque exceeded organiser's expectations, providing an additional oak message board and a replacement for the lectern where Pym often read the day's lesson, sometimes with a writer's ear for economy:

Christmas Eve 1978: I read the epistle – drastically shortening and editing it! St. Paul repeats himself. (MS Pym 80, fol. 19)

The mausoleum in the churchyard reads Du Clos, not de Tankerville, but it dominates the small space as did its fictional counterpart. Recently the remaining family, unhappy about the costs and duties of maintaining the memorial, has petitioned the parish to allow its dismantling – 'What would Barbara have made of that?' smiles Hilary. Many of the graves on the outside of the iron-fenced mausoleum are blanketed with colored marble chips contained by concrete curbs and adorned with vases of artificial flowers, 'surely a disgrace in a rural area' (AFGL, 104) clucks one fictional parishioner and a surviving sister agrees. The stone marker with Pym's name, dates, and the single word 'Writer' sits squarely on the earth, overgrown with long grasses and wildflowers. Hilary tells of complaints from some visitors that the area is unkempt, but both Pyms agreed that graves 'should be allowed to return to the natural state as quickly as possible',[36] and the site is as fittingly unpretentious as her prose.

6
Conclusion

The title image of Pym's final novel, recalling the practical woman's trick of extending the life of a floral arrangement by adding a few fresh green leaves, operates metaphorically not only in that work but throughout Pym's life and canon. The idea had appeared briefly once before in *No Fond Return of Love*: Dulcie Mainwaring hesitates while tossing some half-dead blossoms because 'some of the flowers might still pass, arranged with fresh leaves or massed together in a bowl' (NFRL, 87). Older, familiar material reconstructed and revitalised with slight organic additions for the sake of economy, beauty, pleasure, and simplicity – the description matches Pym's technique in the comic novel of manners.

It is nearly impossible to divorce Pym's own life from any discussion of her work, so imprinted upon her fiction are the details of her experiences. To define her as a novelist of manners requires examining her familiar milieux and their faithful reproduction in her fiction. Her 'observational method' – the careful journal keeping, notebook jottings and diary entries of a lifetime – results in a fictional verisimilitude found usually in historical novels. Indeed, each Pym work is a kind of small-scale historical novel, portraying her vision of the very recent past.

Her work has admitted limitations: there are no successful intimate relationships or compelling sexual attractions between men and women, indeed no strong or sensitive men; her women are seldom wives and almost never mothers, denying the work a marital or maternal perspective; the comforts of satisfying work or of religious faith are negligible; and there is little evidence of contemporary or political issues. This narrow scope could seem to constrict her social novels unduly, but within these limits Pym plays out the familiar conventions of the novel of manners, and adds to the genre her feminine perspective.

Her contribution to the tradition of the genre lies in her unarticulated feminism, delivered from the perspective of a solitary female who measures the moral basis of her world with clear-eyed generosity. Although Hazel Holt insists she has 'fought to keep Barbara out of the hands of the feminists',[1] it is not a battle that requires fighting. In Pym's world a woman need be neither an aggressor nor a victim, since her superiority to the anemic males surrounding her is so clearly understood. There is no anger or stridency in this assumption, and it would be a mistake to label these 'women's novels', either for their point of view or for their abundance of domestic detail. Behind the surface 'cosiness' lies a non-gender-specific awareness of isolation and loneliness, and as Philip Larkin noted of her books, 'no man can read them and be quite the same again'.[2]

The canon consciously continues a literary tradition. She learned from Jane Austen the melding of subject and style, and from Henry James the delineation of complex psychological perceptions through physical detail. Mrs Gaskell, Anthony Trollope, and Charlotte Yonge contributed to her view of life in English villages and vicarages, Dickens to her fondness for eccentrics. Allusions to and quotations from a broad spectrum of British literature fill her novels.

To place her among her English and American contemporaries requires a ranking procedure as subjective as it is futile, but she has admirers among both groups. Anne Tyler shares her penchant for marginal lives and eccentrics, David Lodge her satiric wink at academia and the modern church, and Anita Brookner (although she would chafe at the comparison) her evocation of the solitary life. Her minimalist style aligns her with many current practitioners of the contemporary novel, and the biographical basis of her work has its counterpart in the fictional journalism of the 1980s.

Will the scholarly attention and public acclaim afforded Pym's work over the last decade evaporate? Certainly the weaker novels, the rejected *An Unsuitable Attachment* and those published posthumously without benefit of her final shaping, will find a smaller audience. Several of the novels are currently out of print. On the other hand, two scholarly conferences on her work have been held, the *Barbara Pym Newsletter*[3] is published semi-annually, and critical texts continue to appear. Hazel Holt has recently completed an authorized biography, *A Lot To Ask*, but she plans no further publications from the manuscript collection, so the canon is probably complete.

Pym's choice of a traditional style and form, divorcing her as it did from modern and experimental literary movements, may insulate her work from the whirlpool of contemporary critical theory and insure her alignment with mainstream British fiction. Philip Larkin finds in this traditional quality the touchstone of her talent: 'In all her writing I find a continual perceptive attention to detail which is a joy and a steady background of rueful yet courageous acceptance of things which I think more relevant to life, as most of us have to live it, than spies coming in from the cold.'[4] Barbara Pym refreshed the novel of manners with the addition of a few green leaves gathered from the details of her own life and observations, and her best will continue to be studied and taught by readers with an interest in the mid-twentieth century varieties of the genre.

Notes

CHAPTER 1 MANNERS AND COMEDY

1. Here and throughout, parenthetical notation cites manuscript and folio number from the papers of Barbara Pym collected in the Department of Western Manuscripts, Bodleian Library, Oxford.
2. J. I. M. Stewart, *The Naylors* (London: Victor Gollancz, Ltd, 1985), p. 87.
3. Hazel Holt and Hilary Pym (eds), *A Very Private Eye: An Autobiography in Diaries and Letters* (London: Macmillan, 1984) p. xiii.
4. Barbara Pym, 'A Year in West Oxfordshire', in *Places, an Anthology of Britain*, Ronald Blythe (ed.), (Oxford: Oxford University Press, 1981), p. 120.
5. Personal letter from P. T. W. Baxter, former Director of the International African Insititute, 6 August 1983.
6. Tony Kirk-Greene, 'Barbara Pym 1913–1980', *Africa*, 2 June 1980, pp. 94–5.
7. Caroline Moorehead, 'How Barbara Pym was Rediscovered after 16 Years Out in the Cold', *Times Literary Supplement*, 14 September 1977, p. 11.
8. 'Reputations Revisited', *The Times Literary Supplement*, 21 January 1977, p. 68.
9. E. M. Forster, *Aspects of the Novel* (New York: Harcourt, Brace and World, 1927) p. 6.
10. Lionel Trilling, 'Manners, Morals, and the Novel', *The Liberal Imagination* (New York: Viking, 1951) p. 205.
11. James W. Tuttleton, *The Novel of Manners in America* (Chapel Hill: University of North Carolina Press, 1972) p. 10.
12. Margaret Drabble (ed.), *The Oxford Companion to English Literature*, 5th edn (Oxford: Oxford University Press, 1987).
13. Frederick C. Crews, *The Tragedy of Manners: Moral Drama in the Later Novels of Henry James* (New Haven: Yale University Press, 1957).
14. Gerald Mast, *The Comic Mind: Comedy and the Movies* (Chicago: University of Chicago Press, 1973) p. ix.
15. Richard Poirier, *The Comic Sense of Henry James* (New York: Oxford Universtiy Press, 1960) p. 63.
16. Trilling, p. 222.
17. Trilling, p. 206.
18. Forster, pp. 68–9.
19. Henri Bergson and George Meredith, *Comedy: Meredith's 'An Essay on Comedy and Henri Bergson's "Laughter"'*, Wylie Sypher (ed.) (Garden City: Doubleday, 1956) p. 128.

20. Isa Kapp, 'One Woman's Virtue', *Washington Post*, 14 January 1984, D, 4. p. 3.

CHAPTER 2   THE EARLY WORK – POEMS, STORIES, AND RADIO SCRIPTS

1. Shirley Hazzard, 'Excellent Woman', in Dale Salwak (ed.), *The Life and Work of Barbara Pym* (London: Macmillan, 1987) p. 3.
2. Hazel Holt, personal interview, Tivington Knowle, Somerset, April 1987.
3. David Lodge, *Small World* (New York: Macmillan, 1984) p. 64.
4. Robert Liddell, 'Two Friends: Barbara Pym and Ivy Compton-Burnett', *London Magazine* (August–September 1984) p. 62–3.
5. Somerset interview.
6. Liddell, 'Two Friends', pp. 62–3.
7. Personal letter from Robert S. Smith, 20 August 1983.
8. Anthony Kaufman, 'The Short Fiction of Barbara Pym', *Twentieth Century Literature* (Spring 1986) p. 50–7.
9. Personal letter from Colin Harris, Principal Library Assistant, Bodleian Library, 14 March 1985.
10. Kathleen Browder Heberlein, *Communities of Imaginative Participation: The Novels of Barbara Pym* (Unpublished doctoral dissertation: University of Wisconsin, 1984) p. 20.
11. Kaufman, p. 67.
12. Kaufman, p. 68.

CHAPTER 3   THE EARLY NOVELS

1. Philip Larkin, 'The World of Barbara Pym', *Times Literary Supplement* (11 March 1977) p. 260.
2. Colin Harris, Assistant Librarian, Department of Western Manuscripts, Bodleian Library, Oxford. Personal letter, 14 March 1985.
3. Tony Kirk-Greene, 'Barbara Pym 1913–1980', *Africa* 2 (June 1980) p. 94.
4. Hilary Pym, personal interview, Barn Cottage, Finstock, April 1987.
5. Hazel Holt, personal interview, Tivington Knowle, Somerset, April 1987.
6. Geoffrey Holt, Somerset interview, April 1987.
7. Anita Brookner, 'The Bitter Fruits of Rejection', *The Spectator*, 19 (July 1986) p. 30.
8. Anne Tyler, 'From England to Brooklyn to West Virginia', *New York Times Book Review*, 13 February 1983, p. 1.
9. Lotus Snow, personal letter, April 23, 1988.
10. Robert Liddell, 'Two Friends: Barbara Pym and Ivy Compton-Burnett', *London Magazine* (August–September 1984) p. 61.

11.   'Women of Character', *The Times Literary Supplement*, 7 July 1950, p. 417.
12.   In *Jane and Prudence*, chain-smoking novelist Barbara Bird laughs about a reviewer who complained that her work held 'much incident and little wit' (JP, 117).
13.   Liddell, p. 61.
14.   Robert Emmet Long, *Barbara Pym* (New York: Ungar Publishing, 1986), p. 25.
15.   Elizabeth Gaskell, *Cranford*, Elizabeth Porges Watson (ed.), (London: Oxford University Press, 1972) p. 1.
16.   Jane Nardin, *Barbara Pym* (Boston: Twayne Publishers, 1985) pp. 63–4.
17.   Nardin, p. 67.
18.   Nardin, p. 69.
19.   E. M. Forster, *Aspects of the Novel* (New York: Harcourt, Brace and World, 1927) p. 53.
20.   Alison Lurie, *The Language of Clothes* (New York: Random House, 1981), p. 3.
21.   Lotus Snow, *One Little Room An Everywhere: Barbara Pym's Novels* (Orono, Me.: Puckerbrush Press, 1987) pp. 31–54.
22.   Victoria Glendinning, 'Spontaneous Obsession, Imposed Restraint', *New York Times Book Review*, 8 July 1984, p. 3.
23.   Michele Slung, 'Barbara Pym: the Quiet Pleasure of Her Company,' *Washington Post, Book World*, 17 January 1988, p. 3.
24.   A. N. Wilson, 'Daffodil Yellow and Coral Pink', *The Literary Review*, June 1985, p. 43–4.
25.   Rossen, *The World of Barbara Pym* (New York: St. Martin's Press) p. 181.
26.   Jocelyn McClurg, 'Posthumous Pym: Less Than Others', *The Hartford Courant*, 22 September 1985, G3.
27.   Rossen, p. 32.
28.   Miranda Seymour, 'Spinsters in Their Prime', *Times Literary Supplement*, 28 June 1985, p. 720.

CHAPTER 4   SOMETHING 'VERY BARBARA PYM'

1.   Elizabeth Wilson, *Only Halfway to Paradise: Women in Postwar Britain 1945–1968* (Tavistock Publications: London, 1980) p. 149.
2.   Untitled anonymous review of *Excellent Women, Kirkus Reviews*, 1 August 1978, p. 837.
3.   'Divided Loyalties', Anonymous review of *Excellent Women, Times Literary Supplement*, 28 March 1952, p. 217.
4.   Polly Brodie, untitled review, *Library Journal*, 15 October 1978, p. 2135–6.
5.   Anon., *Kirkus Review* 46, 1 August 1978, p. 837.
6.   Anne Duchêne, 'Brave are the Lonely', *Times Literary Supplement*, 30 September 1977, p. 1096.
7.   Karl Miller, 'Ladies in Distress', *The New York Review of Books*, 9 November 1978, pp. 24–5.

8. John Updike, 'Books: Lem and Pym', *New Yorker*, 55, 26 February 1979, p. 121

9. Robert J. Graham, 'Cumbered with Much Serving: Barbara Pym's "Excellent Women"', *Mosaic* 17 (Spring 1984) p. 145.

10. Updike, 'Books: Lem and Pym', pp. 117–18.

11. John Updike, *Hugging the Shore* (New York: Alfred A. Knopf, 1983), p. 415.

12. Diana Benet, 'The Language of Christianity in Pym's Novels', *Thought* 59, no. 235, December 1984, 505.

13. Benet, p. 507.

14. Robert Smith, 'How Pleasant to Know Miss Pym', *Ariel* 2, no. 4, October 1971, p. 66.

15. Robert Liddell, 'Two Friends: Barbara Pym and Ivy Compton-Burnett', *London Magazine*, August–September, 1984, p. 61.

16. 'Family Failings', *The Times Literary Supplement*, 2 October 1953, p. 625.

17. Joyce Carol Oates, 'Barbara Pym's Novelistic Genius', in *The Life and Work of Barbara Pym*, Dale Salwak (ed.), (London: Macmillian, 1987) p. 43.

18. Anatole Broyard, 'Overflowing Her Situation', *New York Times Book Review*, 15 August, 1982, p. 27.

19. Michael Gorra, 'Restraint is the Point', *New York Times Book Review*, 31 July 1983, p. 18.

20. R. Smith, p. 66.

21. Daniel Snowman, *Britain and America: An Interpretaion of Their Culture 1945–1975* (New York: New York University Press, 1977) p. 84.

22. Rosemary Dinnage, 'Comic, Sad, Indefinite', *New York Review of Books*, 16 August 1984, p. 16.

23. Richard Poirier, *The Comic Sense of Henry James* (New York: Oxford University Press, 1960) p. 23.

24. Benet, p. 6.

25. Barbara Pym, *A Glass of Blessings* (New York: Perennial Library edition, Harper & Row, 1981), back cover.

26. Henry James, as quoted in F. O. Matthiessen, *HJ: the Major Phase* (New York: Oxford University Press, 1944) p. 50.

27. Edmund Fuller, 'Finding a Lifetime Friend in a Writer's Work', *Wall Street Journal*, 20 October 1980, p. 24.

28. Kate Browder Heberlein, *Communities of Imaginative Participation: The Novels of Barbara Pym* (Unpublished doctoral dissertation: University of Wisconsin, 1984) p. 144.

29. Asa Briggs, *A Social History of England* (New York: The Viking Press, 1983) p. 290.

30. Hazel Holt, 'The Novelist in the Field: 1946–1974', in *The Life and Work of Barbara Pym*, Dale Salwak (ed.), (London: Macmillian, 1987) pp. 22–33.

31. Holt, in Salwak, p. 24.

32. Holt, in Salwak, p. 24.

33. Holt, in Salwak, p. 26.

34. Holt, in Salwak, p. 22.

35. Holt, in Salwak, p. 26.
36. Holt, in Salwak, p. 27.
37. Holt, in Salwak, p. 26.
38. Holt, in Salwak, p. 31.
39. Holt, Somerset interview.
40. Holt, in Salwak, p. 23.
41. Holt, in Salwak, p. 28.
42. Tony Kirk-Greene, 'Barbara Pym 1913–1980', *Africa* 2, (1980) p. 94.
43. Kirk-Greene, p. 94.
44. Barbara Pym, 'In Defence of the Novel: Why You Shouldn't Have To Wait Until the Afternoon', *The Times* (London), 22 February 1978, p. 18.
45. Riley Hughes, 'Books', *Catholic World* 185, September 1957, p. 473.
46. Holt, in Salwak, p. 27.
47. Alfred Harris, University of Rochester, Rochester, New York, telephone interview, September, 1988.
48. Rubin Rabinovitz, *The Reaction Against Experiment in the English Novel 1950–1960* (New York: Columbia University Press, 1967) pp. 28–9.
49. Jane Nardin, *Barbara Pym* (Boston: Twayne Publishers, 1985), preface.
50. Lotus Snow, personal interview, Canandaigua, New York, 1988.
51. Janice Rossen, *The World of Barbara Pym*, (New York: St. Martin's Press, 1987) p. 37.
52. Anne Tyler, 'From England to Brooklyn to West Virginia', *New York Times Book Review*, 13 February 1983, p. 1.
53. Pico Iyer, 'Tricks of Self-Consciousness', *Partisan Review* 52, no. 3, 1985, p. 289.
54. Anatole Broyard, 'A Funnier Jane Austen', *New York Times*, 1 January 1983, p. 10.

CHAPTER 5   REJECTION, RESURRECTION, VALEDICTION

1. Robert E. Long, *Barbara Pym* (New York: Ungar Publishing, 1986) p. 148.
2. Marilyn Butler, 'Keeping Up With Jane Austen', *London Review of Books*, 6 May 1982, p. 16.
3. Butler, p. 16.
4. Hazel Holt, Somerset interview, April 1988.
5. Philip Larkin, Foreword to *An Unsuitable Attachment* (London: Macmillan, 1982) p. 5.
6. Larkin, p. 5.
7. Larkin, p. 9.
8. Edmund Fuller, 'Two Remaining Works of a Novelist of the Ordinary', *Wall Street Journal*, 18 July 1983, p. 18.
9. Edith Milton, 'Worlds in Miniature', *The New York Times Book Review*, 20 June 1982, p. 11.
10. James W. Tuttleton, *The Novel of Manners in America* (Chapel Hill: University of North Carolina Press, 1972) p. 188.

11.   Gilbert Phelps, 'Fellow Writers in a Cotswold Village', in *The Life and Work of Barbara Pym*, Dale Salwak (ed.), (London: Macmillan, 1987) p. 35.

12.   Charles Monteith, 'Publishing Larkin', *Times Literary Supplement*, 21 May 1982, p. 552.

13.   Hazel Holt, 'Philip Larkin and Barbara Pym: Two Quiet People', in *Philip Larkin: The Man and His Work*, Dale Salwak (ed.), (London: Macmillan; Iowa City: University of Iowa Press, 1988) p. 59.

14.   Holt, 'Larkin and Pym', pp. 63–4.

15.   Holt, 'Larkin and Pym', p. 63.

16.   Holt, 'Larkin and Pym', p. 66.

17.   Holt, 'Larkin and Pym', p. 66.

18.   Philip Larkin, 'Toad Work', in *The Less Deceived* (East Yorkshire: The Marvell Press, 1955) p. 18 .

19.   Joseph Epstein, 'Miss Pym and Mr. Larkin', *Commentary*, 82, no. 1, July 1986, p. 45.

20.   Gail Pool, 'Excellent Women', *The Nation*, vol. 239, no. 3, 4 August 1984, pp. 88–9.

21.   Larkin, Foreword to *An Unsuitable Attachment*, p. 6.

22.   Robert Liddell, 'A Success Story', in *The Life and Work of Barbara Pym*, Dale Salwak (ed.), (London: Macmillian, 1987) p. 182.

23.   Robert Liddell, 'Two Friends: Barbara Pym and Ivy Compton-Burnett', *London Magazine* 24, August–September, 1984, p. 62.

24.   Liddell, 'A Success Story', p. 182.

25.   Phelps, p. 37.

26.   Barbara Pym, 'Across A Crowded Room', *New Yorker*, 55, 16 July 1979.

27.   Adamson, Lesley. 'Rediscovered after Fourteen Years in the Wilderness'. *Guardian*, 14 September 1977, p. 11.

28.   Wendy Smith, 'Brief Review', *The New Republic*, 16 July 1984, p. 41.

29.   Hazel Holt, 'The Novelist in the Field: 1946–74', in *The Life and Work of Barbara Pym*, Dale Salwak (ed.), (London: Macmillan, 1987) p. 29.

30.   Holt, 'Novelist in the Field', p. 30.

31.   BBC program 'Tea with Miss Pym', which includes David Cecil, was produced by Will Wyatt for *The Book Program* and later included in the videotape 'Barbara Pym: Out of the Wilderness,' produced by Greybirch Productions, Belmont, MA. Radio interviews include 'Finding a Voice' (now included in *Civil To Strangers*) and 'Desert Island Disks' (MS Pym 148 fols 25–6).

32.   Tullia Blundo, 'La narrativa di Barbara Pym,' typescript thesis for the University of Pisa (MS Pym 174).

33.   Holt, Somerset interview, April 1987.

34.   Janice Rossen, *The World of Barbara Pym* (New York: St. Martin's Press, 1987) p. 154.

35.   Barbara Pym, 'A Year in West Oxfordshire', in *Places, an Anthology of Britain*, Ronal Blythe (ed.), (Oxford: Oxford University Press, 1981) p. 119.

36.   Hilary Pym, Finstock interview, April 1987.

CHAPTER 6   CONCLUSION

1. Hazel Holt, personal interview, Tivington Knowle, Somerset, April, 1987.
2. Philip Larkin, 'The World of Barbara Pym', *Times Literary Supplement*, 11 March 1977, p. 260.
3. *Barbara Pym Newsletter*, Mary Anne Schofield, ed. (St. Bonaventure University).
4. Charles Monteith, 'Publishing Larkin', *Times Literary Supplement*, 21 May 1982, p. 552.

Bibliography

PRIMARY SOURCES

I Books

Pym, Barbara. *Some Tame Gazelle*. London: Cape, 1950; Macmillan, 1978; New York: Dutton, 1983.
——, *Excellent Women*. London: Cape, 1952; Macmillan, 1978; New York: Dutton, 1978.
——, *Jane and Prudence*. London: Cape, 1953; Macmillan, 1978; New York: Dutton, 1981.
——, *Less Than Angels*. London: Cape, 1955; Macmillan, 1978; New York: Dutton, 1980.
——, *A Glass of Blessings*. London: Cape, 1958; Macmillan, 1977; New York: Dutton, 1980.
——, *No Fond Return of Love*. London: Cape, 1961; Macmillan, 1979; New York: Dutton, 1982.
——, *Quartet in Autumn*. London: Macmillan, 1977; New York: Dutton, 1978.
——, *The Sweet Dove Died*. London: Macmillan, 1978; New York: Dutton, 1979.
——, *A Few Green Leaves*. London: Macmillan, 1980; New York: Dutton, 1980.
——, *An Unsuitable Attachment*. London: Macmillan, 1982; New York: Dutton, 1982.
——, *A Very Private Eye: An Autobiography in Diaries and Letters*. Hazel Holt and Hilary Pym (eds). London: Macmillan, 1984; New York: Dutton, 1984.
——, *Crampton Hodnet*. London: Macmillan, 1985; New York: Dutton, 1985.
——, *An Academic Question*. London: Macmillan, 1986; New York: Dutton, 1986.
——, *Civil to Strangers and Other Writings*. London: Macmillan, 1987; New York: Dutton, 1987.

II Articles and Stories

The papers of Barbara Pym. Department of Western Manuscripts, Bodleian Library, Oxford, England. Cited in the text by manuscript and folio number.
Pym, Barbara. 'Across A Crowded Room.' *New Yorker*, 55, 16 July 1979,

pp. 34–6.

——, 'In Defence of the Novel: Why You Shouldn't Have To Wait Until the Afternoon.' *The Times* (London), 22 February 1978, 18.

——, 'The State of Fiction: A Symposium.' *The New Review*, vol. 5, no. 1, Summer 1978, 58–9.

——, 'A Year in West Oxfordshire.' *Places: an Anthology of Britain*, Ronald Blythe (ed.). Oxford: Oxford University Press, 1981, 119–25.

SELECTED SECONDARY SOURCES

I   Books

Ackley, Katherine Anne. *The Novels of Barbara Pym*. New York and London: Garland Publishing, Inc., 1989.

Benet, Diana. *Something to Love: Barbara Pym's Novels*. Columbia, Mo: University of Missouri Press, 1986.

Cotsell, Michael. *Modern Novelists: Barbara Pym*. New York: St. Martin's Press, 1989.

Crosland, Margaret. *Beyond the Lighthouse: English Women Novelists in the Twentieth Century*. New York, Taplinger Publishing Co., 1981.

Heberlein, Kathleen Browder. *Communities of Imaginative Participation: The Novels of Barbara Pym*. Unpublished doctoral dissertation: University of Wisconsin, 1984.

Holt, Hazel. *A Lot to Ask: A Life of Barbara Pym*. London: Macmillan Ltd, 1990.

Liddell, Robert. *A Mind at Ease: Barbara Pym and her Novels*. London: Peter Owen Publishers, 1989.

Long, Robert Emmet. *Barbara Pym*. New York: Ungar Publishing, 1986.

Nardin, Jane. *Barbara Pym*. Boston: Twayne Publishers, 1985.

Pym, Hilary and Honor Wyatt. *The Barbara Pym Cookbook*. New York: E.P. Dutton, 1988.

Rossen, Janice, ed. *Independent Women: The Function of Gender in the Novels of Barbara Pym*. Sussex: The Harvester Press and New York: St. Martin's Press, 1988.

——, *The World of Barbara Pym*. New York: St. Martin's Press, 1987.

Salwak, Dale, ed. *The Life and Work of Barbara Pym*. London: Macmillan Ltd, 1987 and Iowa City: University of Iowa Press, 1987.

Snow, Lotus. *One Little Room An Everywhere: Barbara Pym's Novels*. Orono, Me: Puckerbrush Press, 1987.

II   Articles

Ableman, Paul. 'Genteelism.' *Spectator*, vol. 241, 8 July 1978, 26.

Ackroyd, Peter. 'Minor Passion at a Good Address'. *Sunday Times* (London), 16 July 1978, 41.

——, 'Survival of the Faithful.' *Sunday Times* (London), 21 February 1982, 43.

Adamson, Lesley. 'Rediscovered after Fourteen Years in the Wilderness.' *Guardian*, 14 September 1977, 11.

Auchincloss, Eve. 'Surprises of Comedy and Sadness.' *New York Times Book Review*, 1 February 1981, 9.

Bailey, Paul. 'The Art of the Ordinary.' *The Observer*, 27 July 1980, 29.

——, 'A Novelist Rediscovered.' *The Observer*, 25 September 1977, 25.

——, 'Period Hoot.' *The Observer*, 30 June 1985, 23.

Barr, Charles. 'The "Miracle" of Rediscovery.' *The Listener*, 31 July 1986, 24.

Bayley, John. 'Life-Enhancing World Views.' *Times Literary Supplement*, 16 September 1983, 978.

Berndt, Judy. 'Barbara Pym: A Supplementary List of Secondary Sources', *Bulletin of Bibliography*, 43, no. 2, June 1986, 76–80.

Binding, Paul. 'Barbara Pym.' *Dictionary of Literary Biography*. Detroit: Gale Research Co, 1983, 14, pt. 2, 604–7.

Blum, J. M. and L. R. Leans. 'Current Literature 1978', *English Studies*, 60, 5 October 1979, 628.

Boeth, Richard. 'Brief Lives.' *Newsweek*, 92, no. 17, 23 October 1978, 121.

Brookner, Anita. 'The Bitter Fruits of Rejection.' *The Spectator*, 19 July 1986, 30–1.

Brothers, Barbara. 'Women Victimised by Fiction: Living and Loving in the Novels of Barbara Pym.' *Twentieth Century Women Novelists*, Thomas F. Staley, ed. Totawa, NJ: Barnes & Noble Books, 1982, 61–80.

Broyard, Anatole. 'Overflowing Her Situation.' *New York Times Book Review*, 15 August, 1982, 27.

——, 'A Funnier Jane Austen.' *New York Times*, 1 January 1983, 10.

Burkhart, Charles. 'Barbara Pym and the Africans.' *Twentieth Century Literature*, 29, no. 1, Spring, 1983, 45–53.

Butler, Marilyn. 'Keeping Up With Jane Austen.' *London Review of Books*, 6 May, 1982, 16–17.

Calisher, Hortense. 'Enclosures: Barbara Pym.' *The New Criterion*, September, 1982, 53–56.

Campbell, James. 'Kitchen Window.' *New Statesman*, 103, no. 2657, 19 February 1982, 25.

Cantwell, Mary. 'Books of the Times.' *The New York Times*, 10 May 1982, 21.

Catalog of the Papers of Barbara Pym. TS. Department of Western Manuscripts, Bodleian Library, Oxford.

Clapp, Susannah. 'Genteel Reminderrs.' *Times Literary Supplement*, 7 July 1978, 757.

Clemons, Walter. 'A Quiet Life Full of Surprises.' *Newsweek*, 23 July 1984, 64.

——, 'The Pleasures of Miss Pym.' *Newsweek*, 16 April, 1979, 91–2.

Colegate, Isabel and Michael Dirda. 'Tea and Sympathy: Philip Larkin and Barbara Pym.' Book World, *The Washington Post*, 1 July, 1984, 1, 5.

Cooley, Mason. 'The Sexual Politics of Narcissism.' *Twentieth Century Literature*, 32, no. 1, Spring, 1986, 40–49.

Dahlin, Robert. 'How Could I Have Waited So Long, Miss Pym?' *The Christian Science Monitor*, 7 December 1984, B2.

Digillio, Alice.'Teatime at Oxford.' *Book World, The Washington Post*, June 9, 1985, 9.

Dinnage, Rosemary. 'Comic, Sad, Indefinite.' *New York Review of Books*, August 16, 1984, 15–16.

——, 'Spontaneous Obsessions, Imposed Restraint.' *New York Times Book Review*, July 8, 1984, 3.

Donahue, Deirdre. 'The Lost Novel of a Latter-Day Jane Austen.' *Washington Post, Book World*, 20 June 1982, 6.

Donavin, Denise P. Untitled review of *Jane and Prudence. Booklist*, 78, no. 3, 1 October 1981, 179.

Dorris, Michael. 'In Short: Fiction.' *New York Times*, 1 September 1985, sec. 7, 14.

Duchêne, Anne. 'Brave are the Lonely.' *Times Literary Supplement*, 30 September 1977, 1096.

——, 'Handing on Loneliness.' *Times Literary Supplement*, 26 February 1982, 214.

Duffy, Martha. 'In Praise of Excellent Women.' *Time*, 26 September 1983, 70.

——, 'Blue Velvet.' *Time*, 24 June 1985, 81.

Epstein, Joseph. 'Sex and the Single Novel.' *The Hudson Review*, 36, Spring 1983, 185–6.

——, 'Miss Pym and Mr. Larkin.' *Commentary*, July 1986, 82(1), 38–46.

Ezell, Margaret, J. M. 'What Shall We do with our Old Maids?: Barbara Pym and the "Woman's Question".' *International Journal of Women's Studies*, 7, November/December, 1984, 450–65.

Feinstein, Elaine. Untitled review of *A Few Green Leaves. The Times* (London) 17 July 1980, Sect. D, 11.

Fitzgerald, Penelope. 'A Secret Richness.' *London Review of Books*, 20 November–4 December 1980, 19.

Fuller, Edmund. 'Two Remaining Works of a Novelist of the Ordinary.' *Wall Street Journal*, 18 July 1983, p. 18.

——, 'Finding a Lifetime Friend in a Writer's Work.' *Wall Street Journal*, 103, 20 October 1980, 24.

——, 'An Anthropologist of the English Middle Class.' *Wall Street Journal*, 25 May 1982, 30.

——, 'Stylish High Comedy and Astute Perception.' *Wall Street Journal*, 197, 2 March 1981, 16.

——, 'Tale No. 12: Essentially Pym.' *Wall Street Journal*, 9 September 1986, 26.

Glendinning, Victoria. 'The Best High Comedy.' *New York Times Book Review*, 24 December 1978, 8.

——, 'Spontaneous Obsession, Imposed Restraint.' *New York Times Book Review*, 8 July 1984, 3.

Goldstein, William. 'A Novel, a Biography, a Play: A Peek Inside the Pym Estate.' *Publisher's Weekly*, 4 October 1985, 43.

Gorra, Michael. 'Restraint is the Point.' *New York Times Book Review*, 31 July 1983, 12, 18.

Graham, Robert J. 'Cumbered with Much Serving: Barbara Pym's "Excellent Women".' *Mosiac*, 17, Spring 1984, 141–60.

Hills, C. A. R. 'The Bubble, Reputation.' *Encounter*, May 1987, 33–38.

Holt, Hazel. 'Philip Larkin and Barbara Pym: Two Quiet People.' *Philip Larkin: The Man and His Work*, ed. Dale Salwak, (London: Macmillian; Iowa City: University of Iowa Press, 1988), 59–68.

Howard, Philip. Untitled review of *The Sweet Dove Died*. *The Times* (London), 6 July 1978, 14.

Hughes, Riley. 'Books.' *Catholic World*, 185, September 1957, 473.

Iyer, Pico. 'Tricks of Self-Consciousness.' *Partisan Review*, Vol. LII, No. 3, 1985, 286–91.

Kakutani, Michiko. 'Books of the Times: Some Tame Gazelle', *The New York Times*, 5 August 1983, C 22.

Kapp, Isa. 'Out of the Swim with Barbara Pym.' *The American Scholar*, 52, no. 2, Spring 1983, 237–42.

——, 'One Woman's Virtue.' *Washington Post*, January 14, 1984, D 4.

Kaufman, Anthony. 'The Short Fiction of Barbara Pym.' *Twentieth Century Literature*, 32, no. 1, Spring 1986, 50–7.

Keener, Frederick M. 'Barbara Pym Herself and Jane Austen.' *Twentieth Century Literature*, 31, 1985, 89–110.

Kemp, Peter. 'Grave Comedy.' *The Listener*. vol. 104, no. 2670, 17 July 1980, 89.

——, 'One of the Unwanted Lovers of This World.' *The Listener*, vol. 112, no. 2869, 2 August 1984, 23–4.

——, 'Pym's No. 7.' *The Listener*, 18 February 1982, 24.

King, Francis. 'Barbara Pym's Sunlit Garden.' *Books and Bookmen*, vol. 23, July 1978, 8–9.

——, 'Fairly Excellent Woman.' *Spectator*, vol. 245, no. 7932, 19 July 1980, 21.

Kirk-Greene, Tony. 'Barbara Pym 1913–1980.' *Africa*, vol. 2, June 1980, 94–5.

Kubal, David. Untitled review of *Less Than Angels* in *The Hudson Review*, 34, no. 3, Autumn, 1981, 462–63.

Larkin, Philip. Foreword to *An Unsuitable Attachment*. London: Macmillian, 1982, 5–10.

——, 'The World of Barbara Pym,' *Times Literary Supplement*, 11 March 1977, 260.

Larson, Edith S. 'The Celebration of the Ordinary in Barbara Pym's Novels,' *San Jose Studies*, 9, no. 2, 1983, 17–23.

Lenhart, Maria. 'Quiet Novels Earn Belated Applause.' *The Christian Science Monitor*, vol. 70, 8 November 1978, 18.

Levin, Bernard. 'Middle Marches . . .' *Sunday Times* (London), 27 July 1980, 40.

Liddell, Robert. 'Two Friends: Barbara Pym and Ivy Compton-Burnett.' *London Magazine*, 24, August–September 1984, 59–69.

Lively, Penelope. Review of *An Unsuitable Attachment* in *Encounter*, 58, no. 4, April, 1982, 76–8.

Lyles, Jean Caffey. 'Pym's Cup: Anglicans and Anthropologists.' *The Christian Century*, 21 May 1986, 519–22.

Marsh, Pamela. 'Pym – Subtle and Accomplished.' *Christian Science Monitor*, 29 December 1982, 15.

McAleer, John. Untitled review of *Less Than Angels*. *Best Sellers*, vol. 40, no. 12, March 1981, 428.

McClurg, Jocelyn. 'Posthumous Pym: Less Than Others.' *The Hartford Courant*, 22 September 1985, G3.

Mellors, John. 'Bad Trips.' *The Listener*, 17 August 1978, 223.

——, 'Mixed Foursomes.' *The Listener*, 27 October 1977, 550.

Miller, Karl. 'Ladies in Distress,' *The New York Review of Books*, 9 November 1978, 24–5.

Milton, Edith. 'Worlds in Miniature.' *The New York Times Book Review*, 20 June 1982, 11.

'Miss Barbara Pym: Novelist of Distinctive Qualities.' Obituary. London: *The Times*, 14 January, 1980, F 14. Monteith, Charles. 'Publishing Larkin.' *Times Literary Supplement*, 21 May 1982, 552.

Moorehead, Caroline. 'How Barbara Pym was Rediscovered After Sixteen Years Out in the Cold.' *Times* (London), 14 September 1977, 11.

O'Conner, Patricia T. 'Romance Comes To Up Callow.' *New York Times Book Review*, 17 January 1988, 29.

Paulin Tom. 'Talking Transparencies.' *Encounter*, 50, no. 1, January 1978, 72.

Peterson, Lorna. 'Barbara Pym: A Checklist, 1950–1984.' *Bulletin of Bibliography*, 41, no. 4, December 1984, 201–6.

Phillips, Robert. 'Narrow, Splendid Work.' *Commonweal*. 8 May 1981, 284.

Pippett, Aileen. 'Observers Observed.' *New York Times Book Review*, 31 March 1957, 33.

Pool, Gail. 'Doses of Reality.' *New Boston Review*, June/July 1980, 15–16.

——, 'Excellent Women.' *The Nation*, vol. 239, no. 3, 4 August 1984, 88–90.

'Pym's Number One', *The Economist*, 1 September 1984, 73.

Radner, Sanford. 'Barbara Pym's People.' *Western Humanities Review*, 39, no. 2, Summer, 1985, 172–7.

'Reputations Revisited.' *Times Lterary Supplement*, 21 January 1977, 66–7.

Rosenstein, Harriet. 'Have You Discovered Barbara Pym Yet?' *Ms.*, May 1979, 33–5.

Rossen, Janice. 'Love in the Great Libraries: Oxford in the Work of Barbara Pym.' *Journal of Modern Literature*, 12, July 1985, 277–96.

Rowse, A. L. 'Austen Mini?' *Punch*, 273, 19 October 1977, 730–2.

Rubenstein, Jill. '"For the Ovaltine Had Loosened Her Tongue": Failures of Speech in Barbara Pym's Less Than Angels.' *Modern Fiction Studies*, Winter, 1986, 32 (4), 573–80.

Rubin, Merle. 'A Cooler, Tougher Woman.' *New York Times Book Review*, 7 September 1986, 25.

——, Untitled review of *A Very Private Eye*. *The Christian Science Monitor*, 23 August 1984, 21–2.

Schofield, Mary Anne. 'Well-Fed or Well-Loved? – Patterns of Cooking and Eating in the Novels of Barbara Pym.' *University of Windsor Review*, 18, no. 2, Spring/Summer, 1985, 1–8.

Seymour, Miranda. 'Spinsters in Their Prime.' *Times Literary Supplement*, 28 June 1985, 720.

——, Untitled review of *An Unsuitable Attachment*. *The Times* (London), 18 February 1982, 10.

Shapiro, Anna. 'The Resurrection of Barbara Pym.' *Saturday Review*, 9, July–August 1983, 29–31.

Shrimpton, Nicholas. 'Bucolic Bones.' *New Statesman*, 15 August 1980, 17.

Slung, Michele. 'Barbara Pym: the Quiet Pleasure of Her Company.' *Washington Post, Book World*, 17 January 1988, 3.

——, 'Pym's Last Cup.' *Washington Post, Book World*, 12 October 1980, 6.

Smith, Robert. 'How Pleasant to Know Miss Pym.' *Ariel*, 2, no. 4, 1971, 63–8.

Smith, Wendy. 'Brief Review.' *The New Republic*, July 16–24, 1984, 41.

Snow, Lotus. 'The Trivial Round, the Common Task: Barbara Pym's Novels.' *Research Studies*, 48, 1980, 83–93.

Stetz, Margaret Diane, '*Quartet in Autumn*: New Light on Barbara Pym as a Modernist,' *Arizona Quarterly*, 16, 1985, 24–37.

Stewart, Ian. Untitled review of *A Few Green Leaves*. *Illustrated London News*, October 1980, 99.

——, Untitled review of *The Sweet Dove Died*. *Illustrated London News*, 266, August 1978, 103.

Strouse, Jean. 'Elegant Surgery.' *Newsweek*, 97, no. 3, 19 January 1981, 81.

Taliaferro, Frances. 'Some Tame Gazelle.' *Harper's*, 267, no. 1599, August 1983, 74–5.

Thwaite, Anthony. 'Delicate Manoevres.' *The Observer*, 9 July 1978, 25.

Toomey, Philippa. Untitled review of *Quartet in Autumn, Excellent Women* and *A Glass of Blessings*. *Times* (London), 15 September 1977, 18.

Toulson, Shirley. 'The Sweet Dove Died.' *British Book News*, 17 October 1978, 843.

Trease, Geoffrey. Untitled review of *A Few Green Leaves*. *British Book News*, December 1980, 761.

Treglown, Jeremy. 'Puff Puff Puff.' *New Statesman*, 94, 23 September 1977, 418.

——, 'Snob Story.' *New Statesman*, 96, 7 July 1978, 418.

Tyler, Anne. 'From England to Brooklyn to West Virginia.' *New York Times Book Review*, 13 February 1983, 1.

Updike, John. 'Books: Lem and Pym,' *New Yorker*, 55, 26 February 1979, 116–21. Reprinted in *Hugging the Shore: Essays and Criticism*. New York: Alfred A. Knopf, 1983, 516–25.

Vogel, Christine B. 'A Sip of Pym's Number One,' *Book World, Washington Post*, 21 August 1983, 1.

Wade, Rosalind. 'Quarterly Fiction Review.' *Contemporary Review*, 232, January 1978, 45–6.

Wickenden, Dan. 'Fun Among the Anthhropologists.' *New York Herald Tribune Book Review*, 5 May 1957, 3.

Wilce, Gillian. 'Borderland.' *New Statesman*, 24 August 1984, 23.

Wilson, A. N. 'Daffodil Yellow and Coral Pink.' *The Literary Review*, June, 1985, 43–4.

——, 'St Barbara-in-the-Precinct.' *Spectator*, 20 February 1982, 22–3.

——, 'Thinking of Being Them.' *Times Literary Supplement*, 18 July 1980, 799.

Wymard, Eleanor B. 'Secular Faith of Barbara Pym.' *Commonweal*, 13 January 1984, 19–21.

Wyndham, Francis. 'The Gentle Power of Barbara Pym.' *Sunday Times* (London), 18 September 1977, 71.

Index